New Sermons on
Gospel Texts ✚

AUGSBURG
SERMONS 3

✚ Gospels, Series A

Augsburg

MINNEAPOLIS

AUGSBURG SERMONS 3
Gospels, Series A

The sermons by Walter Kortrey for the Second, Fourth, and Fifth Sundays in Lent were previously published in *People around Jesus* (Philadelphia: United Church Press, 1974). Pastor Kortrey's sermons for Maundy Thursday and Good Friday appeared in *In the Eagle's Eye* (Philadelphia: Parish Life Press, 1976).

Interior design: Virginia Aretz, Northwestern Printcrafters
Cover design: Judy Swanson

Library of Congress Cataloging-in-Publication Data

Augsburg sermons 3: Gospels, series A.
  p. cm.
  Includes bibliographical references.
  ISBN 0-8066-2618-6 (alk. paper)
  1. Bible. N.T. Gospels—Sermons.   2. Lutheran Church—Sermons.   3. Church year sermons.   4. Sermons, American.   I. Title: Augsburg sermons three.
BX8066.A1A874   1992   92-12758
252'.6—dc20   CIP

Manufactured in the U.S.A.   AF 9-2618

96   95   94   93   92   1   2   3   4   5   6   7   8   9   10

Contents

4

Richard J. Foss
Trinity Lutheran Church
Moorhead, Minnesota

Walter A. Kortrey
Saint Peter's Lutheran Church
New York, New York

6

Ralph J. Wallace
Faith Lutheran Church
Knoxville, Tennessee

Harry N. Huxhold
Our Redeemer Lutheran Church
Indianapolis, Indiana

7

Phyllis Faaborg Wolkenhauer
Zion Lutheran Church
Oelwein, Iowa

8

Richard L. Schaper
St. Mark's Lutheran Church
San Francisco, California

Roy A. Harrisville III
First Lutheran Church
Litchfield, Minnesota

Preface

The sermons in this volume provide a fresh look at the Gospel of Matthew through the Gospel texts for Series A in the three-year lectionary cycle prepared by the Inter-Lutheran Commission on Worship. These lessons are also included in the Common Lectionary (with minor variations) and are used in the worship services of a number of denominations. *Augsburg Sermons 3*, three volumes of sermons on the Gospel lessons for Series A, B, and C, builds on the widespread acceptance of the previous two Augsburg Sermons series, which were also based on the texts from the three-year lectionary cycle.

The fact that the Gospel lessons in each series focus on one of the Synoptic Gospels (with some lessons from the Gospel of John interwoven) provides continuity throughout the church year. Pastors can study the Gospel from each series with greater thoroughness and can share their insights with their congregations in preaching.

Eight pastors of the Evangelical Lutheran Church in America from different backgrounds and areas of the country wrote the sermons in this volume. We thank them for their contributions.

FIRST SUNDAY IN ADVENT
A New Year's Resolution
MATTHEW 24:37-44

Grace to you and peace from God: Creator, Redeemer, and Sanctifier. Amen.

Let us pray: Gracious God, creator of all life and all our senses, we give you thanks this day for the privilege of coming together in your name. Give to us the ability to hear with your ears, to see with your eyes, to touch with your hands, that we might continue to grow in our knowledge of you and in our love for one another. We pray this in Jesus' name. Amen.

Happy New Year! Today, we begin the celebration of a new church year. What resolutions have you made? We rarely think of the church's new year as a time for new resolutions. Have you resolved not to overindulge during the holy-day festivities? To lose that extra ten pounds? To be a better Christian? Perhaps to be more faithful to your commitment of time, treasure, and talents in your local congregation? Or to be a better parent, child, grandparent, brother, sister, cousin, niece, nephew, aunt, uncle, or friend?

Often we plan to reach new goals based on what we have not accomplished during the previous year, and we become the center of our goals—we focus on ourselves. Yet a new year is an opportunity to focus on Jesus in a new way.

Thus a new year's resolution might be to allow Jesus to have center stage in our lives: to become centered again in Jesus. The gospel for today challenges us to rethink our goals and our orientation.

Matthew was Jewish, and his Gospel was written for the Jewish community. His purpose, as we shall rediscover during this liturgical year, was to present Jesus as the Messiah to the Jewish people, who had been patiently awaiting the coming of the One who would deliver them. Having been trained in the Jewish religious tradition, Matthew was able to make connections between the Old Testament prophecies and the life of Jesus for the masses of first-century Jews who were unable to meet the Messiah in person.

In today's Gospel we are catapulted into the midst of what we understand now as Jesus' description of the end times. In encouraging the people to be prepared for the coming of the Son of Man, Jesus uses three examples of those who were not ready.

First Jesus reminds us of how the Old Testament people in Noah's time did not take God and God's ominous calls to readiness seriously. Like them, we too are relatively unconcerned about being ready for God's coming, and we go on living in a business-as-usual manner, not looking too closely at the wickedness that is running rampant in our times. Many would point to the increase of natural catastrophes, of substance abuse, to the exploitation of people and nature, the general disregard for law and order, our lack of faith and trust in one another, the over-use of the court in settling disputes or imagined disputes, the rumors of war—all of these things suggest a rise in the activity of the demonic. Has anyone in this congregation been guilty of reflecting on these matters? The question with which we are challenged by today's Gospel is, Are you ready?

The second illustration that Jesus uses is that of two people working beside each other. When the Son of Man returns, one will be left and one will be taken, whether working in the fields or in the mill.

The text's final example is the unwary householder who should have made preparations to prevent a break-in.

Does your New Year's resolution prepare you to be ready when Jesus returns?

As we reflect upon the beginning of a new church year, we must ask ourselves if we have made all the preparations necessary for the coming of Jesus. Have we lived every day fully? Have we done the things that we should have? Have we gone the second mile? Have we passed on to the youth the important truths about the Christian faith and given them the spiritual tools they need as they begin to wrestle with the demonic?

How do we place Jesus in the center of our lives again? Perhaps we need to take some time and reflect on what it means to be a Christian. We might want to study anew what Baptism and Holy Communion are all about. We might want to review what the Christian confession of faith and the creeds of the church really do say. We might want to explore again what the ministry of all the baptized, the priesthood of all believers, is about as we pursue our daily vocations. We do need to rediscover what it means to let go and let God.

Not too long ago a young woman I was counseling assured me she had given everything, all the problems with which she was presently wrestling, to God; yet she couldn't sleep at night because she kept worrying about her problems. I suggested to her that she hadn't fully given her problems to God if she was still worrying about them. She had communicated her problems to God in prayer, but she couldn't give them to God. She found it difficult to let God have free rein in solving her personal dilemmas. She had essentially said to God: Here are my problems, but I really don't expect you to solve them, so I will continue to worry with you and in that way I can help you solve them, God. To let go and to let God is to recommit our lives to Jesus; to know that there are no problems that God cannot solve; to struggle every day to place Jesus at the center of our lives, where he rightfully belongs, so that he can direct our lives and our days.

Paul charges us today, in his letter to the church in Rome, to "put on the Lord Jesus Christ, and make no provision for the flesh, to gratify its desires" (Romans 13:14). This is the way to begin this new year: to resolve that Jesus will be the center of our lives, to recommit our lives to Jesus, and to become prepared to receive Jesus, whenever he shows himself.

Happy New Year!

C.S.P.

THE SECOND SUNDAY IN ADVENT
Time for Preparation
MATTHEW 3:1-12

Grace to you and peace from God: Creator, Redeemer, and Sanctifier.

Let us pray: Gracious Lord, you have given to us, your servants, the ministry of service. Give us also the courage and determination to hear your word wherever it is proclaimed and the discernment to see you wherever you appear. Give us the strength and power to continue to be your servants. In your name we pray. Amen.

During the holy-day season most of us will be doing some entertaining. We take certain steps to ready ourselves for the visit of guests. The first thing we work on is the guest list: who can visit together amicably? The invitations are sent out or we make telephone calls; our invitees accept (hooray!)—then we begin the preparations in earnest.

Perhaps the next thing we do is to plan the menu. We think about our guests and their personal likes and dislikes in regard to food. We make our food purchases accordingly.

Then we decide the type of decor we want: red ribbons and twinkling lights and candles, or something else? We dust and vacuum and tidy up. Where should we put all these magazines and the junk mail? We find places to stow the clutter. We scent our home with wonderful fragrances. We pay special attention to the bathroom and put out the best soaps and handtowels. We take time and prepare very carefully for those whom we invite into our home. Thus when the doorbell rings announcing the arrival of our first guests, we are ready.

In today's Gospel we see God going about similar preparations for the arrival of the Christ child. God invites the people by sending out a special courier to announce the event: John the Baptist. Baptism is the way that the invited guests accept the invitation, as well as the way that God begins the process of tidying up. God involves the entire universe in this preparation process: the angels and the rest of the heavenly hosts, the people and their leaders, the earth and all that dwells therein. Human repentance directed by God continues this process. The nourishment that God prepares is very long in the making. It is none less than the Christ child himself. For those who accept God's invitation, the event itself is now and continues to be a wonderful success.

Let us reflect on John the Baptist, a very special participant. Not only was he on God's invitation list, but he also became a host for God. God invited John, prepared him by his wilderness experience while nourishing and tidying him up, commissioned him, and then turned over to John the job for which he had been prepared. John's way was not an easy task. He experienced rejection, persecution, ridicule, humiliation, and indignity, even to the point of imprisonment and beheading. Yet God continued to give John the courage and strength he needed for the task at hand: preparing a way for the Lord. God looks to us to do the same, not just when we feel like doing it, but on a regular basis.

The significant difference between my analogy and the Gospel lesson is that God's invitation is lifelong, while ours is generally for a single party. God's invitation is not a simple once-in-a-lifetime event about which we can reminisce fondly. God's invitation began almost two thousand years ago and continues to draw people of faith to remember and to participate even today. God's invitation calls people of faith to continue to be the couriers today: to prepare for the arrival of the Christ child again and again in our world; to be witnesses to those who are not people of faith; to provide nourishment in a world where people are hungry and thirsty; and to proclaim that Jesus Christ is Lord in the face of those who give their allegiance to things.

We are people of God who have been entrusted with the ministry of servanthood and hospitality; we are to extend God's invitation. We are the witnesses of the incarnation—God should make a difference in our lives. The way is often very difficult, and our invitation is not always received positively. Sometimes it is refused.

Our responsibility is to continue to invite others to the feast: to be faithful to our calling in season and out of season; to ensure that our congregations reflect the open arms of our God, whose desire is that we all have life, and that abundantly; to be ready to love all of God's people with the unconditional love that God is; to embrace and care for the totality of God's creation. We are responsible for preparing ourselves and the world for the advent of Jesus.

During this Advent season let us, like John the Baptist and others who have come before us, prepare ourselves for our ministries and prepare the world, or just our little corner of the world, for the advent of the Lord.

With the help of God we can be voices crying in the wilderness of life in the 1990s. We have been baptized into the body of Christ for this calling. God has done the work of tidying up and preparing the feast. We can deliver the invitations.

C.S.P.

THIRD SUNDAY IN ADVENT
Called to Be Prophets
MATTHEW 11:2-11

Grace to you and peace from God: Creator, Redeemer, and Sanctifier.

Let us pray: Precious Lord, take our hands; lead us on; help us stand; we are tired; we are weak; we are worn, just like your servant John. Give us the guidance and direction to continue to be your people in spite of the difficulties and adversities that face us. We pray this in the name of Jesus. Amen.

In today's Gospel we meet the disciples of John the Baptist. They have just visited him in prison, and he has directed them to go to Jesus and inquire as to who he, Jesus, is. "Are you the one?"

One can easily imagine the frustration of John's disciples. They had been with John while he was proclaiming that the messiah was coming. They had been with John as he was baptizing and preaching about repentance and preparation. Perhaps they had seen many fakes and charlatans declare themselves the messiah.

So when their leader directed them to go and ask Jesus if he was the messiah, they complied. Their fatigue must have been severe.

Their message of preparation must have seemed old. Yet they followed John's directive.

"Are you the one?" Implied in the question is not simply a satisfaction of human curiosity. Matthew draws us into the Old Testament's promises and prophecies that the messiah would come. Neither is the question simply rhetorical. The question is sincere and based on the profound concern of one who is searching for truth, one who is looking for a way to make sense of the nonsense in the world. Imprisoned, John is still looking for the reason for his mission and ministry. Note that John does not direct his disciples to ask Jesus why he, John, is imprisoned. They are simply to ask, "Are you the one?"

Jesus might have told John's disciples, "Yes; I am the one!" But instead Jesus asks them to look at the evidence surrounding him: the blind see, the lame walk, the lepers are cleansed, the deaf hear, the dead are raised, the poor are given good news. What additional testimony is needed in order to announce the presence of the messiah?

Matthew tells us nothing more about the disciples of John at this point. We don't know whether they discussed the Messiah's answer among themselves or pressed Jesus for a more direct answer. All we know from Matthew is that they left, presumably to take Jesus' message back to John the Baptist in prison.

We can surmise from the account in Scripture that people had a field day talking among themselves about John. He apparently attracted lots of attention and visitors when he was in the wilderness eating locusts and wild honey and wearing clothing made of camel hair. Evidently people came from all over to see this weird phenomenon of a man.

Jesus challenged the crowd: Did they expect to find someone who was so fickle that he might be swayed by any new personality and ideology that came along? Did they expect to find someone who was dressed in the finest of clothes? If the people were coming to see John in order to see how a prophet dressed and to hear what his most recent prophecy was, then they were sorely disappointed. If, on the other hand, they came to see John in order to determine what a contemporary first-century prophet was all about and to be challenged to repent, to be saved, and to be baptized, then they came to the right place—the desert of Judea, where John practiced his ministry.

In this way Jesus placed the mantle of authenticity around John's shoulders and helped the crowds to understand that John was even greater than Elijah, that greatest of Old Testament prophets, so revered by the Jewish people. John was great because he did what he was called to do in the face of doubt and loneliness and cynicism. Prophets are not slick people who use PR tactics in order to impress the crowds; on the contrary, they are people of God, and their missions and ministries are a life-style. They are chosen by God and wait on God's timing to reveal God's will. Jesus tells the people that "among those born of woman no one has arisen greater than John the Baptist." Yet the Messiah is even greater than John.

As we gather for worship or meetings or celebrations in our local congregations and catch a glimpse, literally or in our mind's eye, of the tiny figure in the manger, we might ask, with the people of the first century, "Are you the one? Can you possibly be the one? How can you, a powerless baby, be the one?"

Or perhaps it's a glimpse of the empty cross on a chain around someone's neck or on the top of a building or in a chapel: "You died before you changed the world, and it's worse now, almost two thousand years later, than when you were alive. How can you be the one?"

Maybe we are so overwhelmed with bad news in our lives that our faith is in crisis. We are looking to make some sense out of non-sense, some meaning out of meaninglessness. "Are you the one?"

Our Christian community helps us to hear God's answer: the blind see, the lame walk, the lepers are cleansed, the deaf hear, the dead are raised, and the poor are given good news. Our Christian community strengthens us when we feel weak. Our Christian community commissions us to go on when the going is extremely rough. Our Christian community helps to undergird our conviction when our faith wavers. Our Christian community reminds us that we are one with Christ when we feel abandoned and alone. Our Christian community renews us when we are hungry and thirsty. Our Christian community puts us in touch with Jesus, where we are reminded that all we do and all we are about is in the memory of Christ.

We are called to be present-day prophets who are not swayed by every new religious idea that arises in our society nor by those who dress dazzlingly to impress the people. We are to be faithful to God's message of salvation and grace as we prepare the way for Jesus. The way may be difficult and lonely. But we must remember that God is always with us in our mission and ministry. The Holy Spirit will not allow us to falter in our work of spreading the good news. As we prepare to celebrate the arrival of the Christ child, let us remember that God has not abandoned us. We can say with certainty, You are the one!

C.S.P.

The Spirit Prepares Us
MATTHEW 1:18-25

Grace to you and peace from our Lord and Savior, Jesus Christ.

Let us pray: Gracious Lord, continue to prepare us. We need your Holy Spirit to help us mature and become more courageous in order to face the trials yet to come. Prepare us, as you did your servant Joseph. In your name we pray. Amen.

It is very early on Sunday morning; the sun hasn't risen yet. The folks in the apartment across the alley have been going at it tooth and nail all night long, it seems. They were arguing when I drifted off to sleep, and they are still arguing. Their angry voices are clearly discernible in my kitchen and bedroom. The things that they have been saying to each other are things that we might have heard on television or at the movies—accusations of infidelity, ventilations of disappointment and unfulfilled expectations.

Hope and love betrayed seem to be a common litany nowadays. Casual relationships, one-night stands, marriages dissolved or perhaps never really consummated seem to be the order of the day. Are they married, or have they been living together in order to protect themselves from any potential hurt, to avoid vulnerability? Does it make a difference anymore? Are there any guarantees that relationships will last and that people who enter into relationships will work at making them work?

How did Joseph feel? He was engaged to Mary; engagement was the same thing as marriage except for living and sleeping together. The commitment that one gave, one's word, was very important then. Backing out of any commitment that had been announced publicly and celebrated by the community was simply not done, not even considered. But Joseph's fiancée, Mary, was pregnant, and Joseph had not even been with her intimately.

Joseph's thoughts might have followed this train. How can I continue this sham? She must have been sleeping around, and I simply cannot be expected to honor this commitment. But wait—there may be a better way. I will wait until after the baby is born and divorce her then. That will be acceptable. I won't have to consummate the relationship and I won't—wild horses can't make me—marry Mary.

How humble and meek and religious she seems. If people knew the real Mary they would be shocked. I still don't understand how she could have slept with someone else, though. Her family always seems to be around her—she's always chaperoned. Where did she meet someone, and how could she have found time away from her family to sleep with him?

Our families go back so far. They have been looking forward to this marriage for such a long time, and it's come to this. Well, I will not dishonor Mary publicly. Lord, I'm tired. I'd rather not think of this anymore. Maybe if I get some rest everything will look different tomorrow, or at least I'll have a better perspective on all this craziness.

As Joseph slept, an angel of the Lord visited him. Perhaps it was the angel Gabriel or one of those who visited Abram way back before Isaac was conceived. At any rate, Joseph dreamed deeply that night. I speculate that before he fell asleep he gave his concerns to the Lord in prayer, and during his REM period, when scientists say our deepest dreams occur, God's angel visited him and explained that Mary had not been unfaithful to their betrothal. Indeed, Mary had been extremely faithful and not simply to their commitment, their engagement, but mostly to God. Furthermore, the child that she would bear was conceived by the Holy Spirit and would save the people from their sins. Our Gospel writer, Matthew, lets us know that all these incidents were to fulfill what the Old Testament prophet had said (see verse 23). So Joseph was calmed by the visit of God's ambassador, and he married Mary. He did not sleep with her until after the baby was born, and, according to Scripture, when the baby was born they named him Jesus.

What does the story of the trial of Joseph have to do with the couple fighting in the apartment across the alley from mine? Everything! Joseph might have ranted and railed at Mary. Mary would have denied what Joseph was accusing her of, rightfully so. Their argument might have gone on and on, creating a wonderful soap opera on which we could eavesdrop.

But instead Joseph and Mary were focused on God. God was the center of their relationship. They could take their disappointments and frustrations to the Lord in prayer, and lay it on God's altar. The couple across the alley from me couldn't go to God in prayer, evidently. Mary and Joseph looked to God to heal a serious potential rift in their relationship. They saw themselves as servants of God and, as a consequence, accountable to God.

I do not know what my neighbor couple's relationship to God was like. I do know that I raised them up in my prayers for a long time after that night. Because I did not have a relationship with them, this was my way of interceding. How people who do not have God at the center of their relationship resolve conflicts is difficult for me to imagine. If there is no basic understanding that God is at the center of life, how can there be a commitment to conflict resolution based on the certainty that God wants us to be reconciled to one another?

Mary and Joseph perceived themselves as actors in God's play and were able to follow God's directive in bringing God's drama to completion. God spoke to both of them through dreams. The couple across the alley didn't have that advantage. There seemed to be no room for the work of the Holy Spirit because the couple saw themselves as the authors and directors of their own drama, actors on center stage. They could only point the way to themselves, it seems.

God's completion of Mary and Joseph's drama was as exciting as the preface that prepared the audience. Mary and Joseph, with God at the center of their relationship, were able to resolve a conflict in order to point the way to the Christ child. There is little room in God's drama for individualism and egoism.

We remind ourselves today that we are participants in God's drama. All our words and actions are reflections of how we understand God's love and witness to it. Joseph was able to put aside his own ego in relationship to Mary. He was made to understand that there was an important reason to heed the voice of the Lord, and he could do nothing less.

God may not speak to us in dreams today, but the lesson that we learn from Joseph's trials is to put aside our own gratification in order to point the way to Jesus Christ, the Savior. Are we able?

C.S.P.

THE NATIVITY OF OUR LORD, CHRISTMAS DAY

The Christmas Connection
LUKE 2:1-20

Grace and peace to you from God and from our Lord and Savior, Jesus Christ.

Let us pray: How beautiful upon the mountains are the feet of the messenger who announces peace, who brings good news, who announces salvation, who says to Zion, "Your king reigns." Listen! Your sentinels lift up their voices, together they sing for joy; for in plain sight they see the return of the Lord to Zion (Isaiah 52:7-8). Thank you, Lord, for coming back to and for us. Inspire us with your spirit of joy so that we can continually praise your name and be witnesses to your love. In the name of Jesus, the Christ child, we pray. Amen.

I remember preparing for Christmas as a young person, a member of the Walther League and the choirs of St. Paul's Evangelical Lutheran Church of Tremont (LCMS, Bronx, New York). The Walther League had responsibility for decorating the tree before the Christmas service, but after the Fourth Sunday in Advent service, of course. The choirs had spent most of the fall learning the music that we would sing on Christmas Eve and Christmas Day. The Sunday school had prepared its pageant, and most of the youth group were Sunday school teachers, so we were all very involved in preparing for and celebrating Christmas.

My parents encouraged this type of social activity and involvement. So they willingly, along with other parents, took their turn carting us back and forth to church. We had a wonderful time. Most of us in the youth group were also students at Our Saviour's Lutheran High School so we got to see our friends all week long, especially on the weekends.

One year we were taught a new musical selection for Christmas; I can still remember the first line: A child was born in Bethlehem. What was unique about this particular song was that the music was sad and somber and pretty depressing. I really didn't understand why this one wasn't as bright and cheerful as the rest of our Christmas music: "Hark, the Herald Angels Sing"; "The Carol of the Bells"; "O Come, All Ye Faithful"; "It Came upon a Midnight Clear"; "Mary's Boy-Child"; "Sing with Joy, Glad Voices Lift"; "On This Day Earth Shall Ring"; "Angels We Have Heard on High"; "The Snow Lay on the Ground"; "Silent Night"; and especially, "Joy to the World!"

Being of curious mind even then, I did not hesitate to articulate my concerns and questions. This gave our choir director and pastor an excellent opportunity to teach us a little about theology and to help us to continue our lessons in Christian maturity. They showed us the connection between Christmas and Holy Week and Easter: We cannot celebrate Christmas without remembering that Easter is the culmination of Christmas and that Christmas is the beginning of the Easter story. I have never forgotten that lesson, and I clearly remember to this day, in the midst of the joy of celebrating Christ's birthday, that sad and somber music.

In Luke's narrative about the birth of Jesus, we are reminded of this connection between Christmas and Easter. Luke strives to make his story as accurate as possible, so he helps the reader to locate the events during a particular political time with particular rulers. Luke places us in the town of Bethlehem, where those who were descendants of King David were required to register, as the Roman Empire was attempting to find out the actual number of its citizens.

Heavily pregnant Mary and fatigued Joseph have just arrived to register when Mary's labor begins. One of the issues that Luke deems important is hospitality. We find that the town of Bethlehem is not very hospitable to this young couple. They have to settle for bunking down in the stables for the night.

Mary's labor continues, and there, in a manger where the animals' hay was available for the animals' dining pleasure, sharing the animals' body warmth for badly needed heat, she gives birth to her first child. It reminds us of the trials through which this tiny baby was yet to go in fulfillment of God's will for the world. Christmas is a harbinger of Holy Week and Easter.

While Mary is delivering her child to the world, other poor people, the shepherds, are busy doing their jobs, watching their flocks. Suddenly something very unusual happens: An angel of God appears and God's glory lights up the night around them. The shepherds get very frightened very fast because they have never experienced anything like this before. But the angel of the Lord knows this, and the first thing the angel tells them is not to be afraid.

An event so wonderful has occurred that even the heavens have to respond. A child is born. But not simply any child. This is God's child, the one foretold by the prophets, the one for whom all the people are waiting, the one who will deliver his people from bondage and oppression. Such wonderful news calls forth a host of joyous angels who join in a heavenly chorus to sing God's praises: "Glory to God in the highest heaven, and on earth peace among those whom he favors!"

How can these poor shepherds not believe this is group fantasy? But then God provides a sign for them, just as God had provided signs for those who needed them over the centuries: The baby will be found in a stable's manger, wrapped in swaddling clothes. So the shepherds go to find out if what they have been told is really real.

They come to Bethlehem and find everything just as the angels have told them. Proof positive! They are excited. They tell Mary and Joseph what the angels have told them. Then, returning to their fields and flocks and sky, they tell everyone they meet. This news is so good that they can't keep it quiet. "And all who heard it were amazed at what the shepherds told them" (verse 18).

It is interesting to note at this point that Luke tells us, "Mary treasured all these words and pondered them in her heart" (verse 19). We don't hear that Mary was elated and began to tell everyone how lucky she was to be so honored by God. No; she ponders in her heart the information that has been shared with her. This too reminds us of the tribulations that are yet to come for the Christ child, his family and friends, and his followers. We are reminded once again of Holy Week and Easter.

Our hearts filled with joy and excitement of the season, giving gifts and doing extra nice things for others, singing the special songs and hymns. We celebrate the birth of the Christ child, and we proclaim that the world is a different place because of this single birth. The poor and the marginalized and the powerless and the disenfranchised and the powerful and those falling from power and the rich and the middle class and those who appear to have it all together and those searching for meaning can take heart and sing with the angel chorus: Glory to God in the Highest! This is good news!

Let us remember that along with the joys of celebration come the frustrations and trials of being ambassadors of and witnesses to Jesus Christ; that the Nativity of our Lord culminates in the Resurrection of our Lord, and that the Resurrection of our Lord could not have occurred without the Nativity of our Lord; that, finally, God is in control and that's sufficient reason for proclamation. Merry Christmas!

C.S.P.

FIRST SUNDAY AFTER CHRISTMAS
The Story Is about God
MATTHEW 2:13-15, 19-23

Grace, mercy, and peace to you from the Christ Child, our Redeemer.

Let us pray: Blessed are You, O Lord, our God, King of the universe. In your mercy you sent to us your gift of salvation: your son, Jesus Christ. Grant to us the spirit of awe and obedience that, like the family of the baby Jesus, we might ponder your marvelous works in our hearts. Amen.

Our text today takes us to Bethlehem following the visit from the wise men of the East. Most likely, Herod had been informed by his own astrologers of the astral phenomenon of a star passing across the sky. Something of significance is about to occur. There had been rumors for many, many years in and among the Jewish communities that the savior was coming, that the savior would be richer and more powerful than any political ruler to date, that the savior would make all things new and different, that the savior would turn around oppression and disenfranchisement. Herod heard these rumors and feared that the savior would take away his position and authority as king. Herod had to protect himself from any political threats.

The three wise men from the East stopped in Jerusalem and inquired about the whereabouts of the child who had "been born king of the Jews." Herod's treasure and his heart, however, lay in the same place, in the office of king, and he would do all in his power to protect his self-interest. Innocent questions sometimes have horrible consequences, and this is one of those instances. The entire population of the city of Jerusalem was thrown into a fright-night. One can almost hear the whispers and rumors circulating: Has the king an illegitimate son who will usurp the power of the throne? Is there a coup in the making? Who is this pretender to the throne of Jerusalem? Maybe there is some truth to the Jewish belief in Yahweh and the promises that this Jewish God has made to the "chosen" people! How will the Jews escape political reprisal this time? Who is this king of the Jews?

Herod consulted with his chief priests and scribes and was told that the messiah was to be born in Bethlehem of Judea. Herod put on the mask of friendship and assigned the wise men the task of seeking out the child for him so that even Herod could pay homage. The three wise men continued their journey with what they believed was the imprimatur of King Herod. The full account of this passage of Scripture recorded in the Gospel of Matthew will be further remembered and celebrated on Epiphany Sunday. For our purposes, however, this is the background of today's text.

After the wise men departed, we are informed, an angel of the Lord appeared to Joseph in a dream and urged him to get out of Bethlehem as quickly as possible because the paranoia of King Herod would lead him to try to destroy the holy family. Our text does not include verses 16-18, which tell of Herod's massacre of "all the children in and around Bethlehem who were two years old or under." We are reminded of the massacre of male newborns in Egypt at the time when Moses was born. Pharaoh was motivated by a similar fear hundreds of years earlier: fear not that his throne would be usurped, as in Herod's case, but that little Jewish boys would grow up into big Jewish men who might lead their Jewish brothers and sisters into acts of guerilla warfare and insurrection against their Egyptian masters and mistresses. Both Pharaoh's and King Herod's fears were appropriate but misplaced. They did not take seriously the power and wisdom of the Jewish God, Yahweh.

Some months later God communicated to Joseph in a dream and informed him that Herod had died and that the time had come for the holy family to return to Israel, where Joseph would be able to raise the child Jesus in safety. The family traveled to the district of Galilee and made their home in the town of Nazareth.

What lessons does today's Scripture teach us? What does the flight and return of the holy family to Israel tell us about how God operates today? Is today's story about Herod and his misplaced fears, or about the power and strength and wisdom of God? Perhaps it about all of the above.

But God's essential message to us today is that the misdirected power of the human will to survive at all costs and by any means necessary at the expense of others must end up being subjugated to the will of God. Although it appears as if the demonic is converting more and more people, God's will will be done. Today we can say with conviction that good will ultimately triumph over evil because the Bible has told us so and because the Christian community, historically and contemporarily, is God's witness. What Pharaoh and Herod intended for evil, God turned round and made into good, demonstrating once again who was in control.

We are reminded that this is God's world and our story is God's story, of how all things fit into place when God's time of fulfillment finally arrives and of how we are to be obedient to God's will. We are significant witnesses to the power and wisdom and strength of God just as Joseph and Mary, as Herod and the wise men, as the shepherds and the Jewish community in the town of Bethlehem, were witnesses. This Christmas season is a good time to follow the example of Mary to "ponder these things in our hearts" and to discuss these miraculous things in our homes and in our churches.

C.S.P.

SECOND SUNDAY AFTER CHRISTMAS
Glory
JOHN 1:1-18

Grace to you and peace from our brother and Savior, Jesus Christ.

Let us pray: God of wisdom and might, we come to you this morning humbled by the love that you have showed us. We thank you for your gift of love in the baby Jesus and ask this morning that you make us worthy of receiving and sharing your love. Help us to glorify you no matter what the circumstances, as far as our human frailty permits. In the name of Jesus we pray. Amen.

Synonyms for the word *glory* include *fame, eminence, renown, celebrity*. The verb means to exult with triumph, rejoice proudly in something. Often when we use the word it is in conjunction with an awe-filling experience; we exclaim, "Glory be!"

In our society we tend to come to understand the meaning of words and emotions through the media; the movie *Glory* was one such attempt. The only other times we really hear the word *glory* used in all its forms and even in other languages is during this season of the year. We hear about the angels and the shepherds and the entire creation glorifying God.

In today's text we read: "And the Word became flesh and lived among us and we have seen his glory, the glory as of a father's only son, full of grace and truth. . . . The law indeed was given through Moses; grace and truth came through Jesus Christ. No one has ever seen God. It is God the only Son, who is close to the Father's heart, who has made him known" (verses 14, 17-18).

What does this mean? It would be nice to be able to go to a catechism and look up Luther's explanation of what this means. But we are challenged by Scripture to wrestle with texts in our continued growth into Christian maturity. My purpose today is to help us to get a handle on what John is telling us in today's text.

"And the Word became flesh and lived among us, and we have seen his glory." God became human and lived a human existence. These fifteen words sum up both the Advent and Christmas stories, which we have been repeating during the last few weeks. As Christian people we believe that the Word of God was, and continues to be, Jesus Christ. We believe that God loved humanity so much that it was necessary for God to become human in order to demonstrate how we are to live together and care for one another. God became human and lived a struggling human existence.

Throughout human history, we have seen God's fame, eminence, renown, celebrity. We are witnesses, throughout the story of Christianity in the past as well as the present, of the triumph of God, the repeated triumph of love over hate and good over evil, of the proud rejoicing that Christian witnesses have demonstrated.

". . . the glory as of a father's only son, full of grace and truth. . . ." The proud rejoicing of a parent over the success of a child who has achieved a seemingly unattainable goal, who has maintained integrity; in spite of adverse circumstances—this is what John is describing to us. The child has not become haughty and arrogant and cold in attaining the goal; on the contrary, the child is still able to be gracious and truthful.

"The law indeed was given through Moses, grace and truth came through Jesus Christ." Words from on high, articulated by God's chosen servants, in this case the great prophet Moses, and written down for posterity were insufficient. It is better to do what is right and act appropriately out of desire rather than coercion. The law tells us that we often fall short of what we should be about; legislation of behavior creates more resentment and negative attitudes than positive behavior.

But Jesus demonstrated a better way. The old folks (called so lovingly) say that we can catch more flies with honey than with vinegar. Jesus showed us that grace and truth can change behavior better than legislation can. Love transforms other people.

"No one has ever seen God. It is God the only Son, who is close to the Father's heart, who has made him known." Not even Moses, the great lawgiver, was allowed to see Yahweh. Prior to Jesus' advent, all we knew of God through Scripture was how God loved the created order. It is only through Jesus, the God-become-flesh, that we know who God truly is. Because of Jesus, God's incarnation, we can now say with authority, as demonstrated and recorded in the Gospels, that God knows the human condition and desires that we have life, abundant life.

The life God desires for us is not the one that the world defines as successful. On the contrary, to be life-filled in the way God desires is the way of love, the way of servanthood, and, oftentimes, suffering. But in the midst of being faithful disciples we can see the fame, the eminence, the renown, the celebrity of God. We can exult with triumph and rejoice proudly that Jesus is Ruler, that God is Sovereign! With the saints who have gone before us and those who will come after us, we fulfill the vocation to which we have been called: giving God the glory!

Giving God the glory is being so filled with the Holy Spirit that we cannot stop praising God's name, to paraphrase a popular gospel song. Giving God the glory is acknowledging that who we are and what we are about is dependent fully upon God. Whenever we do something well, we recognize and acknowledge that our success is a consequence of God's being totally involved in our enterprise.

When I preach a particularly good sermon and members of the congregation tell me that they really understood what I was saying and that they they learned something from it, I often feel great and would like to take the credit. But I must pause for a moment and give credit where credit is due: the Holy Spirit is responsible for the fact that my words connected with the meditations of the hearts of the congregation. My ego must take a backseat to the movement of the Holy Spirit; I must give God the glory because I simply prepared myself appropriately and opened myself up to the Holy Spirit. The fact that my words connected with members of the congregation is all attributable to the power and work of the Holy Spirit.

Sisters and brothers in Jesus, let us continue to struggle to put off our human ego needs and open ourselves to the movement and work of the Holy Spirit in order to glorify God along with the stars and angel hosts and shepherds and all the regular people. We also come to adore the babe in the Bethlehem manger, the God made flesh.

C.S.P.

THE EPIPHANY OF OUR LORD

Epi-Now I See!-phany: The Dawning Light

MATTHEW 2:1-12

If I asked you to turn to your neighbors in the pew this morning and tell them briefly what Christmas or Lent means to you, I would guess that (if you are comfortable with that sort of thing) you could do it fairly easily. But what if I asked you to share what Epiphany means to you? Or if I asked each adult here this morning to explain Epiphany to a child? How would you do?

I lived through a lot of Epiphany seasons in the church before I even had a clue as to what it was about. And I doubt that I'm alone. This odd word, *Epiphany*, is simply a transliteration from the Greek word *epiphaneia*, which means "revelation," "manifestation," or "appearance." If you look up *epiphany* in your dictionary, you'll find several meanings. The first will probably refer to Epiphany Day (which we are celebrating this morning), a church festival observed on January 6 each year. This commemorates the coming of the Magi (wise men)—a sign that Christ is for all the people, including the Gentiles. The wise men were the first non-Jews to see and respond to Jesus.

A second meaning of *epiphany* in your dictionary will read something like this: "a (usually sudden) perception of the essential nature or meaning of something." I like to think of Epiphany as the church's equivalent of "Aha!" It's a sort of ecclesiastical "Eureka!" Epiphany is not only revelation given but also revelation received. It is the season of the year when the Scripture lessons seek to illuminate just who Jesus is.

On Epiphany Day we read of the Magi, who see not only the star in the East but the hand of God in the manger. They see. They perceive. It is an epiphany moment for them.

The first Sunday after Epiphany tells us of the baptism of Jesus, including the startling words of the Father: "This is my beloved Son, with whom I am well pleased." Again, those around Jesus experienced an epiphany moment, suddenly realizing another dimension of his identity.

The second Sunday after the Epiphany recalls John the Baptist, pointing to Jesus and proclaiming: "Behold, the Lamb of God, who takes away the sin of the world." Again, it was an epiphany moment for Andrew, Peter, James, and John, who saw and heard and followed.

The third Sunday after the Epiphany reminds us of the prophecy that "those who have walked in darkness have seen a great light," discovering that this Jesus is the light that is coming into the world.

And on the texts go, to the end of the Epiphany season—the Transfiguration—when again we hear the words of the Father: "This is my beloved Son; listen to him." All through the Epiphany season we will be reminded of what Jesus' birth in Bethlehem means. Christmas was the event; Epiphany helps us understand it. Thus the strange title to this sermon—"Epi-Now I See!-phany: The Dawning Light"—because an epiphany moment is when the light goes on in your head, when it suddenly clicks, when you say, "*That's* what it's all about."

Epiphany is when you catch on. Even in our daily living we experience little epiphanies. They are the delightful moments when we figure out the plot of a mystery novel, realize what a friend has been trying to tell us, make sense of the teacher's explanation in algebra, or recognize a vaguely familiar face in a crowd.

We also experience larger epiphanies: when a child learns to read, deciphering the meaning of those strange black marks on the page; when you discover that another person loves you, really loves you; when your first child is born, and you begin to see your own life in a radically new light.

How do they happen, these epiphanies? Are they bursts of insight? Or the result of a long, slow process, the cumulative effect of gathered information and experience? The answer is, both. The Pacific Science Center in Seattle has a computer room carefully designed to encourage young and old to experiment with the various computers. In my favorite game, pictures formed by thousands of tiny dots are shown on the screen, but not all at once. The screen starts out blank; then, with a timer running, the dots are randomly filled in, a few at a time. The moment you can recognize the picture, you punch it into the computer; if you are right, the clock stops. The computer then tells you what percentage of the dots you needed to see before you made sense out of the picture. I always needed some of the dots revealed; I never had to see them all. It was a gradual process of narrowing the options, culminated by that "Aha!" epiphany moment when I suddenly realized what it was.

Our faith response is a slow process too, replete with myriad epiphany moments, each clarifying God's grace to us in some way.

They may come through suffering, as the promises of a suffering, crucified Christ take on new meaning; or perhaps in loving another, God's love for you is illumined as never before; or maybe in hearing a word of forgiveness when you rightly expected rejection, God's grace breaks through to you with startling power. These are epiphanies, and they are essential building blocks for us as Christians.

The central epiphany in any life is when we come to know Jesus as our Savior, the moment when we can say yes to our Lord. Yet this cornerstone epiphany is almost always a combination of slow, relational growth and sudden insight.

When Peter, in a sudden burst of recognition, exclaimed, "You are the Christ!" it was only after long exposure to Jesus. Even after that, through the painful experience of Jesus' death and his own denial, Peter discovered how much he still didn't understand about Jesus.

The Roman centurion at the foot of the cross had certainly watched this Jesus for some time before he said in awe, "Surely this was the Son of God." And he undoubtedly stayed close by to learn more about this Jesus in the following days.

How did you (or perhaps the question is, how *will* you) see the light? How did you recognize Jesus as your Savior? Most of us can't point to any particular moment. It's a little like driving in fog and at some point realizing you're no longer in fog, but not knowing exactly when you emerged; or watching a sunrise over the flat prairie horizon, where it's impossible to pinpoint precisely when dark became light.

Yet others of us can point to a more precise event or time, more like suddenly emerging from a fog bank or watching a sunrise come over a nearby mountain peak in a sudden burst of brilliant light. For Martin Luther it was in his study, as he was poring over the Epistle to the Romans, that the darkness of an angry, vengeful God was blotted out by the bright light of a forgiving God of grace. That was his epiphany moment.

Probably only you and God know (or perhaps only God knows) how your epiphany has come, or will come. If it hasn't happened yet, hang in there; God is at work in you, and the time will come. If you have already said yes to Jesus, stay with him, for there are epiphanies yet to come in your walk with your Lord.

The moment of truth—the "mother of all epiphanies"—is to know your Savior. But that doesn't mean you've run out of epiphanies. As you and I live among God's people, as we gather for worship, as we serve God in the church and in the world, as we strive to deepen our relationships and love one another more fully, and as the Holy Spirit continues to work in and through us, we will experience little, and large, epiphanies.

I hope many of you have either read or seen the marvelous little play *The Best Christmas Pageant Ever*, written by Barbara Robinson (Harper & Row, 1972). It is narrated by a child whose mother has to take over the church Christmas pageant because the one who has organized it "forever and ever" had broken her leg; it soon becomes the story about the Herdmans—six rotten, uncontrollable, terrible kids—who had never come to church, but, upon hearing that refreshments were served, showed up at the rehearsals, and, being the neighborhood bullies, grabbed all the good parts.

The Herdmans had the reputation of being the most awful kids in the world. They were all alike except that they had different black-and-blue places where they had hit each other. Everyone knew they had broken most of the commandments; they took the Lord's name in vain, swore at their teachers, lied, stole, talked dirty, were mean to little kids or anyone else they didn't like, and sometimes were mean to adults, too—they even burned down a neighbor's old toolhouse. They did all kinds of things the other children hardly dared to think about—they smoked cigars, even the girls.

They seemed headed straight for hell, that is, until they began to show interest in the church's Christmas pageant. The director, Mrs. Robinson, discovered that the Herdmans knew next to nothing about the Christmas story. They knew Christmas was Jesus' birthday, but nothing about his birth in a stable because the inn was so crowded, or anything about the shepherds, the angels, the star, or the Wise Men. It was all new to them! So Mrs. Robinson decided to begin by reading the Christmas story from the Bible, much to the other children's dismay—they already knew it almost by heart and just needed to know which characters they were and where they should stand. As the story goes on, we find out that Imogene Herdman, who played Mary, bashed people over the head with the baby Jesus doll to keep them in line, and how the Christmas pageant unfolded that night as all the folks flocked in because they had heard how awful it was going to be, and how Imogene burped the baby Jesus in the middle of the pageant because she thought that's what you'd do if you loved the baby, and how the Wise Men brought their Christmas ham that the welfare had given them because they thought Jesus deserved better than this smelly perfume they were supposed to bring.

Many times the people were relieved when it finally was time to sing the last carol, "Silent Night," but that night they seemed to wish the pageant would go on. With the Herdmans in charge, everyone waited in anticipation about what might happen next. The young storyteller mentions that when they came to the line, "Son of God, love's pure light," she happened to look at Imogene and, in her surprise, almost dropped her hymnbook on a small angel. The unexpected had happened, for there was Imogene Herdman, crying!

In the candlelight her face was all shiny with tears and she didn't even bother to wipe them away. She just sat there—awful old Imogene—in her crookedy veil, crying and crying and crying.

Afterwards everyone said it was the best Christmas pageant ever. They weren't sure why, but they knew there was something special about it. The storyteller felt she knew because earlier she had seen Imogene in kind of a daze, as if she had just caught on to the idea of God and the wonder of Christmas. She adds,

For years, I'd thought about the wonder of Christmas, and the mystery of Jesus' birth, and never really understood it. But now, because of the Herdmans, it didn't seem so mysterious after all.

As the storyteller discovered, it wasn't only an epiphany for Imogene, who heard the story of Jesus for the first time; it was an unexpected epiphany for the other kids, as well as for the jaded church members who came expecting to hear the same old thing, only to hear the Christmas story in a way they'd never heard it before.

Today we begin the Epiphany season. Our Savior, the light of the world, has come. Now is a time for epiphanies. May they be many for you, as the light of the world, Jesus Christ our Lord, continues to dawn in your life.

R.J.F.

THE BAPTISM OF OUR LORD, FIRST SUNDAY AFTER THE EPIPHANY
Jesus Was Baptized? Why?
MATTHEW 3:13-17

As a child, when I heard the account of Jesus being baptized in the river Jordan by John the Baptist, it seemed natural. I was baptized; others were baptized; and Jesus had told us to go into all nations, baptizing in the name of the Father, Son, and Holy Spirit. It seemed only natural that Jesus, the one at the center of all this baptizing, was himself baptized. But it wasn't so easy the first time I tried to preach on this text.

It was the second year of my pastoral ministry, and I began to ponder the text far in advance. I read, "In those days John the Baptist appeared in the wilderness of Judea, proclaiming, 'Repent, for the kingdom of heaven has come near,' " and a few verses later, "Then Jesus came from Galilee to John at the Jordan, to be baptized by him." Evidently baptism had a lot to do with repentance; in fact, Mark (1:4) says, "John the baptizer appeared in the wilderness, proclaiming a baptism of repentance for the forgiveness of sins." I had a problem: I couldn't figure out why Jesus would undergo a baptism of repentance. I understood why repentance and forgiveness were necessary in my baptism. But Jesus? Why did he have any need of such forgiveness?

I read the commentaries at my disposal, and they put forth a host of "good reasons" (most of which I relayed to the congregation, in hopes that the reasons might help somebody, even though they weren't doing much for me). But even those commentators had to admit it was a bit of a puzzle—and that it was by no means a new problem. In fact, when Mark wrote his Gospel, he simply wrote down the account of Jesus' baptism without a blush. But a few years later, when Matthew was recounting the same event, it was already problematic. Matthew was familiar with Mark's Gospel, but he decided to add John the Baptist's protest, "I need to be baptized by you, and do you come to me?" to which Jesus responds, "Let it be so now; for it is proper for us in this way to fulfill all righteousness." The whole thing was problematic from the start. Matthew acknowledges that John didn't understand it either: Why should Jesus be baptized with a baptism of repentance when he wasn't guilty?

So there I was, a young pastor, who had read the commentaries, pestered friends and colleagues, and scoured the Bible, hoping to be persuaded. But as Sunday morning approached, I had a serious problem: I still couldn't see any good reason why Jesus should have been baptized.

Well, what do you do then? I surely wasn't going to pretend. It was a little late to preach on the epistle for the day. And I really didn't want to pick a fight with Matthew, Mark, and Jesus about the event. So that day I gave a brief summary of the reasons scholars had given, said I hoped that it might help some people, acknowledged that it wasn't at all persuasive to me, and proceeded to preach on the topic "What does a Christian do when a biblical text makes no sense to him or her?" The next year I preached on "What do you do when you *still* don't understand the text?" The third year it began to make some sense to me, and it still does.

Fortunately, I happened across an unpretentious little book by a theologian named Oscar Cullman, entitled *Baptism in the New Testament*. It is true, he acknowledged, that Jesus submitted to a baptism of repentance to fulfill all righteousness. However, it wasn't a baptism of repentance for *his* sin; it was a baptism of repentance on *my* behalf, and on *your* behalf. Just as he died on the cross, not for his sins, but for yours and mine, so he was baptized in solidarity with, and on behalf of, you and me.

Jesus' baptism was the beginning point of his mission, which culminated on the cross. The words of the Father he heard, "This is my beloved Son, in whom I am well pleased," were particularly poignant. As you may know, that sentence is the joining of two well-known phrases from the Old Testament. One half is from the first song of the Suffering Servant in Isaiah 42; the other is from the coronation hymn of Psalm 2. We have, in effect, an affirmation—a seal of approval—from the Father, pointing Jesus to his mission as the Servant/King.

Or, as Cullman puts it,

> At the moment of his baptism, Jesus received the commission to undertake the role of the suffering servant of God, who takes on himself the sins of his people. Other Jews came to the Jordan to be baptized by John for their own sins. Jesus, on the contrary, at the very moment when he was baptized like other people, hears a voice which fundamentally declares, "Thou art baptized not for thine own sins, but for those of the whole people. For thou art he of whom Isaiah prophesied that he must suffer representatively for the sins of the people." This means that Jesus is baptized in view of his coming death, which effects forgiveness of sins for all. For this reason, Jesus must unite himself in solidarity with his whole people and go down himself to the Jordan that all righteousness might be fulfilled. . . . The baptism of Jesus is related to righteousness—not only his own, but to that of the whole people.[1]

Jesus' baptism has been seen as important for his ministry and mission in various ways, but for me it finally begins to make sense when I remember that, whatever else may or may not be involved, he did it for me.

Jesus made baptism something new. The Jews had for centuries baptized Gentile converts in a ceremony of renewal and cleansing, a grafting into the Jewish community not unlike a modern-day naturalization process for becoming a United States citizen. Jesus, in his final commission to the disciples, called them to "Go therefore and make disciples of all nations, baptizing them in the name of the Father and of the Son and of the Holy Spirit."

Baptism is now something utterly new. Just as he transformed the Passover meal into Holy Communion, just as he transformed and gave new meaning to the Old Testament Scriptures, so he made baptism a new thing.

Now, in obedient response to his command, we are baptized, knowing that in baptism God acts. God is the primary actor; God has promised to initiate and implement a radically new relationship in baptism. Through this sacrament God promises to bind himself to us in love, to bring us within the community of faith, and to adopt us as precious children, whom God will never abandon.

When you and I are baptized, we are not taking out a divine insurance policy that guarantees us a reserved pew in heaven. Instead God establishes a new relationship with us. We are invited and empowered to live within that relationship, yet he still leaves us the capacity—the awful freedom—to try to live outside it. I suppose it's similar to the adoption of a child. When I adopt a child (as Nancy and I have done), I must go through a process. I have to sign papers promising to be a parent to the child, to love, support, nurture, and provide for that child as I would for any other child of mine. But those papers are only as good as my word. The promise behind them is the real power, just as the promise of God is the real power undergirding our baptismal certificates. In baptism, or any other adoption, the act is real. The gift of love is real. The change in relationship is real. But the future of the relationship is not guaranteed.

In adopting a child, the parent has sealed the relationship, from his or her side, with a promise. But the child (who, if old enough, as in our case, has consented; or if younger, is blissfully unaware) still must live in that relationship. Neither notarized papers nor solemn promises are any guarantee that the child will choose to live in response to the love that is offered. It is fully possible for the child to reject the relationship; he or she may choose to live with indifference to, or in rebellion against, the offered love. The only thing outside the child's power is the capacity to kill the love of the parent.

Nancy and I have a child whom you do not know; he does not live with us in this community. This child finds it extremely difficult to live within the relationship established by our promises to be his parents and to love and sustain him within our family. For whatever reasons, he has found it extraordinarily hard to respond to our love. It is even possible that he will continue to fight against it—possible, though we hope and pray he won't. You give a terrible freedom to another when you love him or her. It is the same freedom God has given us: the freedom to reject the lover, the freedom to refuse the love. If you have had a child do this, even for a brief time, then you have had a bitter taste of what God must feel when you or I reject God's love or are indifferent to the divine call.

But there is one thing my child cannot do. He can't make me stop loving him. In my frailty, he can come close. He can alter my feelings; he can precipitate regrettable actions born of my frustration or anger. But in the end he cannot make me stop loving him.

As long as that love continues, there is hope—hope that he, like the prodigal son in Jesus' parable, will find a way to live in that love once again. What truly gives me hope in this life is that if my son, in his rebellion or confusion, cannot make me stop loving him (as sinful and imperfect as I am) when I have promised to be his parent, then I am sure that whatever else I may do in my sin, whatever pain I may cause myself or others in turning away from God, there is one thing I can never do: I cannot make God stop loving me! The hope remains for my reconciliation—always—because at my baptism he has promised to love me and be my God.

It is a profound hope. I know about the pain all too well; so do you. When you or I, for whatever reason, will not live in harmony with those who love us, do not respond to the love of God, there is pain. Real pain. Isolation. Loneliness. And the terrifying possibility of an alienation that endures—tragically—despite the love of God and others. That is real.

But Jesus was baptized—for me. Jesus died—for me. Jesus transformed the rituals of religion into the acts of God—for me. And when I am baptized, he promises that he will be my God and love me, forgive me, nurture me, and stay with me. That is real too. Whatever pain we might perpetrate in this life, neither you nor I can make God stop loving us.

May you live in the relationship God has created with you in your baptism; may you know and respond to the love that is offered; and in it, may you find healing and hope.

R.J.F.

---

1. Oscar Cullman, *Baptism in the New Testament* (Chicago: Henry Regnery, 1950), 18.

SECOND SUNDAY AFTER THE EPIPHANY
Truth to Tell
JOHN 1:29-41

A wise old preacher once said that John the Baptist spoke the whole gospel when he said, "Behold, the Lamb of God, who takes away the sin of the world." Everything else, he said, is ramification or commentary. Well, perhaps. In any case, John is articulating the core of the gospel. Yet it is couched in language and imagery that isn't so familiar to us today, so let's take a closer look.

"The Lamb of God"—a strange image to anyone new to the church, but it has deep roots and would have had tremendous evocative power for its early hearers. The lamb was a Hebrew symbol for purity and innocence, an incarnate image of sinlessness. In addition, the Aramaic word had a double meaning: it could refer either to a lamb or to a servant. The original Aramaic phrase may have had the primary thrust of "Behold, the servant of God, who takes away the sin of the world." However, the Gospel According to John was written in Greek; since Greek has separate words for lamb and servant, the writer had to choose. Why would he have chosen *lamb*?

Not only did *lamb* convey a sense of innocence and purity, not only did *lamb* prick a rich remembrance of the Suffering Servant in Isaiah 53, but Jesus was crucified during the Passover time. Passover, as you know, was the celebration of the Israelites' escape to freedom from Egypt. The lamb was a central symbol of that sacrifice and freedom. Moreover, Jesus had transformed the Passover meal at the last supper so that, through the sacrificial gift of his body and blood, he frees us, not from Egypt, but from sin and death. John, keeping all that in mind, translated the Aramaic word as *lamb*, the Lamb of God who takes away the sin of the world.

" . . . takes away the sin of the world"? *World* is another critical word in that brief sentence. It isn't "takes away the sins of the Jews" or "takes away the sins of the elite" but "takes away the sin of the world." We won't spend much time on that today, since it fits so nicely later in Epiphany, but it is worth noting.

At this time of year our nation commemorates Martin Luther King, Jr., who spent his life to remind us that this Lamb of God takes away the sins not only of whites but also of blacks. Over and over again we need to hear that Jesus came not only for Jew or Greek, not only for male or female, not only for slave or free, not only for rich or poor, but for all. The message is plain: Whoever you are, whatever your sin, however deep the hole you've dug, wherever you find yourself, there is still one who can and will set you free from the suffocation of your sin. It is Jesus, this Lamb of God, who takes away the sin of the world.

John realized that. I don't know whether it was a shock to him to discover that his cousin Jesus was the one he'd been waiting for, or if he had suspected it for some time. I don't know whether the recognition burst upon him suddenly or if it was a slow, dawning realization. But when John came to understand who Jesus was, he did the one sane, rational, faithful thing he could do with that kind of news—he shared it. When he saw Jesus coming, he turned to the people he was with and said, "Behold, the Lamb of God, who takes away the sin of the world."

Because he shared what he knew, Andrew and Peter met Jesus. Because they later said to those they were with, "Behold, the Lamb of God, who takes away the sin of the world," others came to know Jesus. That's the way it happens. Kids gathered around a campfire sing, "It only takes a spark to get a fire going . . . pass it on." It's true. We are called to tell the truth that we know.

Telling the truth involves more than simply not lying. It often means not remaining silent as well. If I am sick and ask a doctor for diagnosis and remedy, the doctor has a responsibility to tell me what he or she discovers. But even beyond that, if I look or act sick, and you have some reason to know of a person who can help me yet remain silent, your silence is at best unhelpful, more likely evil. Your responsibility is not to cure me, of course; but if you know I need help and you know someone who can help me, then you must say so.

If you and I owned the same model car, and I heard that the brakes were prone to locking and that the dealer was offering free repair on all cars of that model to avert potentially fatal accidents; and if I realized you were unaware of the problem and the offer, would you expect me to tell you about it? Of course. If you and I had children with similar reading problems, and I heard about a free program with someone who had been able to help many children with such difficulty, would you expect me to tell you? Yes, you would.

And we do. We're pretty good at it usually. We tell each other about good bargains at a store, about the latest news in nutrition, about a hot tip that helped our golf game, or about a good book or movie. Not that we are responsible for our friends; not that we say, "You must do this," or "You must try that." But because we care about them, we don't keep good news secret; we share it. Neither do we feel that we have to be a professional in a given area to do it. You know, of course, where I'm heading. If we tell other kinds of good news, why not tell the good news of Jesus, the Lamb of God who takes away the sin of the world, to our friends? Not to tell them what they have to do, not to declare our own religiosity from on high, but to articulate, affirm, and bear witness to the love of God active in our own life, to share the promise that the same power of love is offered to them. "Behold, the Lamb of God, who takes away the sin of the world."

I don't have much time for street-corner evangelists who button-hole people or ramble on at passersby about the end of the world. I can't stomach a TV evangelist who slanders God and extorts money from vulnerable, well-intended people with threats that God might "call him home" if enough money isn't raised. I don't care much for Christians who harangue and bedevil co-workers all day long about needing to receive the gift of the Spirit. But I don't think many people here are in danger of these particular pitfalls.

You and I are much more likely to err on the other side, to commit the sin of omission by withholding the word of grace and witness that a friend might desperately need to hear. Maybe we do it out of modesty, perhaps because we're afraid of imposing ourselves on another, maybe because we don't think we can do it as well as someone else, or possibly we might be tempted to think that no one else cares what God does in our lives. This, I think, is a much more common problem for us Lutherans.

I'd like to tell you about a humbling experience I had a few years back. A good friend from college moved to town and joined the congregation I was serving as pastor. Some time later she went through a very painful and difficult experience. We spent time together during those troubled days, and she expressed appreciation for my help as a pastor and friend. Then, about a month after things had returned to a more normal pattern, she phoned, and said, "Rick, you don't need to accept this invitation, but I'd like to take you to lunch. If you are amenable, I'd like to tell you what you did that was helpful to me in my pain, and what you could have done that would have been even more helpful. You'll encounter others in my predicament, and maybe I can help you and them." I said yes.

We went to lunch. She began by telling me all the things I'd done that she had found helpful, and thanked me for them. Then we ate and visited. Finally she said, "Maybe we should just eat and chat; that might be cheerier." I said, "No, I want to hear what I could, or should, have done." (I'm not at all sure I really wanted to hear, but at least that's what I said).

Then she gently said, "When I was at my worst, you weren't of much help. I knew you were available because I know you, and because I trusted you when you told me you were available anytime. I believed you when you said I could call day or night, and you wouldn't consider it an imposition. But at my worst I was unable to do that. I needed something else. For example, one Sunday morning you walked by and realized I was in bad shape. There were people all around, and it was not a good time to talk, but you stopped briefly and said, "Why don't you give me a call in the next day or two?" Do you remember? (I remembered well; she hadn't called).

"Well, a few minutes later your wife, Nancy, came by, looked at me, saw what you had seen, and said, 'I'll call you tomorrow.' She did call the next day. She listened, talked, shared, and listened some more. I came away with a glimmer of hope. Rick, if I had been in a little better shape, I could have responded to you and made the phone call you invited; but as low as I was, I just couldn't do it. As Nancy somehow realized, I was in no shape to reach out, so she reached out to me."

What had happened? At her lowest point, the professional (me, regrettably) was oblivious to the real need. But a friend, a neighbor, who was willing to risk a phone call to listen, who shared her own pain and God's love, was all the help in the world. I learned a lot at that lunch; maybe you too can learn from my failings and from the gentle words of my friend.

Are you willing to take the risk of sharing the good news—and yourself—with another? Does your family know what God means to you? If you have found a word of wisdom, an act of grace, or an insight into Scripture particularly important in your life, has anyone else received the benefit of that experience or insight? We learn from others. We are reassured by others. We are renewed and emboldened by others. And we need each other to be willing to take the necessary risks to reach out.

A friend of mine was talking about a woman who was depressed and lonely, isolated in her gloom. One day she expressed the gloom to an acquaintance and then retreated. But her acquaintance reached out, shared a similar experience of pain, acknowledged the battle, and affirmed God's patient healing power. Today, the woman is in much better health. Why? Because somebody said, "Behold, the Lamb of God, who takes away not only my pain but yours." Well, how do you go about it? How do you tell the truth about God? The same way you tell any other truth: gently; in love; with a lot of listening; from a stance of commonality rather than superiority; honestly; and with (patience-tempered) enthusiasm.

About now you might be thinking, "Well, that sounds great, pastor, but I'd rather live out my faith. Why should I talk about my faith when I can live it out; besides, remember, the old adages, such as 'A picture is worth a thousand words' and 'what you do speaks so loudly I can't hear what you say.' "

True enough. But you have to remember two things. First, I'm not suggesting that you talk about *your faith*; I'm suggesting that you share with others what a gracious God has done in your life. John the Baptist didn't say a thing about himself; he said, "Behold, the Lamb of God, who takes away the sin of the world."

Second, what we do and what we say need to go together, like inhaling and exhaling. Children are great observers but poor interpreters. They see what we do (often much more clearly than we'd like), but they are often greatly mistaken about why we do it. If you've been around children, you are well aware of the need to tell them why you do what you do. Adults aren't much better, except we aren't so transparent about it. We observe what other people do but often don't know why they do it unless they are willing to tell us.

If you live out a Christian life but never utter a word about the love of Jesus Christ that keeps you going in the midst of your troubles, your witness may be lost on most of us. We may assume you are just a better person than we are (which only makes us feel worse about ourselves) or that you are a clever perfectionist putting up a nice facade (which only makes us feel skeptical about your witness). A few well-chosen words now and then could illuminate your life as a witness to God's love.

You see, if you are just a nice guy or a successful manipulator of life's events, that has nothing to do with my life. But if you are enabled to love and thrive through the love of Jesus Christ, who offers the same enlivening love to me, then that does make a difference in my life.

Here are two questions for each of us to ponder this morning: first, What has been particularly important to me as God has lived out God's love in my life? Second, Are there those I care for who could benefit from knowing about it? If so, have I cared enough or been brave enough to tell them?

To withhold the depths of life from those around us is misguided and contrary to the call of Christ. But to share, to witness, to pass on the story is to be faithful to God and to give a precious gift to those we love.

Your story is one of many stories of God's people. But your story is important and needs to be heard, for it tells over and over again, in one way or another, what we need to hear: "Behold, the Lamb of God, who takes away the sin of the world." That's the truth, the truth for us to tell.

R.J.F.

THIRD SUNDAY AFTER THE EPIPHANY
God's Odd Building Material
MATTHEW 4:12-23

When I was a student, the various professors or counselors had reputations (usually warranted) about how they would treat their students. Based on reports of how they had treated other students like me, I would get some indication as to whether they were likely to be kind, patient, and forgiving; terse, legalistic, and harsh; wise or shallow; open or resentful. Almost always the way they had treated others was the way they would treat me.

We usually want to know how a person is likely to respond before we make ourselves vulnerable to them or entrust them with something important. You're likely to ask around before you go to a counselor for help; you will do a little checking before you confide in an acquaintance; you will pay attention to a business associate's track record before entering into significant contracts. You and I want to know something about how people have treated others before us in similar situations. It isn't so much different for us when we consider God and how God will deal with us.

How can we know how God is going to respond to us in any given situation? By what God says and promises, I suppose; yet words are so subjective and open to varying interpretation. Even rigid, unsympathetic people think they treat those around them fairly and gently. What if God says God loves us, but that turns out to be very different from how we understand love? How do we know what God really means? Perhaps one of the best gauges we have is to look at how our Lord had treated others like ourselves, because he is likely to do the same with you and me.

In our Gospel text today, we find Matthew's account of Jesus calling his first disciples: Simon, who was called Peter, Andrew, James, and John. These were the first in a long line of followers that extends to us today, the first building blocks of his church. If I follow Jesus, how will he deal with me? How has he treated others who followed him? We probably have a more complete account of Jesus' interactions with Peter than with any other. Let's see if we can draw any inferences about how God will deal with us.

Over the years Jesus spent with his disciples, we find evidence of gentle teaching, patience, confrontation if or when necessary, and a pervasive love. But we learn the most as we draw near Calvary. In Matthew 16 we read about a retreat Jesus took with his disciples to the picturesque northern countryside, in an area called Caesarea Philippi. At some point in that retreat, Jesus looked at his followers and asked, "Who do people say that I am?" They gave a variety of responses. Then Jesus looked more closely at them and asked, "But who do *you* say that I am?" Among the group was Peter, the impetuous fisherman, whose name in Aramaic was Cephus (the same word as "rock," which made for a natural nickname). He blurted out, "You're the Christ, the Son of the Living God. You're the Savior, the Messiah. You really are, aren't you, Jesus?!"

Jesus looked at Peter (*petros* being the Greek word for "rock" and Simon's transliterated nickname) and said, "Blessed are you, Simon son of Jonah. For flesh and blood has not revealed this to you, but my Father in heaven. And I tell you, you are Peter [Gk. *petros*] and upon this rock [Gk. *petra*] I will build my church." (double or triple entendre clearly intended, especially since they were likely sitting in the grassy brook area below a massive rock outcropping that dominates the area).

Jesus rejoiced with Peter. There must have been love and pleasure in his voice as he reminded Peter that he couldn't really take credit for the insight, but they could all surely give thanks. Jesus received Peter's confession with a loving grace and promised him a significant place in the mission of the church. That is precisely what Jesus will do in response to your confession of faith too.

You could protest. You might say. "Pastor, those are nice words, but you know Peter was special. He was the rock! Peter was a man of deep, abiding faith, who courageously followed Jesus and preached the gospel. I have days when I don't even know if I believe, and I definitely don't always know what it means for me to have Jesus as my Lord. Peter understood, and Peter followed Jesus faithfully, heart and soul. I waver. Some days I'm so tentative nobody would know I'd ever heard of God's love.

"I misunderstand things. I'm ashamed of my behavior, more often than I'd like to admit. When I look back at some of the stances I've taken toward others—especially those different from me in obvious ways—I'm so embarrassed I don't want to talk about it. So

Jesus' response to Peter doesn't really pertain to me. Peter and I are just nothing alike.''

But if you made such a protest, I would say to you, "You don't know Peter very well; you're more like him than you realize.''

Jesus, with an affectionate twinkle in his eye, had just finished telling Peter that he, Jesus, would build his church on this marvelous, rock-solid stance of faith. What did Peter do next? According to Matthew, Jesus began to tell his disciples about the impending events in Jerusalem, where he would suffer and die, and then be raised on the third day. Peter, confident of himself following his insight and Jesus' ensuing approval, took Jesus aside and said, "God forbid. Don't do it!'' Jesus stared at him with a look harder than any Peter would ever see again and growled, "Get behind me, Satan.'' From church pillar to evil incarnate, in one fell swoop.

Peter's first confession, earnest and heartfelt as it was, was no more profound or complete than yours or mine. If someone here this morning has recently taken step in responding to Jesus—perhaps at a Bible camp or retreat or with the encouragement of a friend—then you will most likely experience the same sort of nose-dive that Peter did. You will probably discover that the roots of your faith are still pretty shallow, that they are easily dislodged and need time to grow and deepen.

So what did Jesus do with Peter? Did he harangue him and say, "Well, it looks like that great confession of yours wasn't worth so much after all, was it, Peter?'' No, he didn't. He stayed with Peter, he taught him and nurtured him.

Now, to Peter's credit, he hung in there too. By the time of Jesus' arrest, Peter had recovered some of his equilibrium, so when the soldiers came, Peter jumped up, grabbed a sword, and was going to fight them off. Jesus stopped him cold. Peter had insisted, "I will always be loyal to you.'' But Jesus answered quietly, "Peter, you aren't going to be able to keep that promise.'' Peter said, "Yes I will!'' A few short hours later, a frightened Peter found himself saying, "I don't know him. I'm not one of them. I don't even know the man.'' Then that fateful cockcrow pierced his ear, and Jesus' sorrowful eyes pierced his soul. He must have felt a desolation beyond description.

If anyone here thinks she or he has let Jesus down, has failed our Lord, has flunked God's loyalty test, be assured that none of us has flopped as badly as Peter. What were those around Peter thinking? "Ha, look at Mr. High and Mighty now''; "Yeah, Peter thought he was the rock. Looks more like a pile of gravel to me''; "Well, if that's how Christians react under pressure, God help the church"; "Jesus thought he could make something out of Peter, build his church with guys like him. Looks like he was wrong about that." Peter would have been the first one to agree with those mutterings. A pastor I knew once wrote an autobiography and entitled it, "Heart of an Eagle, Feet of a Chicken." Peter probably would have accepted that description of himself—or worse. But Jesus didn't.

How does Jesus deal with you when you've failed abysmally? Well, what did he do for Peter? The last encounter we know between Peter and Jesus (familiar to most of you) finds Jesus asking, "Peter, do you love me?" He didn't say, "Peter, are you going to do better this time?" or "Peter, have you got your act together now?" or "Peter, give me one good reason why I should give you another chance?" He simply said, "Peter, do you love me?" "Lord, you know I do," responded Peter. "Then feed my sheep, Peter, tend my lambs."

Peter hung in there. He stayed with Jesus, stayed with the other disciples, even in his self-loathing and shame. He asked for forgiveness. Jesus never even hesitated. He told him once again that despite all the failures, despite the goofs, despite the impetuous mistakes, he would still use Peter as a building block in his kingdom. Peter, failure-filled Peter, was entrusted with the care and keeping of God's children and continued to be loved and empowered by his Lord.

So what will God do with you? What will God do with me? If Peter is any indication at all, then despite your failures and foibles, despite my weaknesses and waverings, regardless of our shallowness and betrayals, if we will hang in there and continue to love our Lord ("stay on the vine," in Jesus' words), then he will entrust us with the best that he has. Not only will God forgive you. Not only will God stay with you. This same God will entrust and employ you in the greatest enterprise this world has ever known: the care and keeping of the church.

It isn't somebody else; it isn't somebody better; it isn't somebody more gifted; it isn't somebody more holy. It is you and I who are entrusted with the hopes and dreams of the church. Whether in Sunday school or congregational worship, help for the homeless or a global missions project, or a word of trust and hope to a friend, our Lord has entrusted the task not to "somebody else" but to you and me.

I don't know how you are this morning. I don't know what particular hurts and hopes you bring with you. But whether you are on a high from getting closer to Jesus recently or frustrated with the realization of how shallow your faith really is; whether you're excited about some recent faithful service you've rendered or despondent over a silent betrayal of God; whether you are enthused over renewal in your life or forlorn over a repeated problem you can't seem to lick—whatever your particular circumstances today, Peter has probably been there before you. Jesus has shown us how he responds. So hang in there—you are loved. Stay close—you are needed. Turn over your sins and your sorrows, share your joys and your dreams—you are entrusted with God's work.

Somebody once asked a teacher, "How long will it take you to teach my child?" The teacher said, "It all depends. It takes three weeks to grow a radish, and a lot of years to grow an oak tree. What do you want your child to be?" It takes years to grow into oak-tree proportions as a Christian. Throughout those years, there will be times when you and I will look like Peter the rock. There will be other times when we will look more like Peter the pile of gravel. We constitute some pretty odd building material, but hang in there, and encourage one another. For we have been entrusted with the greatest treasure in creation, as faithful stewards— servants, caretakers—of God's church. God be with us all.

R.J.F.

FOURTH SUNDAY AFTER THE EPIPHANY
To Those Who Mourn
MATTHEW 5:1-12

Jesus said, "Blessed are those who mourn, for they will be comforted."

Not long ago I spent an evening with some close friends whose daughter was pregnant, for whom marriage to the father would probably be the worst of all possible answers and for whom there are no good responses at the moment. They are mourning.

I attended a funeral this past week; that death left a gaping hole in the lives of the family and friends. They are mourning. A little while back I spent part of a day with a young woman who had just been divorced by her husband; she was scared, she is scarred, she was bewildered. She is mourning.

Are you among those who mourn today—who grieve the loss of something or someone precious? If you have lost someone you love in these past few months, you don't have to think twice; you are mourning. If you've suffered deep disappointment or are going through a wrenching separation—whether in family, friendship, job, or even at church—then you too are mourning. In fact, I believe that on any given Sunday a large number of us are mourning. You may be among the mourners today.

What if you aren't mourning? Some of us would say, "Well, actually my life is going pretty well, about as well as I can ever remember." To that I say, "That's wonderful, and I pray that it continues." But we do not only mourn for our own losses or for those close to us. We mourn for our world and for the grief that strikes our neighbor, wherever he or she might be. We read the newspapers and watch TV news. Night after night we sense the deep grief and futile questions in the face of tragic death; we turn away sadly from bloodshed in Europe or the Middle East; we shy away from the carnage in Central America or South Africa; and we are reminded of the seemingly interminable warfare between groups of Christians in Ireland. We almost skim over the reports of violent crimes in our nation or community, but we cannot avoid the realization that there is great pain in our world. We mourn. How could we feel the pain, hear the cries, sense the despair, or come to terms with our own sin—and not mourn?

Yet some would tell us that mourning is weak, unproductive, or foolish. Throughout history some men and women have held to a philosophy that says you can't afford to be overly sensitive. They contend that one should never be too concerned with the plight of other people, especially those on the margins of life, because it will hurt too much. They fear becoming overwhelmed by their grief and claim one person can't do that much good anyway.

It's a common temptation. Haven't you ever thought, "How can I get worked up about every hurt in the world? I don't even know where some of these countries are" or "I only have so much emotional energy; how can you expect me to care about it all?" Haven't you had thoughts like that? I have. One look at the daily news makes it clear that none of us can carry the woes of the world on our own shoulders. Although the answer is not to pull back or withdraw in the face of problems too big to fix quickly, we are repeatedly tempted to say, "I don't care; it's not my problem."

This isn't new. In Jesus' time, when the world was fraught with suffering too, there was a popular school of thought called Stoicism. The Stoics maintained that one should not grieve—should not mourn—in the face of loss. The best response, they said, was self-control. Stuff the feelings inside, and if possible numb yourself into not caring.

A few decades after Jesus, there was a prominent thinker by the name of Epictetus. Among other things (as a logical extension of Stoic thought) this famous man said: "Love your wife and children, but not so much that it will hurt when they die." That is an abhorrent statement, but we still carry traces of it with us.

When I was in seminary, one professor gave us this advice (which I didn't accept then and still don't today), "Don't get too close to the people in the congregation, because if you do, then when the day comes for you to take another call, the separation will hurt too much for you and for them." That's terrible advice.

Yet I can't begin to count the times I've heard someone say, "I've been hurt too badly this time; I won't ever make myself that vulnerable again." It's a thought that may have crossed your mind too. It's nothing but a modern version of Stoicism: Since grieving hurts, I will avoid getting close enough to others to experience pain at their loss. We know better, but the temptation remains. And, although I think we are improving, the phrases we use at funerals betray a similar tendency. We speak about family members "holding up" or "breaking down," as if containing or hiding grief is somehow good, while expressing grief is somehow bad.

Now and then, as a Lutheran of Norwegian heritage, I think my ancestors, the Vikings, got mixed up with the Stoics somewhere along the line. We have a strong tendency toward silent, stoic responses to pain and loss. It is hard for us to mourn; we almost seem to think it is a bad or un-Christian thing to do. But it isn't. Jesus himself was described as a man of sorrows, acquainted with grief. Not that he was some morose moper. He had a sense of humor; he enjoyed things like the wedding celebration at Cana, and he brightened the lives around him. I'm convinced that he had a ready smile and a twinkle in his eye. But he also wept. He wept over Jerusalem. He wept at the death of his friend Lazarus.

When Paul tells us to rejoice with those who rejoice and weep with those who weep, he could well have had Jesus in mind as his model. The strange truth is that when we say yes to Jesus, we say yes to a life of increased joy and of increased mourning. Anyone who tells you that Christian life is all sweetness and smiles is dreadfully mistaken.

Jesus calls us to mourn. His one command to us is "Love one another, as I have loved you." As he spins out what it means for us to love one another, we discover that we are to bear one another's burdens, to care deeply for and about this world, and to extend his love to the farthest reaches of the globe. From the starving child in the sub-Sahara to the lonely widower down the street, we are called to care. When we care, we will do some mourning. Jesus calls us to be deeply engaged in life, to be fully involved with those around us.

A man named James Reid once said, "The saddest thing in all of God's world is not a soul that sorrows. It is a heart so dull that it is incapable of feeling grief at all, a heart so selfish that nothing but what touches its comfort and its ease could move it to a twinge of feeling, for to sorrow means to love. Mourning is but another and deeper side of loving."

It's not surprising that Jesus would say, "Blessed are those who mourn." Mourning is a by-product of loving. The only way to avoid mourning in your life is to stop loving. Vern Bittner, a pastor and counselor who lived a terribly difficult childhood, has written a book entitled *Breaking Free*. The first line of the book is this: "Most of my life I have been afraid to love freely for fear of losing." He goes on to say, "Little did I know that the answer to changing my life did not lie in learning how to protect myself from life. Rather the answer was in learning how to become strong enough to let a bit more of life in!" Bittner knows that mourning hurts. Loss is painful; if you care, it hurts even more. But he had finally discovered what Jesus meant when he said that those who mourn "will be comforted."

Jesus didn't mean comfort*able*, wherein things go smoothly and easily so that you have less pain or stress than the next person. Instead he promised that we will be fortified with God's grace and strength. Rather than pull us out of the turmoil of life, Jesus joins us. Sometimes, rather than lessening the pain of grief, he strengthens us. In fact, one commentator said that although Jesus' words certainly contain an element of sympathy and gentleness, we'd be pretty close to the mark if we translated them, "Blessed are they who mourn, for they shall be made strong."

I have a little plaque on my desk. It simply reads, "Sometimes the Lord calms the storm, but sometimes he lets the storm rage and calms his child." God doesn't want to take us out of the world or to anesthetize us against pain. God calls us to live with one another, and knows what that means—both joy and sorrow. If we allow it, God will comfort us when we mourn. God comforts us in a host of ways, and some of you can bear witness to that far better than I can. God hears our prayers, responds to us out of love, and (perhaps best of all) uses us to comfort one another. You and I are not only comforted when we mourn, we are granted the high privilege of being able to participate as God comforts those around us. This is an essential element in being part of the body of Christ—to enfold one another in times of mourning. You do that. It is sheer joy to see you comforting one another with the comfort of God.

Yet perhaps the deepest comfort is not anything that happens today or tomorrow but what has been called God's ultimate comfort. In the end—through the promise and power of Jesus' resurrection—God will receive us into the kingdom. For you who mourn today, our Lord Jesus gently promises to fortify you here and now with his grace and strength. Yet beyond that is his final word of comfort: the restoration and reconciliation of all his people in a heaven in which he promises to wipe away every tear from our eyes.

When you mourn—and, oh, I hope you love enough to mourn—I pray that you hear and embrace the promise of our Lord, who says, "Blessed are those—no, blessed are *you*—when you mourn, for you will be comforted."

R.J.F.

FIFTH SUNDAY AFTER THE EPIPHANY

Let Your Light Shine . . . in Weakness, Fear, and Trembling
MATTHEW 5:13-20

(This sermon was preached as part of a pulpit exchange in a nearby congregation, on a Sunday designated as Evangelism Sunday.)

You have come today, as you regularly do, to worship God. You have come to pray, to listen to Scripture, to sing hymns of praise, to be reassured by the faith and presence of your neighbor, and some of you may have an added reason today—a little curiosity about this new visiting preacher from a neighboring congregation. "What will he be like? Does he really have that funny quirk my friend says he has? What can he say that will make a difference in my life?"

I too have come today to worship, to pray, to sing praises, to listen to Scripture, to be reassured by the presence and faith of my neighbor. I too have come today with the added questions, What do they expect to hear from me? What kind of congregation is this? How does the gospel manifest itself in this place? Then too I am here fighting the terrible temptation to somehow try to impress you, to leave you with the impression that "that Rick Foss can really preach."

This temptation to "let my light shine to the glory of me instead of the glory of God" isn't a new problem for preachers. Even Paul had to deal with it. Anybody who says, "I didn't come to you preaching lofty words of wisdom" is likely to have tried just that in the past and realized how wrong it was. A preacher who says, "I decided to know nothing among you except Jesus Christ and him crucified," has surely tried all the glossy gimmicks and nuanced arguments, only to find them wanting. A man who says, "I was with you in weakness and in much fear and trembling," has discovered the hollowness of chutzpah and how anemic is the "power" of positive thinking.

He has learned that God uses earthen vessels—vessels whose knees shake, whose stomachs churn, and who despair over ever finding the right words for hurting and hopeful people. A pastor who says, " . . . that your faith might not rest in the wisdom of men but in the power of God," has been led to the heart of the gospel, for it isn't the eloquence of the man or woman in the pulpit that counts, nor is it the urbane manner, dramatic flair, or astute insights; instead, it is the power and promise of the God to whom he or she bears witness.

John the Baptist said of Jesus, "He must increase and I must decrease." If that is true for John, it is true for every preacher, prophet, or pointer-to-God who has come along since, even as we go about "letting our light shine." Paul says, "I preach in weakness, and in fear and trembling." Does that fit your image of Paul? That bold, fearless missionary, going to jail for his faith, standing up to any and all. Yet that's what he says: "I preach in weakness, and in fear and trembling."

What is a preacher? My daughter studied cello for years with an elderly woman who was blunt, loving, irascible, opinionated—and a peerless musician. She said many things I'll remember from the hours I spent in her home during the lessons, but among my most cherished is this: "A performer uses the music to play (or display) their instrument; but a musician uses the instrument to play the music." A performer in the pulpit would try to use the gospel to play his or her instruments (gifts of voice, poise, eloquence, scholarship, etc.); but a preacher in the pulpit uses whatever gifts have been given (and works faithfully to develop them) to "play the music," to share and spin out the incredible message of our Lord Jesus. The preacher uses the given instruments to tell us again and again, with infinite variations on the theme, that the God who made us loves us, calling us to be God's own beloved children, now and forever.

Every once in a while someone will say to me, "I don't see how you can stand up in front of all of us and preach; I'd be so nervous and scared." The truth is, I am too. If the day ever comes when the prospect of preaching doesn't make me a little nervous, then I'll know something is dreadfully wrong. Phillips Brooks once warned preachers never to feel equal to their task, as a way of reminding us that God works in and through our weaknesses, as well as in our supposed strengths. Reuel Howe put it well in his book *Partners in Preaching*:

> The preacher must learn to preach out of the weakness of his [or her] understanding of the gospel and of life, as well as out of his strengths. Then people who are not predisposed toward him may find him to be more authentic. Many people find the pretensions, assumed power, and answers of preachers laughable. They might take the preacher more seriously if he would be honest about what he has to offer, namely, that sometimes he has little to offer, and can only stand humbly before the deep human questions with the hope that God will be able to speak and act out of his honest weakness."[1]

Whatever message the preacher has is given. Whatever skills the preacher has are gifts. However open and exposed the preacher may become, the focus is on Christ and our common humanity before our God. A Dale Carnegie course is not the proper preparation for preaching; confession and forgiveness is. A powerful, self-assured image isn't the essence of a preacher; humble obedience and a trust in the greatness of God is.

You know the difference. It is fun to be entertained. We all enjoy a good show. But week after week that would pale, and you would be sated. You are truly blessed if, week in and week out, your pastors live among you, loving and being loved, lifting up the cross of Christ and saying in every way they know, "Behold the Lamb of God, who takes away the sin of the world." It may be entertaining on a particular Sunday, or it may not be, but you will encounter Christ, even in the midst of the weakness, fear, and trembling going on in the pulpit and in the pew.

Jesus says you are "the salt of the earth, a city on a hill, and the light of the world." Yet as you follow Jesus, living out those magnificent images, the words of Reuel Howe might be profitably paraphrased for each of us: As Christians, we must learn to follow Jesus out of the weakness of our understanding of the gospel and of life, as well as out of our strengths. Then people who are not predisposed toward us may find us to be more authentic. Many people find the pretensions, assumed authority, and easy answers of church folk laughable. They might take us Christians more seriously if we would be honest about what we have to offer, namely, that sometimes we have little to offer and can only stand humbly before the deep human questions with the hope that God will be able to speak and act out of our honest weakness.

You don't need to be superconfident to ask your neighbor to come with you to worship. You can do it faithfully in weakness, and in fear and trembling. You don't need to be brimming with slick ideas of how to get through to seventh graders to teach Sunday school. You can do it in weakness, and in fear and trembling. You don't need to be comfortably sure of what to say in order to visit a fellow member in the hospital. You can do it in weakness, and in fear and trembling. You don't have to be financially secure, guaranteed of a surplus for life, to be a steward who tithes. You can faithfully begin in weakness, and in fear and trembling. You don't need to feel sure of your faith to begin to pray regularly for others. You can stumble over the words, praying in weakness, and in fear and trembling.

And if you do—when you do—you will find not that you miraculously have done everything perfectly, amazing people with your skills. But you will find that your Lord Jesus has been with you, and that somehow the words you stumbled over—the awkward condolence, the wavering word of love, the blurted invitation— found a home in another human heart.

In Ole Rolvaag's epic novel *Giants in the Earth,* we are told of a traveling preacher who stopped at a remote cabin one night. The people in the area gathered themselves into a small congregation, and he led them in worship. As he left, he felt awful, berating himself for not managing to find soothing words and polished prayers for the people; he felt that once more he had failed. But Rolvaag takes us back to the little cabin, where we discover that "something happened," and that, one after another, the people realized they had been deeply moved by the presence of God through that faithful, faltering parson.

On this Evangelism Sunday, we are reminded that we are to "let our light shine" as we reach out with the gospel of Jesus Christ. I don't know precisely what shape that will take for you, what specific opportunities God will lay in your path, or to whom he will lead you. But I pray that as you reach out to those around you, it will not be with absolute self-assurance or an unflappable facade but with weakness, fear and trembling, because then, by the grace of God, "something will happen" in the lives of those you touch.

R.J.F.

---

1. Reuel L. Howe, *Partners in Preaching* (New York: Seabury, 1967), 85.

SIXTH SUNDAY AFTER THE EPIPHANY
You Have Heard It Said . . . But I Say to You
MATTHEW 5:20-37

Our Gospel text for today is not one that many pastors would select as their favorite preaching passage. One of the problems is that Jesus touches on several of the most sensitive, complex, and controversial issues known to humankind, making this a daunting text for any but the most oblivious or foolhardy. But perhaps an even greater problem is that our text is composed of a rapid-fire series of commentaries by Jesus directed to his disciples. Those of us trying to overhear can very easily misconstrue them.

I assume you have all had the misfortune of wandering into the middle of a conversation and completely misunderstanding what is being said because you missed the first part of the exchange. Some of you may have had a misunderstanding while talking with someone of a cultural background different from yours. You may even have had the embarrassment of mistranslating, as one airline did a few years ago when, thinking it was promoting its new leather seats and the airplanes' comfort, enjoined thousands of Spanish-speaking people to "Fly our airline and ride naked."

Well, sometimes the problem is with the speaker; sometimes with the hearer. But misunderstanding is particularly easy when someone is speaking to those with whom they've shared a great deal of common experience, and then another listens in without benefit of the mutual background. It could be a child overhearing a conversation between parents, which she badly misconstrues; or it could be us, two thousand years later and half a world removed, listening in as Jesus talks to his disciples. This is exactly what we are doing today—listening in on an intimate conversation. If we superimpose our own culture and experience onto the translated words, we are likely to draw conclusions that are far from the original intent.

At first glance, it looks like Jesus is instituting a get-tough policy. He appears to be cracking down on the moral codes, tightening up the strictures, saying in effect, "If you thought the rules were rigid before, just wait 'til I get through tightening them up!" But that doesn't fit with what we know of Jesus' life and teachings.

Jesus was attacking what might be called loophole theology. He was zeroing in on the way some of the religious folk of his day had twisted the intent of the law for their own purposes, with no regard for others. He was addressing a situation in which people were very cleverly using the letter of the law to do whatever they wished while covering themselves so they would be blameless under the literal rubric of those laws. The response to God's law had been distorted into "Make sure they can't pin it on you," "Take full advantage of the rules," "Play the system for all it's worth," or "Look out for Number One." Jesus exposed the sham, calling them to return to the original purpose of God's laws, which was to cause them to live together in peace and harmony under God's benevolent reign. He said, in essence, the response should be "Care," "Reach out to others," "Do what is right," or "Love one another."

Our predilection for "loophole living" is an ongoing problem. You know how frustrating it can be when someone finds a loophole, so that completely unethical action—contrary to the true intent of the law—can be carried out with impunity, to the detriment of others. A few years ago there was a scandal in our community. A number of elderly people answered a knock on the door to find a stranger telling them, "I have deed and title to this house. I own it; you'll have to leave." It turns out they had each gotten behind on their property taxes, some without even realizing it. A couple of partners had found a loophole that enabled them to buy the homes for the amount of the taxes due, resell them immediately at a very high profit to someone else (who may or may not have known what was being perpetrated), who then presented the deed and eviction notice to the elderly person. None of those people had any idea that their homes had even been up for sale. Due to a loophole in the law, the entire process was completed before they had any inkling of a problem. All totally within the letter of the law, but certainly not consonant with its intent.

That sort of loophole living can happen in the church too. You might say, "I'm a good Christian; I'm in church every Sunday, so don't lay a guilt trip on me about caring for the less fortunate." Or I might contend, "I'm an ordained pastor and work hard for God; don't bother me with scrupulous details of how I ought to treat people. Obviously I'm righteous and loving, or I wouldn't be a pastor!" But things aren't always what they seem. In our Gospel text today, Jesus points out several glaring examples of religious loophole living, and his warning still packs a punch for us.

Jesus said he came to fulfill the law. He came as the culmination to the law in its original intent: to establish health and wholeness among God's people. Over time, it had been twisted into a tool for self-gain. So Jesus says (if you'll allow me a little preacher's license to expand it), "You know you shouldn't kill; but you think nothing of your anger." (There are two distinct words for *anger* in Greek: one to indicate a quick anger that is soon dissipated; a second to denote an anger that is nursed over a period of time, more like a grudge. The second word is the one Jesus uses.) "You insult one another, you demean your brother, you belittle your sister, you encourage your anger and hold it against one another, and then you say, 'I haven't killed anyone; I'm blameless before the law.'

"But I say to you that if you want to be judged by whether or not you are faithful to God's law, then you will find that insulting, hurting, demeaning, or ignoring your neighbor will be just as damning as killing him, because in killing him you merely finish the job you began with your anger.

"That's not the only havoc you wreak with your loophole theology. Look at the way you treat your women, the way you respond to your wives." (It should be noted that, in such a patriarchal society, Jesus' primary audience would often be men). "You know you aren't supposed to commit adultery. So, when you decide you're tired of your wife and want someone else, you say, 'I'll get rid of her and marry the other one, but I'll do it under the rubric of the law.' So you give her a nicely inscribed certificate of divorce, as prescribed by the letter of the law, and say 'That's the end of my responsibility. Now I can stand blameless before God.'

"But I say to you that you are wrong. If you want to be judged by the law of God, then you have to remember that the law was given so that we could live together in love and care. And if you think you've found a nice loophole for adultery, think again. You may have found a technicality, but God isn't impressed. You have put yourself, and your victimized wife, at odds with what God has intended for you."

Today divorce has touched most of us, one way or another. I cannot ever call it good, although there are times when it is preferable to other, more destructive, alternatives. But it is always a manifestation of our brokenness; it is never a time to stand smugly before God as an innocent party who has followed the letter of the of the law. It is, instead, a time to stand before God as one who is bruised and broken by a severed relationship, one who asks for and receives forgiveness for whatever part one has played, regardless of who was "mostly at fault." It is only in terms of the reconciling power of God's forgiveness that we can deal with divorce and remarriage, not in terms of who was right and who was wrong or whether we followed some set of rules exactly.

But Jesus isn't through. He says, in effect, "Those were exhibit A, and exhibit B. Would you like another example? You know you aren't supposed to swear falsely, to perjure yourself. But you've found a slick loophole here, too. You all say that an oath should be binding, but no more binding than the thing it is sworn by. In other words, your word is dependent upon the worth of the collateral. So if you swear by a minor thing, like a hair on your head, it wouldn't be as binding as if you swore by your whole head. Thus you dicker to try to get others to accept as small an oath as possible from you.

"Then, as if that weren't bad enough, you say that an oath is only truly binding if "the Lord wills," and when you want to break your word, you simply claim that the Lord didn't will it. Then you maintain that you are righteous and honest before God, even as you find ways to be dishonest with your neighbor."

What had happened here, as with the other examples, was that the law designed to encourage truthfulness was being cleverly used to foster deceit. So Jesus says in effect, "Just forget the technical jargon and the fancy doublespeak, and give your word: yes or no."

Do you see what is going on? Jesus wasn't trying to tighten the screws on life. Instead, in these examples (and he could surely find others, for the folks of his day or for us) Jesus was saying, "Return to the original purpose of God's law; don't make a mockery of them. If you know the laws better than others, don't use that to take advantage of them while protesting your innocence. Instead, use your knowledge to serve, to care, and to love, with wisdom and compassion."

If you or I would pursue this conversation with Jesus, sooner or later each of us must inevitably say, "Lord, we are all guilty; who can be saved?" And Jesus would say to us what he said to his first disciples: "With men it is impossible, but with God all things are possible," which is a shortcut for such responses as "Come to me, all you who are weary and heavy-laden, and I will give you rest" or "I forgive you, neither do I condemn you; go and sin no more."

Someone once observed W. C. Fields reading the Bible. Astonished, the person asked, "What are you doing?" "Looking for loopholes," growled Fields.

The poet T. S. Eliot (who probably gleaned his insight looking in a mirror) had us pegged right regarding the way we look for loopholes, the way we want the system to take responsibility for our actions, and the way we so glibly evade the needs of others by pointing to the rules. He wrote, "They constantly try to escape from the darkness outside and within, by dreaming of systems so perfect that no one will need to be good."

But Jesus calls us to be good—to keep our word, to love our spouse, to care for our neighbor. As we struggle to do it, he continues to love and forgive us. I don't know when these issues will hit home for you, but when they do, I pray you hear the loving (albeit with a cutting edge) words of Jesus, "You have heard it said . . . but I say to you . . . " Then, however he may finish that sentence, one way or another he will take you back to the old, old law of God: "I say to you . . . love one another, as I have first loved you."

R.J.F.

SEVENTH SUNDAY AFTER THE EPIPHANY
Pray for Them All?
MATTHEW 5:38-48

Of all the things Jesus asks of us, one of the easiest would seem to be that we should pray. After all, we can pray privately as well as publicly; it doesn't cost any money; no prerequisite for knowledge or study needs to be met before we can pray. It almost seems too easy. But then, to quote from an old Gilbert and Sullivan line, "things are seldom what they seem."

Jesus tells us, in our Gospel text for today, to "pray for those who persecute you." I'm not sure I want to do that. Even at the very low level of persecution most of us experience, we aren't prone to pray for those who do the persecuting. What if you or I had been in the place of the hostages released from the Middle East? Would we have found it within us to pray for our captors? Or the political leaders who set the policies that led to our captivity and torture?

Jesus quietly says, "Pray for those who persecute you." His words are spelled out more fully in the words to Timothy (1 Timothy 2:1ff.), "First of all, I urge that supplications, prayers, intercessions and thanksgivings be made for everyone, for kings and all who are in high positions." That's pretty clear—we are to pray for everyone, including those in power over us, and even those who persecute us. That's not hard to understand. But, recalling Mark Twain's comment (that it wasn't the parts of the Bible he didn't understand that gave him trouble; it was the parts he did understand that were the problem), it may not be so easy to do.

For whom do you pray? Family members? Surely. Friends? Certainly. Those who can influence your life? Probably. Acquaintances whom you know to be hurting? Most likely. Who else? Many of us, I hope, include in our prayers the dozens of people who serve us daily (whose names we may not even know): grocery clerks, bank tellers, road repair crews, flight attendants, mail carriers, busboys, custodians, and countless others who make our lives more manageable and enjoyable. We can pray for people in other parts of the world or for groups of people in particular need or turmoil, even if we don't know them by name. You may pray regularly for the suffering, the hungry, refugees, those embroiled in war, the hospitalized or elderly, both close to home and around the world.

We may find it a little harder to pray for those who are in competition with us, whether in career, music, or sports; it is even more difficult to pray for those who are in competition with those we love, especially our children. (This is really hard! How many of you pray for the opponents before a game in which your child is playing? How often do you pray for the person who is competing with your husband, wife, or child for a job?) It is also hard to pray for those who have hurt us and are likely to hurt us again. Whether the wounds they inflict are intentional or not, it is not easy to pray for such people, who may be your boss, employee, neighbor, teachers, student, or public official. Yet this is precisely what we are called to do.

Jesus said, "Love your enemies and pray for those who persecute you." The words in 1 Timothy 2 explicitly call us to pray for "everyone, [even] for kings and for all who are in high places." I say "even" because at the time the letter to Timothy was written, most kings and rulers were hostile to Christians; they persecuted those who believed in Jesus. This admonition to Timothy was not a matter of saying something like, "Look, the government leaders may not be perfect, they they're really on our side in the long run, so keep them in your prayers." Not at all. They were mostly cruel, brutal men who tortured and killed a lot of Christians and insisted that they themselves rather than God were to be worshiped. Yet we read of the early church leaders repeatedly saying, in effect, "We will not worship you, we will worship God alone; but we will pray for you and respect your authority to govern."

At this point, I really resonate with Mark Twain: It is clear to me what they are saying, but I don't want to do it! It isn't so hard in this nation. I often disagree with the president or other elected officials, but at least I believe they are acting, for the most part, with good intentions and motives, and they certainly don't spend much time persecuting me for my faith in God. I have little trouble praying for men and women in public office, whether or not I agree politically with them; you probably can do this easily too. But God's word isn't limited to the rulers in this country. When was the last time you prayed for Fidel Castro or Saddam Hussein or the death squads in El Salvador? This is not a terribly appealing task; they don't show up much on the lists of the prayer fellowship groups in our churches.

My first impulse is to find a loophole, a way out. I want to say, "Well, what does it mean to 'pray for' them? If I can pray that they be turned around or thrown out of power or rendered harmless, I guess I can do that? But beyond that . . . ?"

However, while Jesus' words ("love and pray") are brief enough to leave us room to wiggle around in our interpretation, the text in 1 Timothy 2:1ff. pulls us up short. Four separate words are used to cover the way in which we ought to pray for those leaders. However you translate those four Greek words into English, two things are clear: first, they are intended to span a broad spectrum of prayer; and second, thanksgiving is included.

Why? When it was clear then, and so clear now, that some people are evil, why? When they knew then about Christians being torn apart by lions; when we read now of terrorist bombings or senseless slaughter, why? Why does God ask us to pray for them all?

Jesus says, "so that you may be children of your father in heaven." In one sense, we can infer that he means this is one of the things we do if we want God to be pleased with us, as children; in another sense (drawing inference from Jesus' words of summation in verse 48, "be perfect, therefore, as your heavenly father is perfect"), we can infer that God prays for all these people, and if we want to emulate God as a child emulates his or her parent, then we need to pray for them all too.

But why would God want to or lead us to pray for them? Again, 1 Timothy 2 makes it more explicit: "God . . . desires everyone to be saved and to come to a knowledge of the truth." They are all

God's children, and God's desire for mercy and salvation is far wider than you or I can easily comprehend. A favorite Bible passage for many of us is the portrait of God that Jesus paints in Luke 15. Do you remember? It is a magnificent triptych of our loving God who seeks out the lost sheep, the lost coin, and the lost son. Jesus unveils a God who searches out the straying, seeks the lost, and waits with patient love for the rebellious. There is something wonderfully consoling about that picture, especially when I mature enough to see myself among the straying, lost, or rebellious. But now, by asking us to pray for even the most repugnant of the alienated, Jesus is asking us to join him—to be part of his incredible mercy—in searching, seeking, and awaiting the waylaid of the world.

I don't know who repulses you. Maybe it is a foreign leader; perhaps people of another nation, creed, or race; it may be the rich; for some it is the transients; or someone who makes life harder for you. Whoever it may be, God has a word for you—and me—about them. It's the same word Jesus spoke having told us to love the Lord our God with all our heart, soul, and mind, and our neighbor as ourselves. Do you recall? The lawyer said, "Yes, of course; but just who is my neighbor?" And Jesus told him the parable of the good Samaritan (or, if you will, the good Libyan, the good Iraqi, the good Cuban, the good alcoholic transient, the good inmate, or the good AIDS patient), who was a member of the most rejected group in Jewish consciousness. He made his point: no one is beyond God's concern. No one falls outside the realm of those for whom we are to care and pray.

But just what do I pray for? I can't believe that I must pray for a thief to be successful or my enemy to triumph in court over me or even for the tolerance to agree with someone when he or she is wrong or the compliance to meekly accept behavior that is contrary to God's will. On the other hand, it isn't appropriate to pray that God will reform them to be just like me or to make them see eye to eye with my views.

I wouldn't presume to tell you exactly what to pray for with regard to your enemies or persecutors. But I do know this: We must pray that God will work in their lives, that they respond to God's will, and that they will be reconciled with God. We can further pray that they be reconciled to us (and we to them) as children of the same heavenly Father; and finally, we need to pray that God will work in our lives to change us in whatever way God sees fit, since you or I might be part of the problem too.

What good will it do if I pray for my competitor, an oppressive ruler, an obstinate neighbor, or an alienated and hurtful family member? What difference will it make? I don't know, not in detail. I doubt that my prayer tonight will alter Fidel Castro's view of the world; but on the other hand, I trust that God will hear my prayer and take it seriously. I believe that God is at work in human history, even if not in the bludgeonlike manner I'd sometimes like to see, so I will add my prayers to the divine work.

I also know that my prayer for one whom I mistrust or dislike will change me. I have discovered that it is terribly difficult to hate someone for whom I am praying. In ways I cannot fully envision or articulate, my prayer, and my subsequent actions and attitudes, will make a difference.

But the question of the results or effectiveness of our prayer is not the issue. We are not asked to guarantee, or even anticipate, the results: we are "only" asked to pray. Beyond that, God will have to (and does) assume responsibility. This is reminiscent of coaching children in sports. They are usually much more concerned with the results—the score—than with the tasks at hand. One of the hardest things is to convince them that if they concentrate on practicing the fundamental tasks at hand rather than speculating on results, they will be much better off.

Unfortunately, we adults aren't much different. I play golf. The worst thing I can do is to begin to speculate on the final score while I'm in the middle of the round. As long as I concentrate on hitting the ball (which is really the only thing one can do to affect the results anyway) things go pretty well. But if I start to think about my score, and what I need to do on the remaining holes to produce a particular result, I'm in big trouble.

You and I could choose to speculate on what will happen if we do or don't pray for any particular person or group; we could focus our energies on debating whether or not our prayers will accomplish anything, but then we would have missed the point at best or been unfaithful at worst. God simply says, "Pray for those who persecute you . . . pray for them all." I still want to protest, "Pray for them all?" But I cannot escape it, and neither can you.

I ask you today to search your hearts. Find those—nearby and far away—for whom you have the hardest time praying. Make a list. Then each day add one of them to your prayers. Don't add them all at once; it would be just too easy to slide over them without any real attention. Just add one a day, with special consideration for that one, praying that both they and you will be reconciled to God, who is the Father of us all. Perhaps in some other place today, another preacher will ask the same thing, and someone will add you or me, or a group to which we belong, to their list; and God will be addressed on your behalf by the very person you have reluctantly added to your list today. Perhaps.

Who knows the results? Only God. But I know, and you know, what we have been commanded to do. As we live out our lives this week, let us pray—and pray for them all!

R.J.F.

EIGHTH SUNDAY AFTER THE EPIPHANY
Don't Be Overanxious
MATTHEW 6:24-34

"Don't worry" (NRSV). "Don't be anxious" (RSV). Whichever way you choose to translate the Greek word *merimnao* into English, you can't help but notice that Jesus repeats it five times in the space of a few short verses.

The sense of the word is "Don't be overanxious." As Rudolf Bultmann writes in Kittel's comprehensive dictionary of the New Testament:

> *In Matthew 6:25-34, there is an explicit discussion of this . . .*
> *self-concern in respect of the future. What makes a proper con-*
> *cern foolish is anxiety. Such anxiety is futile, for the future*
> *which they think they can provide for is not in their hands.*
> *[Jesus' words] in 6:27 refer mockingly to the fact that we can*
> *achieve ridiculously little by our worrying, much less procure*
> *for ourselves security. In any case, such worry is unnecessary;*
> *God has lifted it from his people. . . . While there is uncer-*
> *tainty in life, this uncertainty need not cause us anxiety; what-*
> *ever happens will be under God's control . . . We must make*
> *the lordship of God our first concern, and then anxiety about*
> *our life will wither away.*"[1]

In other words, don't be so concerned with life's results; rather, pay attention to your responsibilities and relationships for today. Live in the love of God, respond with compassion to the needs of your neighbor, and don't worry so much about the outcome of it all.

Roger L. Shinn, an outstanding theologian, has written an insightful little commentary simply entitled *The Sermon on the Mount*, consisting of fifteen brief sections. He arrives at our text for today, labels it "Trust and Anxiety," and begins the section with these words: "Here is the heart of the Sermon on the Mount. Here Jesus confronts life's deepest personal problem."[2]

Five times Jesus tells us, "Don't be overanxious!" Now, we need to be very clear about what he is not saying. He is not saying, "Don't plan ahead." He is not saying, "Don't prepare." He is not saying, "Don't be concerned; you shouldn't care so much about life." That's not it. Shinn puts it this way:

> *Several things Jesus clearly does not mean. He is not patting us on the back and saying, "Don't worry. Everything will come out all right." He knew things do not always turn out "all right." He is not saying that God will step in to correct all our follies and omissions. Sometimes he assumes a place for prudent foresight (cf. Luke 14:28-30). He is not saying that those who trust God will never be injured or persecuted. He has already told his followers to expect . . . persecution. He is not saying we should ignore food. He has bidden us to pray for daily bread and he has never criticized honest work. He is not saying that the lilies and the grass will live happily ever after. As he spoke those words, he probably thought of one of his favorite Old Testament books, which said: "The grass withers, the flower fades; but the word of our God will stand for ever" (Isaiah 40:8).[3]*

What Jesus does say is, "Don't be overanxious."

It is important here that we acknowledge the existence, and common occurrence, of anxiety disorders. Sometimes undue anxiety is the result (and symptom) of a medical illness involving our brain chemistry. Such illness is far more prevalent than we have realized; a recent study by the National Institute of Mental Health showed that "anxiety disorders are the most common psychiatric illnesses today, and that in a given six-month period, at least one out of twenty Americans will suffer from an anxiety disorder severe enough to be treated by a mental health professional."[4] As in the case of related depressive illnesses, an anxiety disorder is a medical (and treatable) illness, and no amount of cajoling or reassuring will be of significant help to one who suffers from it.

A person wishing to regain health in the face of such an illness needs the care of a good physician—an up-to-date psychiatrist or a competent psychopharmacologist, since the most effective treatment includes medicines. *You Mean I Don't Have to Feel This Way?* by Colette Dowling is one of many recent books that explain the chemical basis for such overanxiety. To put it bluntly, if your serotonin (or one of the other chemicals produced in the brain) is out of balance or in short supply, all the religious conviction or moral fiber in the world won't make you well. See a doctor.

But when we are physically well, we need to hear Jesus as he admonishes us not to be so wrapped up in trying to ensure and control the details of our future.

Perhaps the crucial point to recognize is that being overanxious about tomorrow is to be long on the desire to control and short on trust. In fact, it is our inordinate desire to control our lives—to control the future—that gives us so much trouble.

When the disciples asked Jesus about specifics of the future, he always put them off. He reminded them that the key is their relationship with him and others. The specific results will be a matter for God to worry about.

When does appropriate concern turn into overanxiety? How can you tell if you are "worrying too much"? Rabbi Edwin Friedman insists this is one of life's most important issues—how to be fully present to another human being, with compassion and love, without becoming enmeshed in the futile folly of overreactive, overanxious behavior. (He explores this issue in depth in his perceptive book, *Generation to Generation*, and I commend it to you for your reading.)[5] This is hard not only to achieve but even to recognize. What may seem overanxious to one person (deriving simply from their God-given temperament) may seem like appropriate concern to another. We need to acknowledge that.

But enough clues are available. Are you worrying a lot? Does it seem as though others don't worry enough, so you have to do it for them? After all, somebody has to. Do your worries lead to frequent loss of sleep, or despair? Do your anxieties interfere with your relationships? Do others sometimes tell you to relax or try to reassure you that "things will be OK"? Are you often "more concerned" than others around you over circumstances you have in common? If so, then you are probably prone to becoming overanxious in the face of uncertainty or distress.

Some things in life will go well, and some won't. Some things will happen the way you envision them, and others will more closely resemble someone else's vision or plan. Even in the areas of life where we have some influence over the outcome, worrying about the future results is counterproductive. Any singer knows that it is normal, and even helpful, to be a little nervous before a performance; it helps to focus one's concentration and gets the blood flowing. But beyond a certain point—if it becomes excessive—anxiety is disastrously counterproductive. The energizing blood flow becomes a chaotic flood of adrenaline, wreaking havoc with pitch and tone, and could even cause an emotional paralysis that would render performing impossible.

Most of us have experienced the embarrassment of being so anxious to have an evening go well or to have another person like us that we botch the whole business. That is the relational equivalent of wanting to float so badly (and being so afraid we won't float) that we tense every muscle and ensure our sinking. To be overanxious, in any arena of life, is to function as our own worst enemy.

Matthew reminds us too that it is doubly foolish to worry anxiously about tomorrow, since the cares of today will usually provide us with enough to worry about. The millions of twelve-step people who find serenity in the gentle dictum "One day at a time" are echoing the wisdom of our Lord.

Yet as Jesus makes clear to us, most of life is beyond our control. In my better moments I am deeply grateful for this fact; it is far, far better that the mysteries of life be under God's control than under mine. We have a lot to do in this life; after all, Jesus calls us to follow him. But in the end, what we do pales before what God promises to do, and we need to let God do what God promises. Reinhold Niebuhr's now-famous prayer is an eloquent reminder to us all: "God, grant me the serenity to accept the things I cannot change, the courage to change the things I can, and the wisdom to know the difference."

When we consider this prayer in light of Jesus' words in our Gospel text today, we are inevitably drawn to his call to "strive first for the Kingdom of God, and his righteousness, and all these things will be given to you as well." Jesus reminds us that we need to focus on our relationship with God (repent, believe, follow, receive, love, forgive, abide) and let God worry about the details of the future.

Sometimes our popular culture gets hold of this idea, and the results range from overly glib to completely inane. "Qué será, será" went the old pop song, "Whatever will be, will be." Life isn't quite so simplistically deterministic; what we do does matter, and we each make a difference by our choices and responses to life. More recently a popular song reached new lows of banality, repeating over and over again its refrain, "Don't worry, be happy." This is reminiscent of *Mad* magazine's Alfred E. Neuman and his intentionally insipid refrain, "What, me worry?"

But Jesus isn't telling us to disengage from life. He isn't saying, "Just roll with the punches, go with the flow, don't let life affect you." That's not it. He is saying, "Be fully engaged in life, make yourself vulnerable in relationships, be fully present in the turmoils of today, look to the future (especially to God, who is in charge of the future), but don't get tied up in knots with anxiety about how it will all turn out."

Clichés always contain a kernel of truth; otherwise we wouldn't repeat them often enough to turn them into clichés. The adage "I don't know what the future will bring, but I know who brings the future" is true. We don't know the details of tomorrow, let alone a blueprint for heaven. But we do know that our Lord will be with us not only today and tomorrow but for all eternity.

A touching story tells of two dogs on an ocean voyage (a disconcerting event for a dog who's never been to sea). One was in a proper kennel with adequate food and care but spent the entire voyage confused and terrified; after all, he didn't know where he was or where he was going or what it would be like when he got there. A second dog was also on his first voyage; she too was properly kenneled, fed, and cared for. She too had no idea where she was, where she was headed, or what it would be like when she arrived. But she was calm and curious during the entire voyage. Why? Because her master was with her. And while she had no sense of what was ahead, she knew in whose company she would be, and her trust in the master eased her anxiety and fear.

I have a delightful memory that goes back twelve years, to when one of my children was five years old. I was leaving our house to do some errands, when she spied me walking toward the car and yelled, "I want to go too!" I was in a mischievous mood, so I said, "Why in the world would you want to come along? You don't even have any idea where you'd be going." "Yes, I do," she said. "No, you don't," I teased. "Yes, I do!" she insisted. "Where?" I challenged. "I'm going with *you*!" was the triumphant reply. She was right. I had been dealing in superficial terms. In a far deeper sense than I had intended, she was right. She never did really care about the details of itinerary or destination. She simply wanted to go with—and be with—me. She figured (and rightly so) that any other details could be worked out later by the daddy who loved her.

When anxious fears creep into your life, may God grant you the grace to trust in God's providence and steadfast love. May you know the peace of our Lord, who says, "Don't be so anxious; you may not know what tomorrow will bring, but I will bring tomorrow. Whatever else may or may not be true of your life, remember this: you will be with me—always."

And may God hear the reply from our hearts, "I know where I'm going, daddy; I'm going with *you*."

R.J.F.

---

1. Gerhard Kittel, ed., *Theological Dictionary of the New Testament*, vol. 4 (Grand Rapids, Mich.: Wm. B. Eerdmans, 1967), 592.

2. Roger L. Shinn, *The Sermon on the Mount* (Boston: United Church Press, 1954), 61.

3. Shinn, *Sermon on the Mount*, 65.

4. Colette Dowling, *You Mean I Don't Have to Feel This Way?* (New York: Charles Scribner's Sons, 1991), 199.

5. Edwin H. Friedman, *Generation to Generation* (New York: Guilford Press, 1985).

THE TRANSFIGURATION OF OUR LORD,
LAST SUNDAY AFTER THE EPIPHANY

What Is Real?

MATTHEW 17:1-9

What is real? What is "real life"? Is it an intense encounter, a "mountaintop" experience? Or is it the daily grind?

What is real? Is it the promise and hope of salvation, where every tear is wiped away? Or is it the fears and tears that come our way today?

What is real? Is it the dreams and plans we pursue, the high-held goals of life and love? Or is it our repeated failures, the realization that we haven't quite managed to put it all together, that our reach has exceeded our grasp once again?

What is real? Is it the policies of our communities, or our nation? Or is it the man who is at odds with the local zoning ordinance in his attempt to remodel?

What is real? Is it our vows to love and nurture, the fully intended promises to care, the visions of harmony and laughter? Or is it our moments of anger and disappointment, our too-frequent quarrels and sullen silences?

What is real? Are we right when we respond to a disappointment by sighing, "Well, that's life," or is that giving life a bad rap? Are we right when we say, in those precious moments of delighted contentment, "Now this is really living," or is that too charitable a conclusion?

What is real?

In our Gospel text for today we heard Matthew's account of the Transfiguration of Jesus; Mark and Luke also recount it, with minor variations. It is one of those rare mountaintop events of life: a little beyond full explanation, linking us somehow with the mystery of creation and eternity. It offered Jesus a confirmation by the Father on his path of ministry. It gave Peter, James, and John a glimpse of the transcendent, a peek at the reality beyond their everyday lives. But Jesus quickly led them back down off the mountain, back into the daily routines of teaching, preaching, and caring for the hurting. What is real? Is it the mountaintop, with its glimpse of glory? Or the messy muddlings of daily ministry?

What is real in the church? Is it our prayers and worship, our confession of faith, and our hope of heaven one day? Or is it our acts of kindness, words of encouragement, and other concrete expressions of our faith on ordinary days?

I went to a basketball game last night. It was well played. What was real? Was it the long hours of conceiving and practicing the game plans? Or was it the forty minutes of implementing those plans?

In the church, what is real? The prayers, plans, and dreams of the congregation and council? Or the carrying out of those plans?

By now you realize, I'm sure, that again and again the answer has to be, in some sense, "Well, both are real." A game plan without a game isn't much, and a game without a game plan is probably worse. Action without vision is often worse than useless, yet insight without implementation doesn't do anybody any good. Life is much more than its cumulative moments of misery, but life cannot be detached from its burdens and cares. Life surely dwells in the daily grind, yet we may never be so fully alive as when we experience one of those rare, intense, mountaintop moments of life.

"Reality is where Jesus and human beings come into contact." I like that sentence. I stole it from Arndt Halvorson, my former homiletics professor. "Reality is where Jesus and human beings come into contact!" Now, what does that mean? It means, to use the imagery of Paul (see 2 Corinthians 3:14), that when we turn to our Lord, allowing Jesus to be our model and guide, we begin to perceive life with some clarity. The veils that blind us in our self-contained agendas are pulled back. Our vision of reality comes into sharper focus. It means that if we want to get a clear idea of the shape or scope of life—of reality—we do well to look to Jesus.

When we look to Jesus, what do we find? On the one hand we find a Jesus who takes us up to those giddy heights of the mountaintop: those intense moments in the hospital room or Bible camp; or when we fall in love or really feel forgiven. That's real.

But we also find a Jesus who leads us deep into the hearts of children, into the homes of the helpless, to the pain of the wounded, or the routines of tending to one another. Jesus is there in that dirty, foul cot of the paralytic; Jesus is there in the furtive fear of Zaccheus; Jesus is there in the joy of a wedding dance; and Jesus is there in the aching loneliness of a bereaved parent. Jesus is there at the repeated failures of his followers, and he is there in our successes. Wherever the haunts of human living lead us, we soon discover that Jesus is there.

Reality embraces our dreams, our visions, our hopes. I used to think of those old Negro spirituals as a sort of escapism from the terrible reality of slave living. But it was no escape; those songs were powerful and necessary reminders that reality was larger than the cottonfields and chain gangs. They didn't attempt to pretend that the pain and persecution weren't real ("Nobody knows the troubles I've seen" is no Pollyanna pretense); those deep, vibrant songs were a witness to the fact that there was more to reality than the burdens of the day.

Reality is where Jesus and human beings come into contact." As we look closely, we discover that Jesus not only encountered human beings in the extraordinary and in the routine, but he repeatedly led them where they hadn't expected to go. "Behold, I make all things new," and suddenly the ago-old prejudices against Samaritans or children or women or any race or nation cannot be sustained. "Behold, I make all things new," and suddenly all our wonderful plans to earn our way to God are swept away with the promise of grace, the power of the cross, and the offer of salvation as a free gift. "Behold, I make all things new," and suddenly we are supposed to serve those people whom we want to lead, pray for those who hate us, and forgive beyond measure. "Behold, I make all things new," and suddenly people whom I've never seen, living in countries I cannot even pronounce, are declared to be my brothers and sisters in Christ.

Reality is where Jesus and human beings come into contact. Wherever that is, wherever it may lead, we also discover that love is there. "God is love." "God so loved the world, that he gave his Son." "Love one another as I have loved you." Jesus meets us in love; love is the DNA of reality.

There is a wonderful classic children's book—I hope you've read it—entitled *The Velveteen Rabbit*. It's a charming mixture of fable and insight. The chief character is a small stuffed bunny who comes into a little boy's life at Christmas and not long after finds himself discarded. The other primary character is the skin horse, who has been around the nursery for a long, long time. I'd like to read you a bit of the book.

> For a long time [the velveteen Rabbit] lived in the toy cupboard or on the nursery floor, and no one thought very much about him. He was naturally shy, and being only made of velveteen, some of the more expensive toys quite snubbed him. The mechanical toys were very superior and looked down upon everyone else.
>
> . . . Even Timothy, the jointed wooden lion, who was made by the disabled soldiers, and should have had broader views, put on airs and pretended he was connected with Government. Between them all the poor little Rabbit was made to feel himself very insignificant and commonplace, and the only person who was kind to him at all was the Skin Horse.
>
> The Skin Horse had lived longer in the nursery than any of the others. He was so old that his brown coat was bald in patches and showed the seams underneath, and most of the hairs in his tail had been pulled out to string bead necklaces. He was wise, for he had seen a long succession of mechanical toys arrive to boast and swagger, and by-and-by break their mainsprings and pass away, and he knew that they were only toys, and would never turn into anything else. For nursery magic is very strange and wonderful, and only those playthings that are old and wise and experienced like the Skin Horse understand all about it.
>
> "What is REAL?" asked the rabbit one day, when they were lying side by side [in the nursery]. "Does it mean having things that buzz inside you and a stick-out handle?"
>
> "Real isn't how you are made," said the Skin Horse. "It's a thing that happens to you. When a child loves you for a long, long time, not just to play with, but REALLY loves you, then you become Real."
>
> "Does it hurt?" asked the Rabbit.
>
> "Sometimes," said the Skin Horse, for he was always truthful. "When you are Real you don't mind being hurt."
>
> "Does it happen all at once, like being wound up," he asked, "or bit by bit?"

"It doesn't happen all at once," said the Skin Horse. "You become. It takes a long time. That's why it doesn't often happen to people who break easily, or have sharp edges, or who have to be carefully kept. Generally, by the time you are Real, most of your hair has been loved off, and your eyes drop out and you get loose in the joints and very shabby. But these things don't matter at all, because once you are Real you can't be ugly, except to people who don't understand."

"I suppose you are Real?" said the Rabbit. And then he wished he hadn't said it, for he thought the Skin Horse might be sensitive. But the Skin Horse only smiled.

"The Boy's Uncle made me Real," he said. "That was a great many years ago; but once you are Real you can't become unreal again. It lasts for always."

You and I are truly loved. That's what happens when there is contact between Jesus and a human being. Whether it's up on a mountaintop, in the tedium of ordinary life, or down in the pits; whether in crucifixion or resurrection, reality is when Jesus and human beings come into contact. In your pain or in your joy; in your grief or in your celebrations; in your visionary hopes; and in your daily tasks, our Lord is there in love. And, living in his love, we are real.

R.J.F.

ASH WEDNESDAY
Faith Works
MATTHEW 6:1-6, 16-21

Jesus the teacher did not mince words when he spoke to his disciples about their ministry of serving and worship. In effect he told them, "Don't blow your own horn!" In plain, upfront language he warned them against making a show of their good works and parading their prayers and their piety for all the world to hear and see.

You may appear devout, dedicated, and faithful in the eyes of your friends, neighbors, and the community at large, but in the eyes of God, who sees in secret, beware lest your ministry become a self-serving spectacular with little substance.

The Lord God, Jesus said, measures our devotional depth not by external displays of piety and ostentatious offerings but by the soft-spoken petitions of a humble, contrite heart and the unseen mercies of a truly faithful soul. True faith must be expressed in true worship, or, to put it another way, true faith must result in "faith works." Yes, not good works but faith works; and *works* is a noun and *faith* is its descriptive adjective (as in public works or water works, so faith works.)

Here, on Ash Wednesday, at the start of the Lenten time of special devotion, some thought must be given to the genuineness of our serving worship, the purity of our piety, and the faith works of our lives.

But let us be very clear about this: Faith works and good works are two different propositions. They are not synonymous. Although it is proper to say that all faith works are good works, it does not necessarily follow that all good works are faith works.

Do you see? Good works are done for many reasons, some of them quite noble, some not so. Good works are done by Christians and non-Christians alike. In some communities it is often the secular, nonsectarian groups that lead the way in the care of the elderly, in the ministry to unwed mothers, in reaching out to victims of AIDS and their families, and in many other humanitarian causes. Good works are done, quite unselfishly, by many nonbelievers for the sake of their neighbors and the good of the community. Good works are done by the government, and all taxpayers, irrespective of their faith or lack of it, share in them, sometimes in spite of their own hard hearts.

Good works are done for many reasons by many people who are not, never were, and never will be a part of the church. And please understand. In no way should we imply that such good works and the doers of them are in some way inferior. We need to join hands with all people for the common good. But in the community of the Christian faith, and in the declaring of God's word, we must emphasize the clear distinction between good works and faith works.

The faith work has its origin and its eventuality in Christ alone. The singular motivating force of faith works is Jesus the Christ, our crucified and risen Savior. In turn, the singular goal of faith works is to glorify God in Christ.

A Christian performs an act of mercy, a deed of love, a special ministry that is in substance identical to the good work done by her Zen Buddhist or humanistic neighbor. They may work side by side in various community endeavors, as I have seen them doing in many different places. But the Christian's work becomes distinctively a faith work when it is prompted by his faith relationship to the redeeming God in Christ. Christian believers serve as they do because the love of Christ compels them. And if they are asked, "Why do you do that; why do you give yourself, your time, your energy?" the faith worker can only reply, "What else can a Christian do?"

In Christ we are free to choose, but if we are truly Christ's, then we have no choice. Jesus loves us with an everlasting love. Jesus saves us from sin, death, and ourselves. We are baptized. The light of Christ is on our heads. The love of Jesus is in our hearts. We cannot do otherwise.

Faith works are the Christian believer's reflex actions. If you have to think about it before you reach out, if you have to weigh alternatives and consider causes and effects—the chances are you are about to do a good work, but not a faith work. Like the blinking of your eye, faith works happen because they are part of the Christian's nature. Imbued with the Christ spirit, infused with the explosive love of Jesus, the Christian believer in any situation of human need rushes in where even angels hesitate. Faith works are the natural, almost unconscious, conditioned responses of a believing heart to God. It just seems the appropriate thing to do, because God loves you so.

I must say this essential Christian idea of faith works distinct from good works leaves me just a little uneasy. I know very well, if I'm honest with myself, that a lot of what I do in church and community is motivated by something other than my faith relationship with Christ. I do some things because to tell the truth, it's my job.

I think every pastor does. It's expected of me, and sometimes deep within I feel a blush of guilt when someone's lavish praise of my concern interrupts my inward griping over having to take the time.

I do some things because, quite frankly, I need to be liked. My applause sign is always flashing. A lot of people in the church share this affliction.

Finally, I am only too aware that some of my kindnesses are done in compensation for my past and present failures in kindness. I offer myself here, without stint, because my hard heart refuses to budge an inch there.

This examination of motives for discipleship, this probing and proving of our inner promptings could well be the most critical need in our lives during these Lenten days.

Faith works are motivated by the Christ Spirit in our hearts. We act because he acted for us. We love because he first loved us. Faith works begin with Christ.

And they end in him. Faith works ultimately magnify the Lord, not the disciple. Good works almost inevitably always say, "See what we have done, see how much we have given, look at the record of our stewardship." But faith works testify, "See what the Lord has done. See what a grace the Christ has offered. See the sacrifice he made."

Good works, by their very nature, must be seen by others and appreciated. Faith works, by their very nature, are content to be seen of God alone.

If you accept this idea, doesn't it make you a little uneasy when you think of your own life of worship and service? We all like to feel that our good deeds and our offerings of self are recognized and appreciated. It's only human, we say. It's the merit-badge approach to Christian discipleship.

This is only natural. When we do good works we want to get some credit, some appreciation. But let us not make the mistake of confusing good works that massage our own individual or congregational egos with faith works that glorify Jesus alone, the Christ of our lives, the Savior of our souls.

Another and perhaps more serious difficulty with the goods works approach is that it leads to false notions of what constitutes "success" in the kingdom of God.

Faith works are seen and known to God alone, to God who is in secret and who sees in secret; this concept is basic to our life and work and worship as Christians.

The Christ calls us to remember who we are. We are the company of those for whom God came in Christ. For us he lived and suffered and died, and his resurrection is the guarantee of life for us and for all who believe. We belong to Christ Jesus. We are baptized into Christ Jesus. We believe in Christ Jesus, and our faith is given lively expression in the works of love we do in Jesus' name.

W.A.K.

FIRST SUNDAY IN LENT
The Testing Time
MATTHEW 4:1-11

"The last time I saw the devil was in the funnies." So spoke the homeless philosopher who collects my leftover loose change at the newsstand every morning on my way to work. Most of us would probably agree with him. We have been duped into thinking of Satan, the devil, Beelzebub, the spirit of evil in the world, as a comic-strip character, to be taken lightly, to be laughed at—a ridiculous superstition out of an old and primitive time.

Perhaps this is the evil one's greatest achievement. We have been persuaded to believe that evil as a real entity does not exist, and that our shiny, modern, intellectual, sophisticated world will no longer fall for this old prince of darkness with the pitchfork and the flaming eyes.

But the witness of God's word is insistent, that there is an evil force, call it, call him, call her what you will. Daily we are put to the test. The confrontation with evil is as real as it was in Eden, when Eve fell for that slinky line, and Adam, her pushover husband, readily followed suit. Evil in the world is as real today as it was at the start of the human adventure. The testing comes to all of us even as it came to Jesus the Christ, true God and yet truly human and vulnerable.

Matthew's story of Jesus' temptations at the start of his ministry is not to be seen as a literal eyewitness account. It is rather a spiritual portrayal of the confrontation of Christ our Lord by the force of evil that he had been sent to overcome. Inspired by the Holy Spirit, the evangelist describes, in a most dramatic way, the kinds of testing our Lord faced throughout his days on earth, the testing that we have fallen heir to.

Matthew's account, and Luke's shorter version of it, state quite clearly that evil is an actual and powerful reality in the world. Then the accounts unfold the way evil works in the hidden corners of our hearts and minds in our day-by-day lives.

The testing comes to us as it first came to Jesus, through our senses, our appetites, our natural desires. Jesus had gone without food; only now and again a sip of water from a nearby stream. He was hungry, desperately hungry, and therefore most vulnerable at the point of his physical appetite. The testing spirit sought to lure the Lord to use his God-given powers for the satisfaction of his earthly hunger. Basically the proposition was this: Remain true to God and suffer the bitter pangs of hunger, or disobey God, do the devil's bidding, and satisfy yourself.

Whether we "believe in the devil" or not we know by now that one of the areas of our greatest vulnerability is our earthly, sensual appetite and desire. With us as with Jesus, the issue is "Me or God"? On the one hand, the word of God declares, "I am the Lord your God. You shall have no other gods before me." But on the other hand, the enticing voice whispers, "Enjoy yourself, it's later than you think. Life is short, just do it!" On the one hand, God's word lays it out plain, "Love your neighbor as yourself." On the other hand, the testing spirit among us and within us holds an index finger to the sky and cries: "Number one! Look out for number one!" With us, as with Christ our Lord, the luring voice offers the same alternatives: "Satisfy yourself and enjoy! Or follow God's way and go without."

Every day of our lives this test is set before us.

For us, as for the Lord, it comes in another way. Sometimes the testing comes to us through our doubts and fears. Do you remember what happened to the Lord? He was mysteriously, as in a nightmare, carried high upon the pinnacle of the temple. In his humanity, mortal fear for his very life swept over him. And the testing spirit came: "What are you afraid of? If God is God, if God keeps promises, nothing can harm you. If you really believe, God will give you a soft landing."

Basically the test was this: Trust God and believe God's word in spite of the fear and trembling, or call God's bluff and let him prove himself.

Isn't it so? This old test is put on us over and over again. Whenever we cry out in the midst of some spiritual anguish or physical cross-bearing: "If God cared . . . " or "Why does God do this?" Whenever the human spirit trembles in frightened denial of the goodness and mercy of an everlasting God, it is a sure sign that the testing spirit of evil has been slinking about, prodding and poking and challenging the truth of God's existence and word. The testing spirit does not understand and does its most to see what we will not. God's mercy and grace are most surely proved through faith, never through unbelief. Christ's followers must guard against the temptation to say, "If God loves me, God will do this or that for me." They must rather say, "God loves me and will do what is right."

We are tested by the desires of the flesh and our carnal appetites.

We are tested in times of life's extremities, when God's presence and love seem very far away.

And as Jesus was, so are we tested through our human ambition. The testing time for Christ came high on one of the holy mountains, where all the world seemed visible before and beneath him. There Christ, the Son of God, was offered a shortcut to the very prize he had been born to receive. "You came to bring the kingdom, to rule in human hearts, to have yourself and your works made known in the uttermost parts of the earth. See how easy it is. All you have to do is shift your allegiance from God to the godlessness of the world."

Basically the question was this: Does it matter how you achieve God's will for your life? Does it matter what methods you use to realize your ambition? What is more important—the way you live or what you end up with?

We are tested by the evil, grasping, greedy spirit of these days in much the same way. We are repeatedly led to magnify the end and ignore the means by which it is achieved. We are hypnotized by our vision of the crown and the throne—the power and the glory—until they become so important that we seek to gain them without regard for our brothers and sisters and with utter disdain for God's word. If the end can apparently be readily achieved through a little dishonesty and double-dealing, under the influence of the Prince of Avarice we wind our way along a crooked path of self-centeredness and malicious disregard for others that leads finally to destruction. Soon, as the testing times and the moments of failing come and go, we forget that we ever heard God's call to walk the path of righteousness for his name's sake.

The testing time is always and everywhere. What shall we do? To whom shall we go?

The Lord Jesus in his testing time gives the answer: The word of God, the way of God, the truth of God is our only sure defense. Tempted by our appetites, we hear the Lord's reply: Humankind shall not live by bread alone but by the word of God.

Tested by fear and trembling doubt, we hear the Lord's reply: "Into your hands, O father, I commend my spirit—perfect love casts out fear."

Tested by our own ambitious seeking of the kingdoms of the world, we hear the Lord's command. "Strive first for the kingdom of God and his righteousness, and all these things will be given to you as well."

W.A.K.

SECOND SUNDAY IN LENT
Finding Ourselves and God
JOHN 4:5-30

Jacob's well stood at a crossroads outside the town of Sychar in Samaria. Though it still held good, clear water in its reservoir, by the time of Jesus it was more a shrine than a working well. According to tradition, Father Jacob in the ancient past had bought this tract of land, dug the well, and left it to Joseph, his favored son. Joseph, when he died, was carried back from Egypt and buried there. An atmosphere of holy history surrounded this well.

But its sacred past meant nothing to the woman of Sychar. She preferred Jacob's well above the more convenient fountain in the marketplace only because it was remote. She had it all to herself, especially at midday. That's the way she wanted it, far from prying eyes and wagging tongues.

She had made a mess of her life, and she knew it. As far back as she could remember, there had always been a restlessness within her, a nameless, unsatisfied longing, a vague discontent, a thirst that would not be quenched. She went through life as one possessed, seeking her peace in all the wrong places. Thinking her thirst a thing of the senses, she sought relief in sensuality, eating and drinking and trying so hard to be merry. She went from spree to spree, from bed to bed; she made vows and quickly broke them. Her little fibs became outright lies, and all were woven finally into a fabric of infidelity. Loving and being loved gave way to a sordid using and being used. And with it all she became cynical and contemptuous of God and man. She lost her self-esteem. She lost herself.

When she came to Jacob's well that morning, it never occurred to her that the man she saw there would reach out in her direction. He was a man, a Jew, possibly a rabbi. She was a woman, a Samaritan, living in sin. The walls of separation between them were high and wide. And yet . . .

"Give me a drink," he said. And in the confrontation that followed, the woman at the well in Samaria found herself and God.

In Jesus' presence she found herself and the reality of her own sin. He had a way of cutting through the conventional rationalization. He looked her in the eye, and she could not put the guilt off onto someone or something else. Her parents and her early childhood, her first husband and his lack of understanding, her mother-in-law and her intrusions, the "changing morality," "sexual liberation," the community's hypocrisy and prejudice—all these had played a part in shaping her life-style. But in the Lord's presence she saw at last that she was personally accountable for her own condition. With his eyes upon her and his spirit probing hers, she saw the truth about herself as she had never seen it before. In the presence of Jesus, the woman at the well found herself at last, a sinner in need of forgiveness, a sinner in need of God.

When Jesus came, the woman of Sychar found in him peace for her troubled spirit, answers to her anxious questions, and the living water of God's forgiveness and grace for her sin-parched soul. He spoke words of hope to her: "Those who drink of the water that I will give them will never be thirsty. The water that I will give will become in them a spring of water gushing up to eternal life." But more than the words, his very presence—the calm strength, the ring of authority in his voice, the gentle assurance of genuine love—assured her that in Jesus the Christ, mysteriously, she was face-to-face with God.

Few of the people around Jesus have as much to tell about him and his effect upon them as the woman at the well in Samaria. Among the many facets of this story, the most important word for us is this: When the Lord, in word and sacrament, comes in his real presence, sinners find themselves and their God. Face-to-face with Jesus, we are forced to see the reality of our own sinful natures and our personal accountability for the wrong we have done. At the same time, in the presence of Jesus we are assured that God has not forsaken us in our sin. We are forgiven, redeemed, refreshed by the living water of his grace.

W.A.K.

THIRD SUNDAY IN LENT
Why?
JOHN 9:1-41

"As he walked along, [Jesus] saw a man blind from birth. His disciples asked him, 'Rabbi, who sinned, this man or his parents, that he was born blind?' Jesus answered, 'Neither this man nor his parents sinned; he was born blind so that God's works might be revealed in him.' "

When faced with the reality of a personal tragedy that had no sensible explanation, a man blind from birth, the disciples cast about for a reason. Typical of their time and generation, they perceived the blindness as a "casting out into utter darkness," a terrible judgment on the afflicted one.

But they were confused. This blindness had come out of the womb with him. Surely he could not be held responsible for this sentence on him. They jumped to the conclusion that some sinful act, some deeply hidden wickedness, had caused such a calamity. So they asked, "Who sinned, this man or his parents?"

Jesus' answer confused them all the more. "Neither this man nor his parents sinned; he was born blind so that God's works might be revealed in him." Some pain, some agony of the body and the spirit, some cross of suffering, Jesus—who was soon to climb the hill of Calvary—said is but the preparation for some greater good, some greater vision, some greater glory.

But they were still perplexed, and so are we. The troubling *why* questions of life have no satisfactory answer. At the end of the day, we must either accept in faith that one day all things will come to light and truth or turn away in doubt and disillusionment and ultimately unbelief.

"Who sinned that this man was born blind?" If God exists, why is there so much hurting in the world? If God is the creator and sustainer of all things, why the natural disasters? If God is always here, why the malignant tumor, why the death of my child. Why?

These questions are as old as the Bible itself, and older. The psalmist asked, "How long, O Lord, how long?" The people of Israel cried in their wanderings, "Where art thou, O Lord?" Job, in one of the most ancient of biblical writings, screamed his *why* to God in the midst of personal disaster.

Implied in these questions, no matter who asks, are certain universally held perceptions about God: that God is omnipotent, all powerful; that God is holy, absolutely good and just; that God is love, all loving. If God truly loves all creatures, and especially humankind, made in the divine image, or if God is truly just and fair in all dealings with us, and all powerful, why does not this just holiness or holy love persuade God to intervene when trouble comes our way or when evil seems to have the upper hand in the world? The question is posed again and again. One answer in the Old Testament is that our personal and universal calamities are expressions of God's righteous punishment. That was the answer that Job's advisers brought to him. "Surely you must have done something to displease God. Surely you spoke some word, did some secret deed, had some evil thought that has brought God's fierce punishment upon you."

But Job rejected that answer. The Old Testament writers, though they often spoke of God in terms of wrath and vengeance and discipline, continually praised God's "mercy and loving kindness," and they knew finally that punishment was not the whole answer.

What is the answer when Christians, caught in some calamity, anguish, and pain, ask *why?* Surely not that God is punishing or simply absent. Christians too believe that God is all powerful, all holy, all love. We have learned this especially through Jesus Christ, our gracious Lord and Savior. Jesus Christ teaches us that though God is all powerful ("Cannot I appeal to my Father and he will at once send me more than twelve legions of angels?"), God chooses, because of godly holiness and love, to give up that power in order to allow people to make their own choices in life. God's love and justice require the restraint of power in order that we may be free to decide for ourselves between good and evil, between loving and rejecting God.

God chooses not to be all powerful in relationships with us. God chooses not to make people puppets with strings pulled from above.

We Christians have been deluded into believing that being a Christian should automatically make one immune to the slings and arrows of the world's evils. Many Christians equate the Christian life with a carefree, trouble-free, painless life without suffering.

But the God we know in Jesus Christ never promised us a carefree, painless life. Life's problems and puzzles, its inequities and unfair distribution of pain must be worked through, probed, prayed over, if we are to be truly human.

The hard fact is that we are in a world of trouble, sickness, famine, homelessness, much of it deriving from human perversion, greed, and rebellion against God. But Jesus' way was to take on the troubles of this world, to bear the pains and the burdens and, through bearing them, to redeem and save and be glorified. Christians know from the example of Christ that greatness is developed in adversity, calamity, grief. We must accept the fact that we will never understand the mystery of suffering. In humble gratitude we must recognize that strength of character, faith, and genuine compassion for others in suffering develop most certainly in those who have learned, with Christ, to bear the cross and to endure. It is only in the face of calamity that we discover new dimensions to our character.

Through the night of doubt and sorrow the pilgrim band learns to trust in the holy, powerful, loving God we know in Christ. Only when, overwhelmed, we at last admit that we cannot handle our problems alone, only then are we persuaded to say with the prodigal son, "I will go home to my father."

So the question we ask is not *why*. It is rather, What is God doing for me and with me in the midst of this suffering?

Finally, we need to remember that the God we know in Christ is our Father in heaven. Like a true and loving father, he grieves with his grieving children, he feels their pain in his own being. Our cries are heard, and indeed, on the cross in the person of Christ our Lord, God has shared our cry, "My God, My God, why hast thou forsaken me." We cannot understand how God can feel forsaken, but this is part of the mysterious gift of Christ that is most precious to many who name his name.

In an attempt to help people understand how God must sometimes suffer in silence with us, C. S. Lewis once told of an experience he had during the London blitz in World War II while serving as a medical aide and warden. A little girl, perhaps four or five years old, was brought into the makeshift first-aid station badly hurt, in the arms of her father. The doctor on duty quickly diagnosed that to save the child's life, amputation of one of the lower limbs would be necessary and was persuaded that he had no choice but to place the little girl on the table. Lewis told of the excruciating pain in the father's eyes as he pried the child's fingers away from his own jacket and forced her down on the table, screaming. Lewis told of the fear and hate that came into the child's eyes, as she looked at her father, unable to understand why he had turned away and left her to such torment.

God loves us, Christ has shown, as a father loves his children. Sometimes, sometimes, God grieves with us, and our screams of pain and fear and hatred pierce his heart of hearts. God understands when in our extremity we cry out "Why? Who sinned?"

God calls us to trust him and to believe he suffers with us and will see us through.

W.A.K.

FOURTH SUNDAY IN LENT
Whoever Wishes to Be Great
MATTHEW 20:17-28

She was a typical mother. She wanted only the best for her boys. As all mothers do, she sometimes took things into her own hands. They never would have had their own boat and their own place in the Capernaum market had she not insisted. Her husband, Zebedee, was content with the good life of a simple Galilean fisherman. He thought he could want nothing better for his sons. But his wife was ambitious for them. They must have not just a boat but a fleet of boats. They must be not simply fishermen but the founders of a fishing dynasty. When it came to James and John, Salome would settle for nothing but the very best.

That is why she was so disappointed when they took off without warning. They didn't even come to talk it over with her, just dropped everything to follow Mary's oldest boy, that strange one, Jesus. Oh, he was her nephew, and Salome didn't want to hurt Mary's feelings or cause trouble in the family, so she tried to keep her mouth shut. But she couldn't understand how her sister put up with him—his long silences even when he was a boy, his wanderings up in the hills, his constant questioning. When he want away, off into the desert, Salome was relieved, to tell the truth, and she soon forgot all about him.

But then he returned, an itinerant rabbi and a miracle worker, and Salome was dismayed to see how her sons were immediately drawn to him. Impulsive as always, they one day turned their backs on the fishing trade and threw in their lot with Jesus.

Zebedee only wagged his head and tried to philosophize. "They are still fishermen, of a kind," he said. But Salome felt hurt and rejected. "After everything we did for them!"

But time passed and things changed. Soon the news began to filter back to Zebedee and his wife about Jesus' growing popularity among the people. "The whole world is going after him," they said. Salome's pride in her sons returned as she heard their names mentioned too. They had become leaders among Jesus' men. They had taken charge—the "sons of thunder." Salome liked the sound of that, and little by little she found a new dream building in her heart for her boys.

The kingdom of David was coming again! A new nation was soon to rise! And her James and her John could be cabinet officers at the very least, if only they would push themselves a little. "You won't get anywhere if you don't ask. Look at Simon. He's always making noise, talking big, and already he thinks he's boss. Don't wait until everything's settled. Tell Jesus what you want. After all, you're his own cousins. Go to him today. Tomorrow at the latest. If you don't, I'll go myself!"

James and John knew where their thunder came from, and some of the lightning too. They did what their mother told them to do.

The Bible tells this story in two ways. In Matthew's account, the mother of Zebedee's sons makes the first move and speaks to Jesus herself while her boys stand sheepishly alongside. In Mark's version, the two men come to the Master on their own, without their mother. However the request was made, we might guess that their mother's pushing power had a lot to do with it.

"Promise that these two sons of mine will sit at your right and at your left when you are king."

"You don't know what you're asking . . . "

No. She did not know. Salome did not, at the moment, understand the implications of her request, nor did her sons. Jesus was on his way to be a king, that is true, and he had come to put a new law in people's hearts. But his law was love, and his way to the throne was to be a path of painful humiliation, suffering, and self-sacrifice. To follow him and to sit at his side would bring no gold, no glory in the sight of the world, but a casting out, a bitter rejection, and eventually, perhaps, a martyr's death. These were not the jewels that Salome sought for her sons. She did not know what she was asking.

She did not really understand what the Lord meant when he said, "Whoever wants to be great among you must be your servant and whoever wishes to be first among you must be your slave; just as the Son of Man came not to be served but to serve, and to give his life a ransom for many."

The marks of greatness in the kingdom of Jesus are servitude, humility, the contrite heart, the spirit of love that turns the other cheek and goes the second mile. But Salome did not understand— until she stood beneath the cross. There it all came clear at last.

Watching and waiting, her heart breaking for Mary, she heard the words, "Father, forgive," she saw the Savior's total sacrifice, and the blessed truth—the marvelous paradox of the Christian life that is true for us too,—opened up to her: To be alive to God, you must die to self, and the glory of the Christian life is in the love it gives away.

W.A.K.

FIFTH SUNDAY IN LENT
Two Kinds of Faith
JOHN 11:1-53

When you passed through the doorway of the old house in Bethany, you entered Martha's world. Nearly all her years had been spent beneath that roof. There at that hearth Martha knew who she was, and there she was content. She felt at home in her apron and happy in her housework. Making beds, baking bread, trimming lamps, bringing water from the well, sweeping floors, washing clothes, getting ready for company—Martha delighted in all these common tasks. She felt especially called and especially gifted to make a house a home.

So down through the years, although Lazarus and Mary had always lived there too, in that Bethany neighborhood, the little cottage came to be known as "Martha's place," and very early in his ministry Jesus discovered the faith and friendship that would always wait upon him there.

In her little place in Bethany Martha became the Lord's housekeeper. Some women have a sixth sense about the care and feeding of a man, and Martha was one of them. She saw and served the needs of the human Jesus as only her kind of woman could. She knew when he was tired by the look in his eyes and the sigh when he sat down in his favorite chair. She could tell when he was hungry. She knew when to distract him and ease his mind with small talk about the new buds in her garden or the cloak she was weaving for Lazarus. She had the rare insight to know when to leave him alone, with his feet up. In her special way, Martha made a home for the man Jesus, possibly the only real home he knew through those turbulent years of his preaching ministry.

Martha's discipleship was a serving of the Lord's humanity. With her brother and sister, Martha had come to a deep and abiding faith in Jesus the Christ. Her life had been changed by his friendship. To be sure, there was much that she did not understand about him and his way, but it was not in her to press and probe. Sometimes, in the stillness, she sensed that she had not yet uncovered the whole truth and wonder of the word in him. She had questions about life and death that must one day be answered, but for now it was enough to wait on him and to serve him as she could. Martha trusted in the person of Jesus—"I know God will give *you* whatever you ask." Hers was a simple faith that manifested itself in a service of simplicity.

The little house in Bethany was Martha's world. To live and work and serve the Lord within its walls was all and enough for her. But she could not understand why it was not enough for her sister. She found it hard to see that there might be another way.

From Luke 10:38-42, we can see that Mary shared Martha's faith in Jesus, but she was not content with a discipleship of sitting and knitting. This sister also had a deep hunger for the truth in Christ, but she needed more than small talk with him or the challenge of household chores for her expression of it. For Mary, the better part of serving was to listen and to learn and to seek out the revealed word of God in Jesus. As Martha kept house for his humanity, Mary anointed his divinity. Each in her own way gave an offering of self, but they found it difficult to understand and accept each other.

Martha's way troubled Mary. "Why is she always so busy with things that don't matter? When will she learn to go beyond the pots and pans, the pillow under his head, and the constant cup of tea? How can I make her stop fussing to listen and learn the truth with me?"

Mary's way troubled Martha. "Why can't she accept him as he is and wait on him? He'll show his mystery to us in his own good time, in his own way. Why can't she simply trust him as I trust him—and help me with the dishes?"

You recognize these sisters, don't you? Their separate devotion to Jesus the Christ is still seen in the church today among men and women. There are people in every congregation who are chiefly concerned about the church's housekeeping. Bills must be paid, the altar must look just right, buildings must be kept in good repair, things should be kept in order. They give themselves to this task with a selfless devotion, and their service of simple things is a necessary part of the church's life.

Then there are those who would look deeper into life and the meaning of things. They are concerned about explorations of faith and a study of its affirmations. With an equally selfless dedication, they give themselves to the task of learning the truth and witnessing to it at home with the family and out in the hostile world.

In some places, thanks be to God, Martha and Mary have rubbed off on each other, and their ways are no longer separate or mutually exclusive. More and more these days you will find Martha leading a study group and Mary with a paintbrush in her hand.

But in too many parts of the church, Martha still fusses in her kitchen, Mary still insists on "in-depth discussion"; sisters and brothers in the faith have not yet learned that Martha needs Mary, Mary needs Martha, and the Lord loves each one and needs them all in the whole work of his church.

W.A.K.

SUNDAY OF THE PASSION, PALM SUNDAY
Mockery of Christ
MATTHEW 27:11-54

Huge letters, streaky-scrawled on the cliff rock along the highway: JESUS LIVES! An irreverent hand has added, IN CLEVELAND! On the blackened wall beneath a railroad trestle: JESUS SAVES! AT LINCOLN SAVINGS. And in one of the men's rooms in a university library: JESUS NEVER FAILS—HE'S GOT SOMETHING ON THE DEAN!

We don't know whether to laugh or cry out in anger. We find ourselves with mixed emotions—caught between. On the one hand we reject the extreme Christolatry and the fanaticism of the rock painters. But on the other hand we are troubled and uneasy when the graffiti sophisticate tromps with muddy shoes on holy ground and makes light of the name which is above every name.

Either way something about it seems sacrilegious; either way we sense a distortion of the gospel truth and a mockery of Christ the Savior.

Either way it is nothing new to him. Look at the story of Christ on his way to the cross. Let your eyes run at random through the lines and see how he is doubly mocked by the scorn of strangers and the desertion of his own loved ones. The words sting your eyes and your heart. They took Jesus and mocked him. The men who were guarding Jesus made fun of him and beat him. They blindfolded him and asked him, "Who hit you? Guess!" They said many other insulting things to him. They made a crown of thorny branches and put it on his head; they put a purple robe on him and said, "Long live the king of the Jews." They went up and slapped him.

He went out carrying his own cross. Peter said, "I don't even know him." All the disciples left him and ran away. "They all forsook him and fled."

A dark thread of contempt and scorn runs through the story of the Lord's passion from beginning to end. Humankind's bitter refusal to open its heart to the God who saves through sacrifice—this, it seems to me, is the real tragedy of our Lord's passion and suffering.

Christ had power to redeem their souls if they would let him. In his hands he had life for them, not only life after death but life in this world, more abundant, with more love, more peace. But they mocked him, reviled him, turned their backs on him. The blood they trampled in the dust of Calvary was God's gift to them, but they simply refused to accept it. This is the real tragedy and passion of our Lord—then and now—our rejection of the grace of God.

Hard-hearted or fainthearted, we will not have him if it means that such sacrifice must come alive in us. We call ourselves by his name, we observe the holy days, we wear the cross around our necks and over our hearts, but when you come right down to it, we still reject the Lord of the cross and passion. We scorn him, we forsake him by the way we live our lives, by the attitudes, the prejudices, the little hates, the good we refuse to do for one another, the good we refuse to think about one another. By our motivations and desires, our little envies and our huge jealousies, we mock Christ just as surely as if we had slapped his face or written a dirty word across his picture on the wall.

He is despised and rejected today as in Jerusalem long ago. The cross he carries to Golgotha is not nearly the cruel weight, the overburdening sorrow, that our betrayal and denial are.

Just think it over. Your life in all its various parts. Your family life, your business life, your social life, your inner, personal life. Do you live too often in a state of Christ-mockery? The passionately self-giving Christ, the Lord and Savior who always returns with love—should he not inspire in us a returning, a forgiving, and a great constancy? But no. We are stiff-necked in our own kitchens, most unforgiving with the one who sleeps beside us. We hold back our love, and in so doing, we mock the cross-bearing Lord. We turn our backs upon him.

If we truly accepted the Lord's sacrificial way as our own life-style, certain things would happen in our lives with one another and with the world. Go the second mile. Forgive seventy times seven times. Turn the other cheek. Love one another. Take up your cross—ah. But no. In our ledgers, in our job descriptions, in our corporate policy, in our personnel practices, the reality is too frequently a mockery of Christ the cross bearer. Well he knows, there beneath his cross on his road of sorrows, that we have all denied him.

The sad truth is, Christ's passion doesn't mean a thing to us in the lives we live between Sundays. We know what he wants us to be in our relationships with other people. Love your neighbor, he said. Go out of your way to help someone in trouble. Don't look at your neighbor's spouse that way at parties. Keep your imagination clean. We know what the Lord wants. We know what he demands. But in so many things, our reply is really, "Not yet Lord" or "Not all the way."

You know what I'm talking about, don't you? We are unwilling to face up to his call to take up the cross. Our indifference, our mocking pretense of love and loyalty prolongs his passion and suffering. He agonizes more deeply under the shame of our nominal Christianity that makes an idol out of him, or that slathers pious obscenities over his name, than he ever did beneath the lash and the thorns. Sooner or later we must all see that before the cross there can really be no halfway devotion. It is either passionate commitment or contempt. We accept Christ and go his way of love and utter self-giving where we are, as we are. Or we mock him and turn away.

Christian discipleship calls for passionate devotion to the Lord in these days of remembering his passion and death.

W.A.K.

MAUNDY THURSDAY
As One Who Serves
JOHN 13:1-17, 34

Jesus' teaching that the one who would lead must humbly serve—that God's victories are won through submission and surrender—is not easily learned. All of the apostles found it difficult to understand and accept. To tell the truth, the Lord's parable about the dinner party and taking the lowest place probably annoyed them when they first heard it. They shrugged off his words about the cost of discipleship, and, no doubt for a long time, they simply would not accept his prediction that to follow him would mean ostracism and oppression.

John in particular found all this talk of humility especially hard to take. Strong-willed, forceful, ambitious, he simply was not the humble type. In his early days of walking with the Lord, John made no secret of his desire for a place of prominence and power in the company of Jesus. He had come with the direct request for special recognition as the Master's right-hand man. After all, wasn't he one of the inner circle? Didn't he have the right to expect some special consideration?

Jesus told him that although the world may measure greatness that way, "not so with you; rather the greatest among you must become like the youngest, and the leader like one who serves. . . . I am among you as one who serves" (Luke 22:26-27).

As if to make his words come to life, on the night of his betrayal, Jesus washed the disciples' feet. Foot washing was a commonplace task in Palestine in the time of Jesus. Nearly every house had large waterpots or basins at the entranceway for family members and guests to use to wash their feet before entering the house. Sometimes a servant or slave was assigned the job. In poorer families the children took turns at the foot washing. Whoever did it, it was an undesirable, menial task. In that society, the foot-washing chore became a symbol of the lowest form of humiliating servitude.

When Jesus took this task upon himself in behalf of his disciples, he gave them a stunning object lesson. Taking the basin of water, Jesus went to each disciple, one by one, kneeled before him, washed his feet, and dried them with a towel tied at Jesus' waist. When he had finished, he made sure they understood just what had happened: "Do you know what I have done to you?"

As their Master-Teacher, he had served them in one of the lowliest and most servile ways. He had given himself willingly in this meanest service for their benefit. He showed them the way they must act toward one another. "I have set an example for you, so that you will do just what I have done for you."

To be a disciple of Christ means to give yourself in lowly tasks and ordinary servitude to other human beings in their wants and needs. It is in the humbling of yourself for Christ's sake, in behalf of others, that you shall be exalted. In lowly giving is your glory.

The hard lesson of humble, serving discipleship came alive for John when Jesus washed his feet. But as the days and years of his life went on, the apostle began to see deeper meanings in what the Lord had done.

Looking back, John saw Jesus' act of serving love as another certain sign of God's humiliation of himself. Their Lord, kneeling before each one of them in an abject offering of himself, was God reaching down, humbling himself in his unspeakable love for all humanity. In Jesus' washing of the disciples' feet, John saw the major theme of his gospel revealed anew. God was in Christ, humbling himself. God was in Christ, in the form of a servant. God was in Christ, reconciling.

In the act of washing his disciples' feet, Jesus showed John the kind of humility in serving others that God expects of all Christians and especially of those who lead the way. In addition, John saw in the Master's menial act a living parable of God's humiliation of himself for all humankind. God loved the world so much that he gave his only son, who kneeling before us, washing our feet, shows us what it means to truly love one another.

But John saw still another important lesson for Christians in the foot-washing event. Recalling that upper-room experience in later years and seeing it again in the context of the church's developing life and mission, the Lord's words to Peter on that occasion took on new and special significance.

When Jesus came to Peter with the basin and the towel, the big man at first refused to let his Lord demean himself so. And Jesus said, "You do not know now what I am doing, but later you will understand."

Peter declared "You will never wash my feet!"

Whereupon Jesus answered in effect, "If I do not wash your feet, you will no longer be my disciple."

Remembering that dramatic exchange between Peter and the Lord, surely John must have recalled how puzzled and disturbed he had been. What did it all mean? Neither John nor any of the others understood what Jesus was doing then. But perhaps in retrospect it all came clear. "If I do not wash your feet . . . " At a later time it is conceivable that John, more mature in his faith with a new Spirit-inspired insight, saw the foot washing in the upper room as a kind of baptism at Jesus' hands.

In the Lord's words to Peter, John may have seen the verification of baptism in the name of Jesus as the essential washing of entry into the Christian life and faith. Peter, like so many people in the church, then and now, was inclined to think of himself as a do-it-yourself Christian. I accepted the Lord Jesus Christ. I gave up my old life. I saw the light, and I dedicated myself to God. I come, O Lamb of God. I come.

John realized how critical it was for all Christians to understand that being part of God's kingdom in Christ, sharing in God's love and grace, is the result of God's humiliation of himself in Jesus, the Savior who cleanses us from all sin. To be sure, the Christian must accept, respond, and come, but it is vital to see the primacy of God's act of grace in Jesus: "If *I* do not wash your feet, you will no longer by my disciple."

In humility and serving love, the Christ comes to us in the sacrament of Holy Baptism. His grace cleanses us. His love flows over us. We rise to a newness of life in him.

W.A.K.

GOOD FRIDAY
God Knows
JOHN 19:17-30

These opening words have such a feeling of realism that, as we read them, whatever their source, we can sense the presence of the apostle in and between the lines.

After Jesus' capture in the Garden of Gethsemane, John had run off in fear with all the other disciples. They all "forsook him and fled" (Matthew 26:56, RSV). But John returned to stand the death-watch beneath the cross. This is a significant fact. Of all the apostles and evangelists, John was the only eyewitness of the death of the suffering God in Christ. He was the "disciple standing by, whom Jesus loved." With him was Mary, the mother of Jesus, leaning on him for support. The voice from the cross, John felt, spoke directly to him: "Here is your mother."

The concern of Jesus for his mother in that moment of his suffering is touching, and John was greatly moved by it. He saw it in later years as evidence of God's loving concern for each sinner in his or her own need and place. Jesus the Christ, the Son of God, is the Savior and the lover of all. On the cross, he died for all. But his eye of grace is ever upon the individual; his concern manifests itself continually in answers to specific prayers, personal petitions, singular necessities.

The next utterance of Jesus from the cross that John records is "I thirst!" Here again the apostle shows his deep personal, emotional involvement in Jesus' suffering. Years after, as he wrote, he still felt his own throat parched, and he relived the Savior's agony.

John remembered these words of Jesus as yet another verification of his promise, "I go before you." For John, "I thirst" revealed Jesus' humanity. Jesus' tongue was swollen, the roof of his mouth was like sand, his throat was crusty dry. He was flesh and blood. He was tested in all points as we are. He became obedient unto death. He went before us. He knows.

The remembrance of Jesus' words "I thirst" brought a stinging pain to the heart of John as long as he lived. But they also brought the assurance that God knows, in Christ, what it is like to be a human being, to be in a crowd and lonely, to feel forsaken by loved ones and seemingly forsaken by God as well.

God was in Jesus Christ on the cross of Calvary. That is John's message. God was in Jesus, trembling with fear, sweating blood, and dying of thirst. God in Christ knows what power the body can have over the spirit. He knows how hard it is to keep the things of God in view when the eyes swim in the dizziness of fever. God in Christ knows how hard it is to listen for the voice of God when the blood pressure is pounding, pounding, pounding in your ears. He knows how hard it is to speak words of faith when you gasp to breathe and every breath is possibly the last. God knows in Christ that a person is soul and body and, if that person is to be saved, it must be in body as well as in soul.

John could never forget the personal wrenching of his own being when Jesus cried, "I thirst!" But with the agony came the comfort of knowing that God in Christ knows what we are up against. God knows what we face—all the pain, all the fears, the worries, the sadness, the aggravations, the pressures, the tension, the thirst. God knows it all. And knowing, God understands and judges mercifully.

The last words of the Lord in John's memory were, "It is finished!" A short and simple phrase like *The End* at the close of a story. But John and all the Gospel writers make one thing very clear: The last words of Jesus were not spoken in gasping resignation and defeat. They were not the words of a disenchanted martyr, dying without a cause. He cried "with a loud voice," Luke said (Luke 23:46), as a soldier cries when the battle is done and the victory won, as a mother sings when her child is born and the pangs are gone and the sweet joy has come. It is finished!

It is fairly obvious that, as John recorded these last words of Jesus, he was already looking ahead to the resurrection account. For John, the words "It is finished" were the first signal from the Savior that salvation is assured. All he came to do is surely done.

All that he came to be according to his Father's will, he has surely been.

He is the incarnate God, the Word made flesh who dwelled among us. He is the humiliated, reconciling God. "He humbled himself and became obedient unto death, even death on a cross" (Philippians 2:8, RSV). He is the atoning Lamb of God.

It is finished! The word in all its parts is now fulfilled. In John's view, these words of Christ, "It is finished," were spoken in triumph from the cross and were meant to be his signal of victory to all the world and to everyone. It is finished. Your sins are forgiven. And that's final. God was in Christ reconciling the world to himself. It is finished. It is done. It is true.

You are born again. You have a new life, and it is eternal. "For God so loved the world, that he gave his only begotten Son, that whosoever believeth in him should not perish, but have everlasting life" (John 3:16, KJV). It is finished. It is fulfilled. It is true.

John's record of his deathwatch beneath the cross of Jesus is a treasure to the seeking Christian. It brings us into close personal proximity to that ugly, glorious hour. With him we see and feel in our own flesh and bone the brutality and the mocking. With John we hear the women wailing. With him we remember Mary's sobbing. She rests her head on us; we feel her trembling in our own spirits. With John, through his Gospel, we see the pain in Jesus' eyes, the fear, the forgiveness, and at last the triumph.

W.A.K.

The Impossible Dawn
MATTHEW 28:1-10

The grieving women of the first Easter vigil were wise in their grief; they kept busy. That way they stopped despair from settling in. Life must go on, tomorrow will come, and time heals all wounds. Keep busy.

So very early in the morning—although they had hardly slept the night before, or the night before that—they gathered their stuff together and went out to do for him the only thing that was left to do: prepare his body for its final burial.

On their way to the tomb, they talked about everything but the one thing that was on their hearts. They talked about the bright, sunny morning, the bird song, the springtime blossoms along the way. They talked about his mother and how well she was taking it. The talked about Peter staring at the wall, inconsolable.

Not one of them dared touch upon the feeble hope each held in her heart. To utter it would be to destroy it. Secretly they tried to put it out of their minds as they drew nearer to the burial garden. But the words kept coming back: "After three days he will rise again."

The grim Friday was past—the first day. Saturday had come and gone—the second day. And now it was Sunday—the third day. The Impossible Dawn had come! Impossible. They knew it could not be. Had they not seen the great eyes glazed with death— staring, staring? Had they not shuddered at the strange coldness of his flesh when hurriedly they had washed his wounds before the Sabbath fell? Had they not listened at his breast for one fluttering heartbeat—and only silence, silence? They were not children. This was not the first time that death had come into their lives.

The scent of the spices in their hands brought back the heavy memory of other anointings, other funerals. They knew how final and fearful the grip of death was. They wanted to believe the Lord's incredible promise, but it was too much to ask. Unthinkable, incomprehensible.

Then suddenly, in one luminescent moment, they learned what humankind must ever learn anew: all things are possible with God!

He is risen! He is not here! Jesus Christ is risen from the dead! The ground beneath their feet became suffused with a strange radiance. Their hearts beat faster, their voices choked to silence in their throats as they tried to expand their minds high and wide and deep enough to take the new thought in. The Christ who was dead is alive!

His silent heart, in an exalted moment of mystery, has taken up its beat again. His holy blood, miraculously restored, kindles warm life in the cold ashes of his flesh. The death veil has fallen from his eyes and Christ our crucified Lord has seen the sunrise of this Impossible Dawn. He is risen. Christ is risen from the dead. The Impossible Dawn is made possible by the power of the living God.

How many times we face impossible dawns in the passing of a lifetime. I'm not talking to myself, am I? You know what I mean? The long and sleepless night when the words you spoke in a moment of angry tension keep coming back like fiery darts in your brain, and you toss and turn with the knowledge of the harm you have done, the bitterness you have given birth to. If only when the morning comes and you wash your face you could wash away what you said. If only in the morning it all could be as before. But no. An impossible dawn.

You do know what I mean, don't you? As life goes on in its confusions of love and hate, humility and pride, giving and taking, wanting and rejecting, it happens, rarely for some, too frequently for others; the unredeemable deed committed, the unhealable wound inflicted, the irreparable damage done. If only we could wake to a new morning with that blunder forgotten, forgotten in our own minds and in the hearts of those we have hurt. Oh, if only a day would come when we could say, "Today is a new beginning, I start out fresh, the road is clear before me, clear of all the pitfalls of the past!" If only, if only. Sin dogs our footsteps. The guilt hangs on, and that new day seems an impossible dawn.

When will we learn what this true story in the Gospel means? When will we learn that in the resurrection of Christ our Lord God is telling us that all things are possible with him. No guilt is unconquerable. No sin beyond absolution. God has raised up and given new life to the corpse of Christ, and the God who did that can and does have power to forgive all sins, to redeem all souls. No one is beyond the reach of a God whose hands can extend into the grave. When will we learn that this is what the resurrection is all about? God loves me. God loves me, with a love that can move in my life and forgive my sin and turn me around and make me new. The Impossible Dawn of redemption and forgiveness is made possible by the power of God, who raised Jesus from the dead.

Impossible dawns. Yes there are other impossible dawns. Is it only me, or do you feel it too—the disintegration around you of old values and ideals held dear since childhood? And the accompanying weakening of faith and Christian resolve. So many things that were once solid truths in our homes and in our church are questioned today by the young because they have noticed that we older people don't seem so convinced ourselves anymore. How we long for a morning when we could awaken to the confident singing in our heart: Jesus loves me, this I know; My hope is built on nothing less than Jesus' blood; I know that my Redeemer lives. No. We have all become doubting Thomases. A cold doubt has fallen on our Easter vigil.

When will we learn that God understands, indeed expects a frigid response from our faithless hearts. God knows that faith can come truly only as the Spirit pours it forth on us. The resurrection tells us that God who brought the Impossible Dawn of Christ's new life out of death can quicken our dying faith, roll away the stone of our doubt, and make the sun shine through the icy cold of our unbelief. Christ is risen. God has acted, God can act, God does act now and will in you and me.

There is still another impossible dawn. My mother died when I was a little boy. I remember waking up on the day that followed and thinking, in a half-asleep, childish way, that the sad news of Sunday night was all a mistake. I would be conscious of a hoping against hope that the new day had brought her back to me, to us. "When I get my pants and my socks on, I'll go down and there she'll be!"

Surely everyone who has known the passing of a loved one has known this vague hope and this real despair. It is impossible.

When will we learn what this true story in the Bible means for our lives and death in our loves? All things are possible with God. What does the Scripture say? God, who raised Christ from the dead, shall also quicken your mortal bodies by the indwelling Spirit.

What did the Savior promise? "He that believeth in me, though he were dead, yet shall he live!" (KJV). What did Saint Paul write? "If we believe that Jesus died and rose again, even so them also which sleep in Jesus will God raise with him" (1 Thessalonians 4:14, KJV).

The Impossible Dawn is possible by the power of God. My loved ones are dead, but they are alive in the Lord. I have said farewell— *auf Wiedersehen*—but we will meet again in the glory of his resurrection.

Have you heard the good news?

Jesus who died on Friday is alive.

Christ who was crucified is risen from the dead.

God has made known his power over your sin, your guilt.

God can resurrect you to a new and better life from now on.

God has made known his victory over your death—in God's
  eyes, if you believe, you are already in the everlasting arms.

The Impossible Dawn is possible!

Christ is risen! Thank God!

W.A.K.

THE RESURRECTION OF OUR LORD, EASTER DAY
Belief Bridges the Breach
JOHN 20:1-9, 10-18

In his book *Easter Gospels*, Robert H. Smith says that the postresurrection Christians increasingly felt abandoned, forsaken, and orphaned by God. Dr. Smith believes that John wrote his account of the resurrection to combat those feelings, to bridge the breach by focusing on the belief of some disciples, particularly Mary Magdalene and the beloved disciple.

At first the Christians were permitted to share the synagogues, keeping the Torah and insisting that Jesus was God's Messiah who had come to deliver Israel. But arguments began to develop about baptism and circumcision, about whether Gentiles—even Samaritans—should be permitted in the synagogues. After the destruction of Jerusalem and the temple in 70 A.D., the Pharisees began to include in their prayers a new petition against Christians and "other heretics." Christians felt cast out, orphaned, and forsaken.

As time passed and those who had experienced Christ firsthand began to die without the resurrected Lord's return, the Christians felt more and more separated from God. First Stephen was martyred, then the brother of John, then Peter and Paul and James, the brother of Jesus.

In today's Gospel, John focuses on the blossoming belief of Christ's disciples in order to convince us that the feelings of abandonment and forsakenness are overcome by that belief.

Mary Magdalene was a puzzle. She believed yet she didn't believe. She was a picture of attentiveness and devotion to Jesus Christ. She wanted to anoint him again, to complete the burial routine, to do some good deed for the one whom she called my Lord.

Yet Mary Magdalene was convinced that Jesus was dead. She was so convinced that she mistook the risen Lord for the gardener and asked him where the body of Jesus had been placed. Mary believed, but her belief was incomplete. She believed in a Lord but in one who could be so firmly caught in a cold grave that she would be left to search and grieve and weep.

Mary's conflicting beliefs had to be changed. She had to get beyond her preoccupation with nard and linen. She had to see not a gardener but the risen Lord. When that had happened, when Mary looked at the stranger in the garden and recognized him as the resurrected rabbi, she did not feel lonely again. To death and through it she would feel accompanied by the risen Christ. Her belief bridged the breach between her Lord and herself.

The beloved disciple's belief was not in conflict with itself. It was straightforward. It was immediate. It was mature. It was like the beloved disciple always had been: open and uncomplicated, warm and quick to respond. The beloved disciple outran Peter, peered into the empty tomb, saw the evidence of abandonment, and immediately believed. Without worrying and wrestling with misconceptions, the beloved disciple believed. Without agony and anxiety, the beloved disciple believed and went home to wait for the living Lord to come near.

One of John's primary goals in his Easter story seems to be to convince us that belief bridges the breach, to show us that persons do not feel abandoned but accepted, not forsaken but faithfully held on to, not orphaned but welcomed home when they believe that Jesus Christ has risen from the dead.

Robert Smith's analysis of John's Easter Gospel appeals to me precisely because I am of the opinion that *our setting for experiencing the resurrection of Jesus Christ is felt to be one of abandonment.* On Easter we too feel forsaken, abandoned, and orphaned.

Easter doesn't prevent a Texas mother from plotting the death of another mother in order for her own daughter to have a better chance of being elected a cheerleader. Easter doesn't prevent a meat-plant manager from insisting that a fire door be locked to discourage theft, causing twenty-five persons to die of smoke inhalation. Easter doesn't prevent senators from airing negative ads to prevent the confirmation of a Supreme Court nominee. Easter doesn't prevent the collapse of the Union of Soviet Socialist Republics and the shortage of basic necessities that could turn central Europe into a churning cauldron again. Easter doesn't prevent the government from having to spend $100 billion over the next thirty years to clean up thirty-seven hundred hazardous waste sites. Easter doesn't prevent the corruption that occurs when organized crime infiltrates the justice system and manages much of the economy.

At best, Easter seems to put a new face on an old world only momentarily. It briefly covers the decay with flowers that fade and new apparel that grows old quickly and a passing joy that sees cool spring become sweltering July. For an instant this Easter environment makes us feel better: hopeful, uplifted, joyful. But the feeling passes, and tomorrow we feel as abandoned as ever. Tomorrow, when life starts with its sticks and stones and pain again, we feel bereft.

Easter's environment—forsakenness—doesn't change. But the truth of Easter, when it is believed, does change things. *The fact of Easter, when it is believed, bridges the breach between God and us.* Once Mary Magdalene had made that long and difficult journey from misunderstanding to understanding, from focusing on the physical to the spiritual, from clamoring for the temporal to the eternal, from tears of sorrow and loss to tears of joy and heavenly gain; once Mary Magdalene believed that Jesus Christ had been raised from the dead, she could join the upper-room band of disciples in the changing world. Now she could go about ordinary life in an extraordinary way. Now she could see everything from the perspective of Christ's victory. Truly he was where she and two or three others were gathered. Always he was there to enable her to realize that she was in the kingdom of God.

Once the beloved disciple perceived the point of his peering, once John began to comprehend what the discarded grave clothes meant, life became a different matter. Now his competition with Peter was a memory. Now he was in a harmonious and lasting relationship with not only the Rock but also the risen Christ. Like the thief on the cross, he was in paradise with Christ.

This is what belief in the resurrection of Jesus Christ means to you and me. It bridges the breach. It reaches across all those barriers that banish us to a life of loneliness and misery. It bridges those barriers that make life feel hopeless and unhappy, that makes us feel awful. It places us in an enduring and eternal relationship with God.

When we believe in the resurrected Christ, we are not orphaned, we are adopted. We are not forsaken, we are fortified by a familial relationship with God. We are not abandoned, we are advanced in an association with the living Christ that gives us a different motivation and a different appreciation for all that we do. Our belief in Christ's resurrection bridges the breach.

Easter can be one of two things for persons like you and me. It can be a nice ritual of spring that brings a momentary breath of freshness to an otherwise dull year, a happy face momentarily painted on a pained life, a short season of smiles succeeded by more sadness. Or it can be a magnificent and lasting comfort that colors and changes everything experienced during the remainder of eternity. Which Easter it is depends to some extent on you and me. Our belief in the resurrection of Jesus Christ, founded and fostered by the Holy Spirit through the word and sacraments, can bridge the breach and enable us to live.

R.J.W.

SECOND SUNDAY OF EASTER
Christ Gives Peace and Power to the Incapacitated
JOHN 30:19-31

How different and deflated this day seems to be. One week ago we sparkled and smiled. One week ago we filed in and filled most every pew. One week ago we sang and soared. One week ago we were surrounded by the sights and sounds of a great festival. But today, today seems to be just another Sunday. Reed baskets have been reduced to little pieces of stiff splinter. Toy chickens have lost their pipe-cleaner legs and felt wings. Chocolate bunnies have been consumed. Jelly beans have been mashed into the carpet and removed. Gaily colored eggs have been hidden, found, and eaten. Today the children were just as much trouble to rouse from bed as ever.

Our cameras have no film in them. Front steps did not serve as a stage for family portraits. Fathers did not fuss with details like hand positions, facial expressions, and child placements. Today dad was not the patient photographer. He was the impatient chauffeur as usual.

Gone is the stirring contrast between the somber sanctuary of Good Friday and the beautifully arrayed altar of Easter Day. Gone is the aroma of lilies. Gone is the joyful sound of resurrection hymns that tingled our spines. Gone is the exciting expectation with which we awaited the good news after forty days of preparation. Today it is as if Easter has not come.

Indeed, we feel as though we are right back where we were, fighting familiar frustrations and bearing well-known burdens. This is precisely why we need to grasp the message of the Second Sunday of Easter. It parallels and supports that of the resurrection. It assures us that *Christ gives peace and power to the incapacitated.*

In the Gospel appointed for this day we first see Christ giving peace to helpless and defeated people.

It was late on the day of resurrection. Long since the women had reported the empty tomb. Peter and John had run to the grave and returned with verification of the women's report. But the disciples still hid. They were petrified by the possibility of persecution. They were incapacitated by the prospect of facing those who had remained faithful.

The little band was broken and cowering behind closed doors. Their consciences were condemning them for running out on their Master. Had Peter not said, "Even though I must die with you, I will not deny you?" Had they not sworn to his statement? How could they present themselves for positions of leadership?

The self-respect of those rueful persons was being rubbed raw. Boldly they had broken ties with their former lives when the Master had called. Courageously they had caused miracles when sent on a preaching mission. One of them had walked on water. Another had brought a meager meal for multiplication. And yet, when the showdown came, all but one had melted into the darkness of Gethsemane. And that one had kept a safe distance.

Perhaps they were attempting to hide from themselves. Perhaps they were like Adam, unable to face the betrayed God. Perhaps that is why they did not to go Galilee as Christ had directed and as the women had encouraged them to do.

Suddenly the perplexity of this demoralized group was broken. Christ was in the midst of them saying, "Peace be with you." He was showing them the credentials of the Crucified and saying, "Peace be with you."

If they would not go to meet him, he would come to them. He would show them that he still trusted them, that he still believed in them, regardless of what they had done, regardless of what they had become. He said, "As the Father has sent me, so I send you." In other words, those desperate disciples did not need to despair. God's love was great enough to cover their case. Though they had been unfaithful, God loved them and was willing to forgive them. Christ gave that peace to the incapacitated.

You and I often share the feeling of hopelessness of those persons who huddled in the upper room. Sometimes contemporary disciples are shattered by the strain of battle too. When we are, *Christ gives us peace.*

The battalion of believers gathered here for worship today has won its share of campaign ribbons. Its regulars have recruited replacements, raised a roof over its headquarters, and rendered support to the division of the church to which it belongs. Its representatives have engaged grief in the homes of fellow workers. They have confronted confusion in the lives of troubled travelers.

Then it happens. The regulars are cornered by situations that are too strong for them. We are swept away by fear that presses us to defect. So we flee the fortifying presence of Christ.

Now the conscience begins to churn. Like a computer, it plays back every detail of the recorded sin. Like a microscope, it enlarges every aspect of our secret. Like an amplifier, it fills our awareness with guilt.

Our sense of failure flourishes and our self-respect withers. All mirrors should be turned to the wall and all pools should be avoided, for in them is reflected one who betrayed God's dying Son, who betrayed the confidence of others, who betrayed himself. We cannot bear to look at ourselves. And yet we cannot escape the preoccupation with our defeat.

The atmosphere in the room was almost unbearable. It was thickened with exclamations of guilt, self-deprecation, and fear from a young man whose alcoholism had, the night before, reproduced in his home the same violent and abusive actions he and his wife had experienced in their childhood homes. He had sworn it wouldn't happen. He had sworn he'd never threaten his wife and drive his child out the door. But he had. He had, and he crumpled into a corner of the sofa and sobbed. He felt helpless in the face of a monster that had been devouring him since his adolescence.

What was that? Who said, "Peace be with you?" Ah yes, now we recognize you. That scar and those nail prints identify you. But what do you mean, "Peace be with you?" Don't you see what we have done? Don't you believe our betrayal? "As the Father has sent me, so I send you?" Do you know what you are doing? You are blowing our faithlessness away like a feather. You are waiving the weight of our guilt. You are making our mistakes meaningless by your mercy. You are asking us to take up where we left off, as if nothing had happened.

Indeed, such a request produces peace for us demoralized disciples. Now we know that we have another opportunity.

Moreover, the Gospel teaches us that *Christ gives power to the powerless.* It was not enough to absolve the blunder of the disciples and to set them straight with new instructions. Our Lord had done that before, and it had not been sufficient. He had told them about the upcoming trip to Jerusalem, and they had tried to divert him. He had explained again, and one of them had played the devil. He had warned them to watch and wait in Gethsemane, but they had slept. He had shaken them and said, "Stay awake and pray that you may not come into the time of trial," and they had gone to sleep again.

These were powerless people who had received peace. They could not make themselves do that which Christ commanded. Their frail faith could not be made formidable simply by declaring, "We have seen the Lord." They could not be made strong by another requirement from the Redeemer. They could not be made dedicated through demands. Certainly Jesus Christ knew that. So he did something else. He breathed on them and said, "Receive the Holy Spirit." He gave power to the powerless.

Here is a picture that parallels the Genesis account of creation. On the sixth day God made inanimate Adam. Humans had potential, but they were prostrate. That is, until God breathed the breath of life into them. Just so with our text. Christ re-created the disciples. He broke into their primitive world of spiritual darkness and gave them something that he could not pass on before his resurrection. He gave them a bit of himself, an aspect of God, the Holy Spirit. He gave them new life.

The self-imposed banishment was broken. After the ascension the disciples returned to Jerusalem, chose a replacement for Judas, and began to turn the world upside down while it hurled persecutions at them. Isn't it amazing? They were given power by Christ. That power or new life enabled them to raise a structure called the church, and the course of human history was changed.

Even more amazing is the fact that *Christ still gives power to the powerless.* You and I are chips off the old apostolic blocks. We share their post-Easter demoralization, their sin-caused hangover, and it takes much more than a repeated recitation of Christ's commission to coax us out of our downheartedness.

We know that we are sent to others as Christ came to us. We acknowledge our need to restrain our retaliation for wrongs done to us. But we have failed to show restraint, and we admit that we probably shall fail again. After all, we are only human, and we are driven deeper into despair when we are asked to do something superhuman. We accept the requirement of a carefully controlled temper. But things strike us sharply, spark us, and make us explode. It has happened, and in all probability the fire will flash again.

We don't need to be told that such a condition should not exist. We need to be shown how to change it. We understand that love is the central motivation of a Christlike life. But we get hung up on hatred again and again. Why, we even hate the insignificant habits of those we love the most. We argue about stockings hanging in the bathroom and tops being left off toothpaste tubes. It helps not at all to be harassed because we hate. We need to be helped in handling the hatred.

Here is what I am trying to say. You and I are helpless. Christ gives us peace when he calls us again. However, you and I are incapable of responding to the call. His goodness only goads us into greater depression. So Christ does something else. He breathes the

Holy Spirit into willing people. He gives power to the powerless today.

Our world again begins to be turned upside down. That little bit of Christ in us is heard to say, "What does it matter that someone has done you dirt? Don't stoop to throw mud this time. Don't soil your hands with insignificance."That new life in us bubbles up and counsels, "Easy, easy! A neighbor's dog in the trash barrel doesn't really necessitate the construction of a fence and the fracture of a friendship." The Holy Spirit makes his presence plainly known when he gives us pause with, "What kind of love is it that gets upset over trivialities?"

More magnificent than the peace Christ gives is the power he gives to those who are incapacitated. Not only does our Lord offer a second chance, he helps us grasp it.

Once a fine young sergeant failed in the face of the enemy. He was court-martialed and punished. His captain said to his lieutenant, "We must show the lad that we continue to trust him or he will go to pieces." The two soldiers stuck by the sergeant, never alluding to the unhappy event but always treating him with the old respect and friendliness. A few weeks later when the company was in a tight situation, the captain put the sergeant in charge of the same group he had been with when he failed. In a few days of grim fighting the lad won honor after honor and a promotion for gallantry in the field. "What else could I do," he said to the lieutenant. "I had failed him: he trusted me, he encouraged me. I could not fail him again."

We have failed Christ; often, wretchedly, without excuse. Repeatedly we are as defeated and dejected as the young lad. But even then Christ gives us peace and power. He calls us again and breathes the Holy Spirit into us.

R.J.W.

THIRD SUNDAY OF EASTER
Everyone's Emmaus
LUKE 24:13-35

Somewhere in me there is a disquieting rumble of rebellion when I hear someone begin a prayer with "Lord, we are here in your house on Christmas Eve" or "Lord, we are the delegates of your Southeastern Lutheran Church gathered in the synodical assembly in Atlanta, Georgia" or "Lord, it is the third Thursday, and circle seventy-five has come together and has eaten and is now ready to talk to you about our sick sister." It is all I can do to shift my feet instead of letting a scream shatter the peace of prayer.

Why in the world do worship leaders have to say on Easter, "Lord, we are here to celebrate your resurrection," or on Pentecost, "Lord, we are here to celebrate the gift of your Spirit," or on Mother's Day, "Lord, we are here to celebrate your gift of motherhood," or on the Fourth of July, "Father, we are here to celebrate our freedom," and on and on? I really do not understand how tiny human beings, standing on a particle of cosmic dust, can think it necessary to inform the omniscient God just where we are and what we are doing and what time it is. Talk about irony. Talk about creatures confusing themselves with the Creator. Talk about persons getting things backwards.

Emmaus was like that: the epitome of irony—people trying to tell the only one who knows what is going on.

Our Emmauses are just as ironic. The first irony of everyone's Emmaus is *the irony of trying to tell the only one who really knows what is going on.* According to the text, Cleopas was not following directions. He was neither going to Galilee to meet the risen Christ nor staying in Jerusalem to receive the gift of the Holy Spirit. According to tradition, either Peter or James, the brother of Christ, may have been the other disciple of disobedience. As they made their way from the highest city in Judaism and the highest festival in Judaism, they were joined by a talkative stranger who invited himself into their conversation.

Immediately Cleopas and his friend stopped and began to describe in detail the destruction of their dream. They had been convinced that Jesus was a great prophet, a prophet of marvelous deeds, a prophet who gave great promise of delivering Israel to the golden age that would surpass Solomon's. With sadness they spoke of the travesty perpetrated by the church and state, the torture and death of Jesus of Nazareth. Now the rumor was that he had risen.

"Are you the only stranger in Jerusalem who does not know the things that have taken place there in these days?" asked Cleopas. Are you the only one who can be surrounded by significant historical events and not perceive them? Here, let us inform you.

What irony. Cleopas and his friend were talking to the only one who knew what really happened on those three days. They were talking to the prisoner interrogated, to the king mocked, to the Son of God who knew all too well what it felt like to be scourged. They were talking to the only one who had seen the possibilities in Pilate and the fear in Peter and the desire to do in Joseph and Nicode-mus. They were talking to the only one who could describe death, death by crucifixion, death from the victim's point of view. The irony was that they thought they were informing him, telling him what he needed to know.

There is everyone's Emmaus! Always we are telling the only one who really knows what is going on. It was evident in the calling of the disciples that Jesus knew all that was to be known. He saw Nathaniel while he stood under the fig tree. It was evident in his announcing the future that Jesus knew all that was to be known about going up to Jerusalem and suffering many things at the hands of the elders, chief priests, and scribes and dying and rising again. It was evident in his teaching the disciples how to pray that Jesus knew all about the needs of petitioners before they formu-lated a statement of their needs.

He knows! He knows more than the surface and the significant needs that we call to his attention. He knows the most secret and explosive needs, those most carefully guarded and seldom admit-ted, those absolutely protected needs that bring tears to our eyes when we think we are alone and unnoticed.

He knows that we need to be appreciated, not criticized; under-stood, not ignored; forgiven, not judged; lifted up and loved be-cause we are, not put down because we forgot to pick up some orange juice. He knows! He knows that you and I will not let out of our hearts to anyone. And here we are, thinking that we need to fill him in on all the trivial details. The irony of everyone's Emmaus is that we think we understand what is going on more than the only one who really knows.

The second irony of everyone's Emmaus is *the irony of not listen-ing to the only one who knows what is going on.* Luke is not telling us something new when he says in our text, "Then beginning with Moses and all the prophets, he interpreted to them the things about himself in all the scriptures." Jesus had been doing that, pre-cisely that, for three long years. In his first sermon in the syna-gogue of his hometown, Nazareth, he quoted a passage from Isaiah that described the work of the messiah and then declared that that passage was fulfilled by himself. In his farewell discourse in the upper room he again made it perfectly clear that the events of the day were his fulfillment of Scripture. At his Ascension Christ again explained what was happening in terms of that which had been proclaimed in Scripture. He knew! He knew what was hap-pening. He had told them. He was telling them. He was beginning with Moses and going through the whole word.

But the filters of all communication were working very effectively. Cleopas and Peter, or the brother of Jesus, whichever, listened without hearing the one who really knew what was happening. They listened to the truth, but they heard so little of it that the day almost ended without their recognizing the risen Christ. There is everyone's Emmaus. It is the irony of not really hearing the only one who knows what is going on.

Jesus clearly tells us what is going on now. He says where two or three are gathered in his name "I am there among them." He says, "As the Father has sent me, so I send you." He says, "But you will receive power when the Holy Spirit has come upon you; and you will be my witnesses."

Clearly Jesus tells us what is going on. The only one who really knows says that he is coming among us; to call us, to prepare us, to empower us, and to send us out as witnesses. This is not some optional entertainment to be taken or left, to be relieved by intermissions to the rest rooms and water fountains. This is not one of life's extras that we can give our children if we feel like it. This is not one of those take-it-or-leave-it occasions placed low on the summer's priorities. Oh no.

The risen Christ says that this is his coming among us to complete the call to us and to set a fire in our bones that won't be quenched until we are covering the earth with the good news. Everyone's Emmaus is that we come here again and again without hearing the only one who really can tell us what is going on.

Now, thanks be to God, *the ironies of everyone's Emmaus are removed in a sacramental moment.* Something clicked for Cleopas and his companion when "he took bread, blessed and broke it, and gave it to them." It was as if scales fell from their eyes. It was as if they had an extraordinary flashback to the upper room. Perhaps their memories were finally fighting through the pain and disappointment of the Jerusalem days. It was a very rare moment indeed, a sacramental moment in which they realized that something had been building for the last hours. A revelation was rising. Their reception was increasing. Now they knew. The one they had been telling about the Jerusalem days was the only one who really knew what the Jerusalem days were all about. He was recognizably with them in the breaking of the bread. What a moment. The living Christ was present and perceived.

In everyone's Emmaus the ironies are removed in a sacramental moment. Once in a great, great while—when the broken bread is being placed in our hands—we know that he knows. We know that he knows our fathomless fatigue, our shapeless sorrow, and our deepening depression. When the bread is being broken and placed in our hands, our spirit formulates prayers too complicated to express in words. We give a guttural groan and know that he understands.

Once in a great, great while, when the poured-out wine is being placed in our trembling hands, we are actually able to hear him. Perhaps faintly at first but more and firmly we hear the only one who really knows what happened on Good Friday and Easter and in between saying, "This cup is the new covenant in my blood. Do this, as often as you drink it, in remembrance of me." Everyone's Emmaus is that rare moment in which our despair is sacramentally shattered.

Through the breaking of bread we realize that he knows the truth. Through the pouring out of the wine we hear him whispering to us. Although he may disappear quickly, we know that we have experienced the risen Lord and leave the table to tell the world.

R.J.W.

FOURTH SUNDAY OF EASTER
The Door Makes the Coming and Going a Delight
JOHN 10:1-10

Youth and adults experience tremendously different degrees of delight in their comings and goings. Youth bound blithely back and forth. The basketball has to be exchanged for a bicycle as quickly as possible. Clothes have to be changed to accommodate mall meandering instead of dog washing. Kool-aid has to be downed to slake the thirst of one young person, sometimes of thirteen, and a handful of Oreos has to be grabbed to tide one, sometimes thirteen, over to the dinner hour.

So here they come and there they go: skipping over the doormat that is supposed to collect the abrasive mud from their shoes; pausing too briefly in the bathroom and leaving an abused towel almost on the rack; jogging through the den and down the hall without regard for the shouted restrictions of the parents; making a sharp turn into their rooms by hooking the door facing and pretending that they are safely tethered. Youth bound blithely back and forth through doors and homes. They come chuckling and go good-naturedly because they know that someone else will vacuum the doormats and clean the carpets and hang up the abused towel and scrub the door facings and moldings. Their comings and goings are made a delight by someone else.

The passage of us older persons is different. In fact the difference is so great that it must be measured by more than degrees. Our comings and goings are brisk but not blithe, brisk and businesslike but not jocular. The briefcase has to be exchanged for the P.T.A. gavel. The conservative costume of the workaday world has to be traded for the turtleneck that communicates casual approachability so that opposition at the garden club won't be interpreted as obstinacy. The overcoat is put into the closet and the jeans are taken out because the lawn mower has to be repaired and the kitchen drain has to be cleaned and the utility room has to be painted. We adults don't assault doors like John Wayne sauntering through the swingers of a saloon with the absolute assurance that we can handle whatever lies inside or outside. No, we come and go with greater and greater difficulty until we see ourselves as Arthur Miller's salesman who can come and go no more.

The difference between the comings and goings of adults and youth is that we are aware of the grit on the doormat and see that it's gnawing the wax we put on the tile or that it's being ground into the Indian rug for which we saved. We see the abused towel and the cookie tracks and the broken lawn mower and the vacancies on the P.T.A. board. We come and we see needs. We go and we hear demands. We come and go in a cacophony of claims without ever being given the impression that someone else supports us, without being reminded that someone else makes our comings and goings a delight.

In our Gospel lesson for today you and I are pictured in the traditional position of God's people. Isaiah told Hezekiah that God knew his sitting down and his going out and coming in and his raging against God. The psalmist wrote, "The Lord will keep your going out and your coming in from this time forth and for evermore." Those assurances, those marvelous assurances of a concerned God who captures and encapsulates our comings and goings in God's good will, are crowned by a Christ who presents himself as *the Door who makes our comings and goings a delight*.

The first of two basic points made by our text is *that the Door makes the comings and goings of the shepherds a delight*.

In the first two-thirds of our text John is talking about a city corral into which many flocks were placed at the end of a day and from which the flocks came at the beginning of the next day when their particular shepherd called. First we see the picture of the Door's permitting the legitimate shepherds to go into the corral and call out their sheep while preventing the hireling or the thieves or the false shepherds from getting into the corral at all. Another way to describe the first six verses of our text is to suggest that they are an attack by Christ on the Pharisees. The Pharisees were supposed to be among the most significant shepherds of God's people. They were charged with responsibilities for heading Israel into the way of truth. But in the immediate past they had condemned a man born blind and had excommunicated him from the synagogue because he said that Jesus had restored his sight and that Jesus was a prophet.

The Pharisees were the fence climbers and the gate-crashers and the back-door users whose lives were going to be made miserable by the Door. The Jesus-recognized shepherds were those for whom the coming in and going out was going to be a pleasurable experience, a securing and deeply satisfying experience of meaningfulness and confidence.

Now contemporary shepherds could be seen as members of the clergy, church staff persons, and other leaders. If I read this first point correctly, the Door makes the comings and goings of pastors, staff persons, and leaders a delight.

Perhaps you will be surprised to hear that the delight of a shepherd, whether that person is ordained or not, does not come from a well-turned sermon or a workshop for teachers of three-year-olds that produces oohs and aahs from participants. Delight doesn't spring from being perceived as a paragon of purity or from being patted on the back as an unflappable Jane who can cope with anyone or from overflowing the shoes of the predecessor or from outshining the illustrious saints who have gone before.

No, the delight depends on the Door. It depends on the Door who has opened to us. It depends on that Christ who has invited us to come in among his persons for the purpose of calling them out. The delight is in having a legitimate call to walk unopposed into Christ's world not worrying about the possibility of being a gate-crasher or fence climber.

Neither does the delight of shepherds and shepherdesses spring from the involvement of large numbers of persons. Surface impressions notwithstanding, our spirits don't soar the sharpest and float the highest because we have found a responsive chord and played it until the whole family has been rejuvenated. Not at all. The delight depends on the acceptance of the Door's doings. Like some poorly pivoted bi-fold or some derailed pocket door that seems to have a mind of its own, Christ moves and turns toward the good for those who love him. It is the delightfully demanding responsibility of the leaders to learn that love of the Lord and to help it happen. The delight is in ascertaining and accepting the openings and closings and crackings and creakings of the Door that controls the comings and goings.

Nor does the delight of pastors, professional church workers, and other leaders soar with self-confidence and sag with a sense of personal inadequacy. Shepherds and shepherdesses may feel capable and inadequate at the same time. We may feel defeated because an honest and sincere effort at the improvement of stewardship and evangelism has failed, but we are not without delight. We are not without delight because we have confidence in the fact that the Door's doings will lead to a good pasture. Somewhere in that supposed defeat, somewhere in those trying circumstances, are the shaking signals of the Savior. And he is pointing toward pastures. Those doings of the Door, those magnificent doings of the Door make the coming and going of shepherds a delight.

Although two-thirds of our text deals with shepherds, and although we do need to understand Christ's commendable shepherds in order to be able to work with them more successfully, one-third of our text deals with sheep, Christ's sheep. We learn from it our second point, *that the Door makes the comings and goings of the sheep a delight too.*

In that last third of our text John is using the image of a country corral. The country corral was neither communal nor cloistering, neither high walled nor safely locked. The country corral was a low, circular wall or fence with an opening for passage that was about as wide as a man is tall. In the evening the sheep were driven through the passage, under the shepherd's staff and veterinarian's eye, and when all the sheep had been inspected, the shepherd lay down across the entrance. He literally became the Door.

Now John is suggesting that the members of the church are the sheep; that the laity, the baptized and unordained, the bleating and braying believers, are those who are collected continuously by Christ. John is suggesting that the Door makes *your* coming and going a delight.

The Door permits your passage. The shepherd-shaped Door, with his rod or club of defense and his staff for hooking errant legs and his sling for directing the pinpoint placement of stones and his willingness to be battered down in your behalf—this shepherd-shaped Door is the one who delights. You simply don't have to be anxious about baring your blemishes or doing something to be recognized or building your own walls of defense or hanging your own door. Your coming and going depends on someone else, on the Door. It is acceptance of the Door's doings that delights. Perhaps sheep are despised for their stupidity and docility. Those defenseless and timid creatures didn't fit the frontier spirit of this land, and they still don't seem significant to bullish Americans. We want to achieve, not accept; to advance, not acquiesce; to acquire, not amble along depending on some shepherd's call for our security. But in fact that is where security is found, in the doings of another.

Your safety is in many ways beyond your control. Others could confirm or destroy everything that you have done for yourself. That is the scandal of life. That is the scandal of the cross. But something has been done *for you by someone else*. The Door has flung himself wide when you wouldn't think to knock. The Door has closed himself against Satan after your passage and without your knowing that you were being followed by him. And like the popping-in-and-out child, your coming and going is a pure delight when you accept the Door's doings to such a complete extent that you don't give them particular thought.

Almighty God stirred himself and called the cosmos into being. He paced impatiently and planted his Son in the nature of human beings. God restlessly raised Christ from the grave in order that he and you might be together in indescribable love, harmony, and peace. All his coming and going has been designed to produce that green pasture, and God's shepherd-Son's purpose is to provide present passage to it.

Your comings and goings can be plagued by the pain of lovelessness, frustration, and resentment; they can be cluttered with crimes, complaints, and criticisms of you and against you; they can be traumatized by calamity. But every time the shepherd-Door stands up, shakes the stiffness out, and starts to move, he is leading us to green pastures. That is the delight of you sheep. The Door's doings lead to pasture, and your confidence in that fact delights your coming and going.

When you follow your child or grandchild into your home and notice a difference in the joy of *your* coming and going, pause and review today's parable. The coming and going of that child is delightful because she or he depends on someone else and accepts the doings of that someone and has confidence in the doings of that someone else to produce peace. So it is with the children of God. So it is with shepherds and sheep.

R.J.W.

FIFTH SUNDAY OF EASTER
Two Peculiarities
of the Peace Place
JOHN 14:1-12

If I were a layperson and walked into the church on the Fifth Sunday of Easter and heard the Gospel reading, "Do not let your hearts be troubled," I would understand that as a statement from one who has been raised from death to a suprahuman place. There it makes sense to say, "Let the dead bury their own dead; do not worry about your life; carry no purse, no bag, no sandals; if anyone wants to sue you and take your coat, give your cloak as well." We picture Jesus in heaven, where it really doesn't matter whether the family pet has run away or whether the twins have left their headgears in the school cafeteria to be thrown out with the uneaten lunches or whether Mom's Pap smear was positive or Dad was passed over when promotions were awarded. He is the untroubled Prince of Peace because it is after Easter and he is above all that.

If I as a layperson walked into the church and heard, "Do not let your hearts be troubled," I would think of the Prince of Peace as being raised to a heavenly time warp from which he can appropriately say things like, "One's life does not consist in the abundance of possessions; love your enemies and pray for those who persecute you; if anyone strikes you on the right cheek, turn the other also." We imagine Jesus in a situation where it doesn't really matter that aged parents still don't understand the dreams of their children, that children continue to be bitter because they were not parented better, that death comes before rebellion can become reconciliation, before ugliness can become understanding, before loathesomeness can become love.

When we hear Jesus Christ say, "Do not let your hearts be troubled," we have a tendency to think of him as the post-Easter Christ, the Christ raised above us and our time, the Christ of some Peace Place as yet unknown to us. This is a misconception on our part. It was in the middle of his last week of passion that Christ said, "Do not let your hearts be troubled." It was in the upper room, at the last supper, that Christ said, "Do not let your hearts be troubled." It was when he was troubled in spirit because he had to hand the sop to Judas and tell him to act quickly that he said, "Do not let your hearts be troubled." It was while he watched the twelve go pale and heard them anxiously ask, "Lord, who is it?" that he said, "Do not let your hearts be troubled." It was to a confused and consternated Peter that Christ said, "Do not let your hearts be troubled."

Our Lord was not above the human condition when he talked about peace. He was at its most corrupt core. He wasn't above time. He was in the worst of times. To think otherwise is a terrible misconception.

I believe that today's Gospel corrects two other misconceptions that you and I may have. I want us to see that by taking a look at two peculiarities of the Peace Place.

We usually suppose that the Peace Place is a never-known place in a never-experienced time. Let me attempt to explain that.

The most common reading of today's Gospel is in connection with funerals, where the assumption is made that the deceased's immortal soul has been freed from the prison house of the flesh, finally to go off to some never-before-experienced place that has been prepared for those who love the Lord. That place is thought to be built up there or out there somewhere by the triune God. It is imagined to be a place of fellowship, not exile; of smiles, not threats; of peace, not pain. It is conceived to be a repository of rewards for all those who have done good, and the chief reward is thought to be freedom from the myriad mundane motions on which one has depended for meaning.

There will be no work or drudgery that makes persons salty with perspiration. There will be no temptation to be wrestled. There will be only streets of gold to be strolled and harps to be plucked and endless light that reveals complete happiness. That never visited Place of Peace is up there somewhere, since Christ ascended; and after the purgation of the earth on the last day, that Place of Peace will descend to this orb as the New Jerusalem, as the city of God under a new heaven and on a new earth.

Isn't that what we think when we hear Christ say at one funeral after another, "Do not let your hearts be troubled. . . . In my Father's house there are many dwelling places. If it were not so, would I have told you that I go to prepare a place for you?" For us the Place of Peace is, at worst, some never visited place until death and, at best, some never visited place until Christ's return.

If the Peace Place is a never visited place, it also is in a never experienced time. When we talk about crossing the bar at funerals, at least one of those bars is the time bar. At death, we assume, you and I step over into eternity, over into endless, unmeasured time. The clock isn't important. Deadlines do not exist. How much time a person has or doesn't have isn't a matter of concern simply because everyone has so much of it.

The never experienced dimension of time is where the Peace Place is. It is a separated place to which the risen Christ goes for the purpose of making preparation. It is a separated place from which Christ comes for us when he is ready. It is a place in never experienced time. That is why you and I do not know much peace. Our understanding usually is that the Peace Place is a never known place, in a never experienced time. The Peace Place is heaven after death.

Now I would like to suggest that we attempt to see this passage in a little different light. I have pointed out that Jesus was saying, "Do not let your hearts be troubled," in a time and place in which trouble definitely was being experienced and known. His own heart was troubled. Judas's heart was troubled. Peter's heart was troubled. The hearts of all gathered in the upper room were troubled. That was why Christ was talking about a Peace Place that is very much known, *and the Peace Place was with him.*

This Gospel isn't about a mansion in the sky by and by. This Gospel really is about Jesus Christ; fifteen times in it Jesus says, "I." If you study the I's you cannot miss the point that the Peace Place is with Christ and through Christ with God. If he goes to prepare a place, he comes back to take us to be with him. He is the way to the Peace Place, so being with him is being on the way to and in the Peace Place. Being in him in belief and baptism is being with God, being with God now.

That is what Philip did not understand and what you and I have some difficulty understanding. The Peace Place can be in a tumultuous and torturous upper room if we are in it with Christ who says, "Do not let your hearts be troubled." The Peace Place can be on a cross if we are on the cross with Christ who says, "Today you will be with me in paradise." The Peace Place can be where disillusioned disciples are ready to run away if we are there with Christ who says, "Peace be with you."

The Peace Place is where Christ is, and we know it very well. We know it when we receive the bread and the wine and give the cup of cold water. We know it when we receive the word and become some person's manna. We know it when we receive the yoke and look over our shoulder and find that our yokemate is none other than the Christ. *The Peace Place is the oft-known presence of God in Christ.*

Christ is talking about a Peace Place that is often and widely experienced. The Peace Place is in this time. If he does step out of our time, he will step back into it for the purpose of bringing us into his presence. If he does step out of our time, he will send the Holy Spirit until he steps back into it. He has stepped into our time in order that we see God in him, God in our presence, God in our time. He will step back into our time to complete that concern with an eternal seal.

The point is the present presence of Christ. The Peace Place is in experienced time. It is being in Christ and having Christ in us right now.

The two peculiarities of the Peace Place are: it is in a known place and in an experienced time. *The Peace Place is being with Christ now.*

R.J.W.

You Can't Have the Promise without the Premise
JOHN 14:15-21

Promises are possibilities to which premises have been added. Promises are propositions to which some proof of past performance has been joined. If that sounds complicated, let me attempt to clarify it. A fact is a fact. It never becomes anything but a fact unless something makes its factuality useful. A fact is just a fact unless it is joined by some power or purpose. But when the fact is founded on some premise of power and purpose it can become a promise.

You and I might be passing our neighbor's house at an unusual hour, when we hear the glass in the kitchen door being broken and see strange men gaining entry and carrying out television sets and sound systems to a van marked "Ned's TV and Repair." Those are observable facts. If we are there with other neighbors or sheriff's deputies who are armed with statutes against illegal entry and grand larceny, the facts have the promise of something happening. We will catch the culprits.

Love is a marvelous reality. It can keep a baby from dying and a woman from withering and a man from surrendering to the madness of the workaday world. Love can form resilient relationships and eternal identifications and unbreakable understandings. Those are the promises of love if there is the premise of persons who are willing to give and receive that love.

What I have said to you is this: *You can't have the promise without the premise.* That is one of the points made by Jesus Christ in the Gospel appointed for this day.

We first see the promise that each one of us wants. The scene was the upper room. The time was pre-Gethsemane and pre-Golgotha. The occasion was the Passover, and the dinner-table subject was the departure of Christ. Lovingly our Lord was preparing his disciples for what lay ahead. He knew that they soon would feel abandoned, separated from him and the Father and therefore at their wits' end.

The Greek word used to describe their coming condition is *orphanos*—similar to our word "orphan." It means without a father. The word was used to describe disciples who were bereft of the presence and teaching of a beloved master. Plato said that when Socrates died, his disciples thought "that they would have to spend the rest of their lives as forlorn, as children bereft of a father, and they did not know what to do about it." This is precisely what Jesus thought would happen to his faithful followers after his death. So he said, "And I will ask the Father, and he will give you another Advocate, to be with you forever."

Jesus made a promise. He promised a *paraklētos:* one who was called in as a favorable witness for the defense; one who was called in to give advice or to revitalize depressed and dispirited soldiers or to assist those in trouble or doubt or distress or disbelief. Christ was promising a Comforter, but not a Comforter in the sense of someone who would sympathize and pat muddled heads and weak backs and say "There, there, everything is going to be all right." No, Christ was promising a called-in one who would enable the disciples to be courageous enough to cope. That was to be the work of the Holy Spirit. He was to come and empower the disciples to cope with the consequences of their Christianity. Unless I read the signs with total misunderstanding, that is the promise you and I want.

To be parentless is the plight you and I fear most in our spiritual life. We dread the desolation of being fatherless, the dark and forlorn feeling of being alone in a world that is determined to wrest our witness from our hands and render it worthless. We don't want to be *orphanos*, orphans at the mercy of a sin-crazed cosmos.

Guilt gnaws at us because fatigue, frustration, the foolishness of colleagues, and the thoughtlessness of strangers constantly beset those who are trying to find their way through the world's trials.

Guilt gnaws because ordinary people cannot be Haim Ginott's paragons of parenthood. So we want a favorable witness who will come in and plead our case and let us know that we are not condemned.

Difficult decisions are demanded of us every day. Not all of them revolve around simple economic questions about affording vacations and trading automobiles. Some of them have to do with discovering how to love that changing spouse or how to guide those maturing children or how to give to those aging parents or what to do with problematical opportunities. Every day someone is called on to make decisions about divorce, disease, death, and a whole host of such situations. So we desire a called-in one who will give advice in difficulty.

Not the least of our difficulties is being depressed. Tight schedules, uncooperative persons, little accidents, faulty machinery, missed goals—all darken more than just our Mondays. We long for a called-in one who will do something to revitalize us. We pray the presence of one who will get us up by his power and make us courageous enough for another gallop through the gauntlet. With envious eyes we look at the promise of a *parakletos* given to the disciples. That is the promise we want. And Christ gives it.

But there is a second point we must grasp. There is a premise. *The promise is meaningless without the premise.* At this point it is important to remember that Jesus Christ is the gracious Son of an all-loving Father. In a broad sense this means that the gifts of God's love through Jesus Christ are available to all persons at all times without any personal worthiness or merit. In other words, neither God nor his Son makes deals with us.

Yet our Lord said to his disciples, "If you love me, you will keep my commandments. And I will ask the Father, and he will give you another Advocate, to be with you forever. . . . They who have my commandments and keep them are those who love me; and those who love me will be loved by my Father, and I will love them and reveal myself to them."

Jesus' comment sounds as though he had a prerequisite for giving the parakletos. "If you love me, you will keep my commandments. And I will ask the Father . . . " "They who have my commandments and keep them are those who love me; and those who love me will be loved by my Father." Indeed! Jesus' promise to the disciples did depend on a premise—their willingness to receive what he offers. They had to be loving and obeying the Lord Christ in order that they might be in a position to recognize the parakletos and respond to the coming one whom Christ freely sends.

You and I must remember that we think of love in terms quite different from those used by Jesus. For us love is an emotion, a feeling, a sentiment. Love is the warmth and comfort that permeates our relationship with each other. Love is the soft and cuddly ease with which we do things together. Love is security that springs from strong commitment and throws up an impenetrable wall of defense. Love is the knowledge that we and our well-being are first in the consideration of some other creature and that that creature will go to any lengths to make us happy.

But to Jesus Christ love is much simpler than that. For him love is primarily commitment to the commandments that call us to serve him and our neighbor. For him love is obedience. For him love is being the kind of person God wants us to be and doing that which God's law lays down as being good for us.

Do you remember how Saint Paul speaks of Christ's kind of love in the thirteenth chapter of First Corinthians? There love is patience and kindness, not arrogance or rudeness or selfishness or resentfulness. There love is a rejoicing in the right that bears all things and believes all things and hopes all things and endures all things. There love is commitment to Christ's commandments or obedience to God's law as it is revealed in Christ. Being that kind of person, through the working of God's spirit in us, having that kind of obedience, is what opens one's eyes and ears and heart and soul to the parakletos.

When Jesus talked about the Spirit of truth whom the world cannot see because it neither sees him nor knows him, he was making a comment on the denseness of the worldling's mind and the emptiness of his religion. Those who were not looking forward to receiving the Spirit because of their love for Christ and their obedience to his commandments wouldn't recognize the Spirit if he sat on their doorstep waiting for them when they returned from work. Love expressed in obedience paved the way for the disciples to recognize and receive the gift that is available to all.

Neither can we have the promise without this premise. How utterly ridiculous we sometimes are. We know that picking out the dippers in a summer sky doesn't make us astronomers, nor does looking for golf balls in a hedgerow make us botanists, nor does the study of the centerfold of *Playboy* make us doctors. Yet when we get into the area of religion, we seem to expect a marching-in defender against all guilt and damnation, a sweeping-in wisdom for taking the reins out of these dumb little hands, and a lifting-up renewer who can make us new creatures without any love or labor, compliance or cooperation on our part.

That isn't exactly the way God-in-Christ operates. You can't have the promise without the premise. Our Lord gives the Comforter. He gives the Comforter successfully and freely. He gives the Comforter in order that we might have the love with which to receive him. But the Comforter is received by those who are receptive.

In the church you and I are subject to the gracious ministrations of God through Christ. In the church we are exposed to the means of grace. In the church the initiative-taking God comes to us in Word and Sacraments, in the Bible and sermons, in Baptism and Holy Communion. What promise is here for you and me! But there is a premise too. The sacraments must be seized in seriousness. The Word must be heard with willingness. The means of grace must be grasped with love for the one who climbed Calvary and laid down his life for us; love that is expressed in obedience, obedience that paves the way for the promise to be fulfilled. *You just can't have the promise without the premise.*

R.J.W.

THE ASCENSION OF OUR LORD
The People of God Wait and Witness
LUKE 24:44-53

Christians resemble the maestro's baton that beats the rhythm of salvation's song. Our faces are upturned in eager waiting, and then they are lowered in energetic witnessing: from heaven to earth, from divinity to humanity, from the Father through his children to those whom he is attempting to adopt. Christians are seen as the hungry refugees of the world who wait to be fed and who want to become witnesses for the one who has fed them. Repeatedly we congregate to receive God's word and regularly we go out to share that bread of life with starving souls. Christians are complex creatures who abound in ability and potential.

Yet we creatures of cosmic capabilities sit still, waiting to be motivated, waiting to be touched by the Master's hand, waiting to be made witnesses. Often Christians are the distraught patients of the

Great Physician. But then, once he has come, once he has restored our physical health, as well as our spiritual strength, we witness to others concerning his marvelous ability. The people of God spend most of their time doing two things: *We wait and witness.*

Perhaps it sounds strange to say that the people of God wait. *But one half of the total responsibility of the people of God is waiting, waiting for God to act.* We must be careful, however, to understand what is meant by waiting. To say that the people of God wait is not to indicate that we should be idle procrastinators who put off responsibilities or detour around opportunities. To be the waiting children of the heavenly Father does not mean that we reply to every request with, "Wait a minute," as our children do.

Our texts for today help us understand what is meant by the statement that the people of God wait.

The disciples had waited before. They had waited in the Garden of Gethsemane while Christ prayed, and in spite of his admonition to set up a prayer defense against temptation, they took the opportunity to catch a few winks. The disciples waited in the secrecy of their hideaway to await the clouded future. Today we see the disciples waiting again. They face another wait of undetermined duration. Christ has ascended and the Holy Spirit is awaited.

But this time the scene is different. Luke tells us that the disciples returned to Jerusalem to wait joyfully. As they came away from the scene of Christ's ascension, smiles replaced frowns, assurance dispelled doubts, and question marks became exclamation points. The disciples chuckled in relief. They laughed in happy release. They had not been deceived or deserted. Their worries were wasted, and now they could be joyful. They had Christ's word that the Comforter would come. They now knew that the cause for which they had sacrificed so much would lead to complete victory. They had seen the Son ascend. He was at the right hand of the Father. The disciples felt that they had a guarantee. So they waited happily for God to act.

Luke also tells us that the disciples were waiting in the temple. They were continually in the temple blessing God. The disciples were finished with their despondent brooding. They were finished with the fear that had kept them in back alleys and shadowy doorways. They began to ignore the possibility of arrest and persecution. They spent the interval between Christ's ascension and Pentecost where the people of God should be, and they spent that interval doing what the people of God should be doing. They waited in the temple, and while they waited they worshiped God.

John tells us that the disciples were waiting for Christ to fulfill his promise. They were waiting for the outpouring of the Holy Spirit. The twelve had been taught to subordinate their desires and to submit to the will of God. For three years they had willingly rested on the leadership of the Messiah. They had been pulled along by his perseverance and dogged by his determination. They had been conditioned for the coming of the Comforter, and now the eleven awaited the enlightenment and the encouragement of the Holy Spirit.

In the waiting of the apostles we see the form that our waiting should take. Like the apostles, you and I are to await the revelation of God's will joyfully. Certainly our difficulties make us desperate, our problems seem insurmountable, and our disappointments drag us into despair. Surely doubts threaten the foundation of our faith and unanswered questions crack the pillars of our support. But those are not valid reasons for wearing the black shroud of the dejected. We too know that Christ is on the throne and that he will direct all things in accord with his merciful purposes. With that guarantee we joyfully wait.

Our waiting also needs to be done in the temple of the Lord. Certainly God can speak in the darkness of a den or in the confusion of a kitchen or in the loneliness of bedrooms or even in the stillness of a secluded forest. But what greater opportunities God has to speak to you and me if we come from our self-imposed exile, from our silent staring into space, from our private conversations with ourselves into the temple of the Lord to wait and to pray and to praise.

The word of God is in the temple. The sacraments are in the temple. The love and concern of other Christians are in the temple. The greatest opportunity for God to speak to you and me is in the temple. Since the ascension of Christ, the church has been the tool of the Comforter. Through it he speaks his most audible words. Therefore it is only reasonable that you and I wait for God's revelation in his church, and that as we wait we give our praise to him.

We wait not only joyfully but also with a purpose. We cannot muster our energy, release our intellect, and unshackle our spirits so that we continually fulfill God's commands. Perhaps more than the disciples, we are conditioned by the world to do the opposite of God's will. We have no earthly Jesus to depend on for leadership. If we were walking in Christ's most obvious footprints, it is highly quetionable whether we would choose to follow his leadership. Without the Comforter we are the unmotivated fumblers who frustrate the purposes of God. But with the Comforter we become the gloves on the hands of God. So you and I have to wait with a purpose, with our eyes wide and our hearts open, looking for the Holy Spirit.

When we say, therefore, that the people of God wait, we do not mean that we sit back in comfortable complacency. Rather, we wait joyfully, we wait in God's house with praise and worship, and we wait with craned necks and eager eyes as we look for the fulfilled promise, the presence of the Holy Spirit.

The second half of the responsibility of the people of God is witnessing. Again we are indebted to Luke, who recorded Christ's last earthly wish, for making this clear to us. He indicated that the apostolic band was to remain assembled until it was clothed with the Holy Spirit. Then it was to disperse, taking the good news to every nation. The apostles waited until Pentecost, and then they began their witnessing.

Peter witnessed to the Gentiles in Antioch, Asia Minor, and Rome. John remained in Jerusalem tending the mother of Jesus until she died. Then he bore witness in Rome, Patmos, and Ephesus. Andrew bore witness to the barbarous tribes of northern Russia and died a martyr's death in Greece. Thomas became Christ's witness in Mesopotamia and southern India. Tradition asserts that Matthew was responsible for the witness in Ethiopia, Persia, and Macedonia. Each one of these persons of God had his sphere of influence, and each raised the flag of Christ there.

You and I are the people of God, and like the disciples we must bear our witness. But, again, we must be careful to understand the nature of the witnessing. Most of our actions seem to indicate that we understand our witnessing to be work among the religious or work done within the earthly church. We witness to each other during the services of God's sanctuary, in the living rooms of local Christians, on the patios of the pious, or in the gardens of the good.

We restrict the glow of the good news to a holy hill because we believe in the separation of the church and the state, and the cutting off of the church from social conflicts. We leave the areas soiled by sin and move our congregations to the suburbs because that is where the Christians live. Many of us are good Romanists of the Dark Ages. We want our witness walled in a monastery called the megachurch, sealing us in security and against the secular.

This witnessing is witnessing primarily to our own shortcomings. Christ was born in a stable, not in a sanctuary. The Great Physician went to the spiritually diseased. He did not cater to those who needed no help. The Son of God confronted thieves. He did not coddle them and use their laundered money. The Messiah bore witness to the secular. He did not scurry away from it.

As the people of God, you and I are to take up our cross and witness. That means that you and I represent Christ in the crowded line of the grocery checkout, where impatient people run into our heels with shopping carts. It means that you and I take down the off-limits signs that we have hung on unkempt persons, undesirable neighborhoods, and unsolved social problems; that we own our social responsibility and Christian nature and show Christ to these persons in these places with these problems.

To witness means that members of our church should be less concerned about white collars and more determined to roll up their sleeves, less concerned about where their offerings are sent and more concerned about the amount they give. To witness means that you and I forget about separating the secular and the religious, that we remember that all persons and all things belong to God, and that we set ourselves to the task of returning them to their rightful owner. The second half of our responsibility as the people of God is to witness.

The church is the throbbing heart of Almighty God. Between beats it pauses. It waits to be refreshed. Then it contracts to send its witnesses to every dismal corner of existence and to every confused creature who crouches there. The people of God are the life-blood that is pumped by this mighty organ. We are gathered to wait, to worship joyfully, to be infused with the Holy Spirit. Then we are sent flowing forth with vital sustenance as witnesses. You and I are the people of God. We have two primary responsibilities; to wait and to witness.

R.J.W.

SEVENTH SUNDAY OF EASTER
Eternal Life Is Knowing God and Christ
JOHN 17:1-11

The "theologians" who sit listening in the pews commonly define eternal life as escape. Eternal life is escaping the boundaries of beginnings and endings. It is escaping from measurable time to immeasurable time, from limited time to unlimited time, from finite to infinite. Eternal life is escaping to a fourth dimension where days and months and years have no meaning. Eternal life is escaping the grave. It is escaping the mortality all human beings face and being placed on a plane that is untouchable by physical death.

Eternal life is escaping separation from God. It is escaping the horror of hell and the abandonment of the Almighty. It is escaping from the absence of God to the presence of God, from no home to a heavenly mansion, from torment to the throne of the Lamb. Most of us commonly define eternal life as escape. But in the Gospel appointed for this day, *eternal life is knowing God and Christ.*

Eternal life is knowing. Knowing is an Old Testament characteristic of God's people. Knowing is the tree of life. Knowing is the root of immortality. Knowing is the means of righteousness. That is why the law was so important to the Hebrew people. It was a means, the best means by which one could know God. So if one kept the law he or she was acting in accord with the knowledge of God and was considered righteous and acceptable to God.

In the Old Testament the word *know* is regularly used also to convey the idea of sexual intercourse. "Now the man knew his wife Eve, and she conceived and bore Cain." That knowledge between husband and wife is the most intimate there can be. It is the outward and physical manifestation of the meshing of two minds and spirits and bodies. It is the coming together of two persons in perfect, if momentary, understanding with each other. It is the expression of the most perfect union of which human beings are capable. So eternal life is knowing, having the deepest and most totally integrated and personal relationship with God and expressing it in deeds that comply with God's will.

Eternal life is knowing. Eternal life is knowing God. To be sure, knowing God in the biblical sense means knowing that Yahweh is the one, true, living God and that there are no others. Knowing God means being able to admit that Buddha and all the other supreme beings of other religions are not mere manifestations of the true God. Knowing God means a rejection of pantheism. It means seeing God as the Creator and Sustainer of all things, as one above and beyond all things instead of being in brooks and boulders and trees.

But knowing God also means having an acceptable and proper understanding of God's nature. Knowing God is grasping the righteousness that makes God hate sin and love the sinner. It is appreciating divine justice that delivers us up to death because we are corrupt and that defeats our death because we are loved. It is believing God's unselfishness that permits us the freedom of choice,

God's humility that permits the Son to leave God's right hand for the purpose of becoming one of us, God's generosity in giving the Son up to death, and God's patience that waits for a deathbed conversion.

Knowing God is being accurately apprised of who and what he is through his self-revelation in his word. So eternal life is being convinced that the all-powerful is all-loving, that the all-knowing is all-suffering, that the all-present is all-patient, that the Lord of the universe is willing to be laid out on a cross in order that we might be at peace with him and ourselves.

Eternal life is knowing. Eternal life is knowing God. *Eternal life is knowing God and Christ.* As we have often heard from pulpits, the best way to know God is to know God's Son. The best way to be intimate with God is to be intimate with Jesus Christ. The best way to be inescapably intertwined with God is to live in the Savior whom God has sent and to have that Savior living in us. Christ's being born in a barn had the effect of bringing God down from the lofty heights of Mount Sinai into the meanest and lowliest of conditions. Christ's choosing his disciples from all sorts and conditions of persons had the effect of bringing God from prophets and priests and kings into the life of every human being who can become one of his witnesses. Christ's teaching from boats and synagogues and mountainsides had the effect of moving God's emphasis from the law to the motivation behind keeping it.

Christ's coming to the cross like a lamb before the shearers had the effect of bringing God from the position of being the demanding Master to the position of being the Suffering Servant. Christ's sending the Holy Spirit had the effect of bringing God from the place of the Creator to the place of the Counselor and Comforter. Everything that Christ said and did uncovered and brought home with new clarity the Old Testament fact that God is a covenant maker who condescends in love. Accepting that which Christ has done, being convinced that his revelation is the truth about the heavenly Father, believing what he has shown us, to the point that it becomes the basis of our being and doing, is eternal life. *Eternal life is knowing God and Christ.*

As you and I participate in the Sacrament of Holy Communion, we are privileged to participate in an occasion of eternal life. As you and I celebrate the sacrament we are doing nothing more or less than knowing God and Christ in a unique way. At the table of the Lord we are met by the bread and wine, the body broken and the blood outpoured, by the total presence of the Savior who speaks to us of forgiveness and strength. On our knees at the altar, you and I are told with earthly elements who God is and what God has done for us through the Son. We are reminded that we are loved, forgiven, and fortified. If we believe that; if we know that; if we are convinced of that to the point that we act on it, we have eternal life. The communion has become for us an occasion of eternal life.

No, dear theologians who twist and turn in the pews, eternal life is not an escape from anything, let alone temporal death or physical death or spiritual death. Eternal life is far more positive than that. *Eternal life is knowing God and Christ.*

R.J.W.

THE DAY OF PENTECOST
The Power of the Spirit
JOHN 20:19-23

A grand Negro spiritual, familiar to most of us, is titled "I Want to be a Christian in My Heart." The suggestion is beautiful. Our faith should reveal emotion. Our Christian experiences should stir some feeling. Our Christian expressions should not simply be something out of the book, something we have learned in catechetical classes or memorized by rote. On the other hand, much damage has been done when people rely on their emotions to give them assurance of faith. We cannot rely on our emotions because those feelings are quite apt to pass.

We must also be Christians in the mind. The apostle Paul says we are to have the mind of Christ. Christ must also rule the mind. To be a Christian in the mind is to be able to think through problems to solutions, to create strategies for dealing with the puzzles of life, and to plan for whatever eventualities come to us. If we are only sentimentalists or romanticists, we shall find it difficult to deal with reality. If we are Christians only in the heart, we shall have trouble when depression comes to us. Yet being Christians only in the mind can lead to colorless, sterile, and mechanical views. The better way, of course, is to be Christians in both the heart and the head. We should exhibit a Christianity that is both heady and full of heart.

God Does It

A balance of the emotional and intellectual is not easily achieved. The history of the Christian church is filled with evidence that at different periods Christians leaned too heavily on an emotional religion of the heart and at other times depended only on religion of the head. How can we keep the balance? How do we keep the proper blend of being Christians in the heart and in the head? The truth is that we do not have the answer. It is God who gives the answer. That is what Pentecost is all about.

In the Pentecost event we learn that becoming a Christian is not being made over in our own image. God makes Christians through the gift of the Spirit. God makes Christians what God wants them to be. Pentecost is really the story of the unexpected. The people who saw what happened to the disciples could not make out what was going on. The disciples themselves were surprised at their own ability to witness as they did. They had no idea that things would turn out this way. They had been Christians of the heart as they followed the Christ. Now they were Christians of the mind also, who could enunciate what Christ meant to them. They did this by the power of the Spirit.

An Easter Blessing

The holy Gospel appointed for today does not elaborate on the event of Pentecost. It is an Easter text relating what happened the first Easter evening. But what happened Easter evening was the beginning of Pentecost. This Gospel tells us what transpires in the giving of the gift of the Spirit. Pentecost did not just happen. It developed with the giving of the Spirit. Jesus did not give the gift of the Spirit to the disciples for the first time at Pentecost. During his ministry he had already indicated to the disciples that they were drawn to him by the Spirit. At Easter he gave the gift of the Spirit when he breathed on the disciples. This scene reminds us of how God breathed into the nostrils of Adam in the Garden of Eden that humans might become living beings.

Jesus breathes his Spirit, the Spirit of God, on the disciples. The Holy Spirit is Christ's gift, his gift of himself to us. In the giving of himself through the Spirit to the disciples things began to happen to them. The gift sparked great changes in their lives. At Pentecost we hear they were "filled with the Holy Spirit." What Christ had given them at Easter came to fullness at Pentecost.

Jesus Explains

What the gift of the Holy Spirit meant for the disciples Jesus explained immediately for them. "Receive the Holy Spirit. If you forgive the sins of any, they are forgiven; if you retain the sins of any, they are retained." To have the gift of the Spirit is to experience God's power, which is to forgive or withhold the forgiveness of sins. The manner in which the Holy Spirit grabs hold of our lives is to refashion us and make us over by forgiving our sins. The way in which the Holy Spirit makes new people out of us is to apply to us the fruits of the life, death, and resurrection of Jesus Christ. To forgive us, the Holy Spirit applies the holiness of Christ to us.This means God views us as innocent and holy, like the Christ himself.

This unexpected gift of the Holy Spirit performs the unexpected in us too. We would like to think that somehow we can patch up this old self that we are or redesign or refashion it to make it acceptable to God. But that is not how it works. To receive the Holy Spirit is to get a new birth through the forgiveness of sins. The new birth is not some new determination to live a new life-style that will be pleasing to God. Rather, God gives the totally new life through this risen Jesus Christ, who left all of our sins back on the cross and in the empty tomb. That is the power of the Spirit. It is the power to change people by the total and complete act of the forgiveness of sins. As the apostle Paul states, "So if anyone is in Christ, there is a new creation: everything old has passed away; see, everything has become new" (2 Corinthians 5:17).

God Makes Us Over

After a performance of Benjamin Britten's opera *Peter Grimes,* John Vickers, who sang the role of Peter Grimes, was asked how he could fuse himself so well into that role. It was quite obvious that Mr. Vickers sang not only with his head, through the fine tenor voice that God had given him, but that he sang from the heart as though he himself were Peter Grimes. Mr. Vickers quoted from the Gospels our Lord's saying that unless a grain of wheat falls into the ground and dies, it remains alone; but if it dies it bears much fruit (John 12:24). Mr. Vickers said that he had to die in order that the role he sang could live. "The art form is greater than the artist," even as he believed that the opera is greater than the composer.

In a small way Mr. Vickers' explanation illustrates the power of the Spirit in our lives to put to death the old self in us that the new self may come forth and live. What the Holy Spirit makes us is greater than what we are. Of ourselves we are sinners, but the Holy Spirit puts us to death in Christ that Christ might live in us. Yet it is we who live, just as Mr. Vickers lived and sang yet lost himself in the role to which he had been called. We live with our heart and mind captive to the Lord Jesus Christ. We put on the mind of Christ and we have his heart.

God Makes Us Grow

When Jesus greeted the disciples on that Easter evening, he said, "Peace be with you." The peace that Jesus brings is the binding together of mind and heart in himself. That peace is *shalom.* Shalom is the integrating of the heart and mind under the persuasion of the Holy Spirit. That integration of mind and spirit permits the growth that God expects of us. The fifty-day period between

Easter evening and Pentecost was a time of real growth for the disciples.

With the mind the apostles recalled all that Jesus had done for them and taught them. With the mind they searched the Scriptures and discovered, as Jesus had taught them, that his whole life was the fulfillment of what the prophets had taught of old. With the heart they cherished anew all that Jesus had been to them. Their loyalties were restored. But above all they emerged from their timidity and fear. They developed confidence as they grasped with the mind what really had transpired. The dawning of ideas in the mind was matched with the renewal of fiery emotions. The Holy Spirit had taken over the total being of these people. They were completely submerged in the power of the Spirit. All this happened because the Holy Spirit had furnished them with the power to forgive sins as well as the power not to forgive sins.

God Gives Us Power

The disciples were forgiven and restored by the risen Christ. He forgave them for their desertion from his side and for their denial of him. By granting them peace and forgiveness, he made them new. "If you forgive the sins of any, they are forgiven."

This newness of the Spirit, however, was not limited to the disciples. Christians are empowered by the Holy Spirit to be reconciled to those with whom they must share life. But more, they have power to pass on the very power of God through the forgiveness of sins. They can confer newness on others. Think of what this means in our homes. Today we observe how the home, marriage, and family life are being ravaged by social forces around them. Yet here is power for the restoration of the home, the renewal of marriage, the strengthening of daily life.

Newness is offered daily to husband and wife, to parents and children, through the application of the forgiveness of sins. This power can be stretched to all human relations. How badly we live with one another in our communities is obvious at every level of society. But that does not have to be. Christians who live by the power of the Spirit can be that force for change in the world. They can transform all kinds of human situations by granting the forgiveness of sins. They can offer newness, restoration, reconciliation, renewal, and new life to the world by the very same gift they have received from Christ in the power of the Spirit. That is what Pentecost means to us.

Jesus Stands among Us

The shame of it is that we all too often fail to realize what power is at our disposal. How easy it is for us to forget what our God has done for us. Some people think that renewal will come with new emphasis on what we experience in our feelings. Others aim to keep the church pure with the emphasis on what we know. Yet here at our disposal is the real power to get the job done in the power of the Spirit.

Our Gospel reminds us that on that Easter evening, the disciples were hiding out of fear. They did not know what to do next. How their teeth must have chattered and their knees knocked while they tried to figure out on their own what they could do with the news that Jesus was risen from the dead.

The Gospel says, "Jesus came and stood among them." That is how we get it all together. When we realize that Jesus stands among us, we are graced with the power and the gift of the Spirit. The power is not in us but in the Christ who stands among us. In his presence we receive that gift which is power to change and transform our lives.

May this Feast of Pentecost be a time of renewal for us. Today we pray that we may always live in the power of the Spirit who makes us Christians both in the head and in the heart.

H.N.H.

THE HOLY TRINITY, FIRST SUNDAY AFTER PENTECOST

The Feast of The Holy Trinity
MATTHEW 28:16-20

The Feast of the Holy Trinity that we celebrate today was introduced into the church year at a comparatively late date. In the eleventh century, local dioceses observed the festival. In the twelfth century Pope Alexander II discouraged the observance of the day; he believed it unnecessary, because each day of the church's worship was occasion to proclaim the holy Trinity. In 1332, however, Pope John XXII ordered the festival to be observed universally on this Sunday. It has been observed annually ever since. With good reason the church has continued the liturgical tradition.

The doctrine of the holy Trinity has often been challenged. Moderns may argue that the doctrine really belongs to earlier times when people tried to define as carefully as they could the finer points of theology. They claim contemporary folk neither care for these theological refinements nor accept teachings that do not lend themselves to scientific proof. However, Christian theology is not so naive as to create doctrine simply for the sake of argument or refinement. Nor is it true that people today are so advanced that they have outgrown the need for the comfort that the doctrine of the holy Trinity provides. There is good reason for us to celebrate this day, with gusto and great joy, and to meditate on the holy Trinity.

The Problem

Some zealous sects and expressions of faith are vehement in their denunciation of the doctrine of the Trinity. A major reason for questioning this doctrine is that no Bible passage expresses it in the words in which we confess it; namely, that there is only one God and yet there are three distinct persons, equal in every respect yet different. We cannot point to chapter and verse where this teaching is spelled out. All of this can be rather unsettling when we realize that the doctrine is not only under attack by intellectuals who make reason their god but also by serious and devout people who base their lives on faith. In the holy Gospel appointed for today we do have the baptismal formula as expressed by our Lord. God is named as the Trinity, "Father, Son and Holy Spirit"; however, this is not explained

Overstating the Case

We arrive at the doctrine of the Trinity by deduction, because the truth is well substantiated in Scripture in many places and in various ways. What is more important, the entire biblical treatment of the Trinity takes the doctrine out of the realm of speculation and makes it wholly practical. When Christians defend the doctrine in parlor discussions, they often do give the impression that they have three gods. Criticisms are quite proper if Christians, in their desire to be right about the faith, overstate their case and say things about God that the Scriptures do not say.

Sometimes the argument is so strained that they seem to make God little more than an intellectual proposition. That kind of defense of God as holy Trinity robs God of all warmth, love, and care. We should do everything we can to discourage such an apology for the Trinity. It is a poor witness to what God really is and is more offensive than helpful. Faith is never to be reduced to intellectual exercises that make the mind jump through certain hoops to arrive at some conclusions about God. When we detect people doing this to the faith, we ought to recognize immediately that this is not language about a God who was willing to be born of a virgin and go to the cross to die for humankind.

The Clues

In trying to explore the doctrine of the Trinity, we can take our clues from Scripture passages that are loaded with trinitarian symbols, language, confession, and illustrations and yet are never reduced to propositions about God. We ought to begin with scriptural proclamations about God as a God who seeks to relate to humanity. Our lessons for today do just that. The first lesson reminds us that as we celebrate the Feast of the Holy Trinity we celebrate our confession of God.

To be Trinitarian is to acknowledge the uniqueness of God, that there is no other beside God, and there is none like God. Although we speak and confess that there are three persons, we also confess that God is one. We cannot break God up or make God into segments. We are tempted always to try to rationalize how God does certain things as only Father, as only Son, or as only Spirit. Then we tend to see this in a disjointed way, as though the Father and the Son or the Holy Spirit are not united. The better way is simply to recognize the unity of God in what God does. In the lesson Moses asks, "Has anything so great as this happened or has its like ever been heard of?"

The Work of God

The second think to note about the Feast of the Holy Trinity is that it celebrates the works of God. This is the way the Scriptures reveal and unfold the holy Trinity to us. We never hear of the nature of God in Scripture unless it is somehow related to us. The lessons make the point. There is no philosophical explanation here about God. Rather, God is affirmed as the only one who has a right to first place in our lives. We are to be related to God in love.

The second lesson underscores this love. These words are from Paul's second letter to the church at Corinth. In that letter he scolded the Corinthians for their failure to take seriously his first letter, and he chided them for their lack of respect for his office and authority. But his last appeal was that they find their way back to unity through the God of love and peace. In God, who is one, they could be restored to unity. He concluded the whole appeal with the words "The grace of the Lord Jesus Christ and the love of God and the communion of the Holy Spirit be with you all." We know this as the apostolic greeting or blessing, and it has been used countless times in Christian communities as the expression of our trinitarian confession and our understanding of a trinitarian blessing.

God's Redeeming Work

In this blessing we hear once more that God is not to be understood apart from God's work. The apostles as well as the prophets of old made no assumptions about God apart from the divine work. It was only because God was revealed that people could speak about God. The unique aspect of God's self-revelation was that it was always in relationship to people. From the beginning of the history of Israel with Abraham, the children of Israel discovered God's uniqueness in God's oneness; there was no other to whom they should go.

Equally important to Israel was God's revelation as Redeemer, the one who chose this people in spite of their failures and sins, in spite of their unbelief and rebellion. God saved them over and over again. He was their Redeemer God. Yet they could not know God apart from what God revealed. The Israelites could never be so presumptuous as to think they could figure God out. God would do the revealing in what God did for them. They were reminded again and again that God had delivered them at the Red Sea, fed them in the wilderness, and brought them into the promised land. The Israelites could do the believing and thus be related to God by faith.

The Ultimate Work

The apostle Paul saw this revelation of God come to its fullest expression in Jesus Christ. His letters are filled with glowing doxologies in which he praises God for these revelations. Sometimes in the midst of explaining what God has done, Paul simply explodes into a hymn of praise to this God who surpasses description. It does not surprise us then that Paul should demonstrate the practical nature of the holy Trinity by his repeated phrases of praise for the gracious, almighty God of heaven and earth.

In our second lesson Paul links it all together. The Lord Jesus Christ is present in our lives by grace. He is present not because we know how to make him present by incantations, good works, or mental exercises. Christ is present because he embodies the God of grace and because, as John reminded us, God is love.

God is not some almighty power we can engineer or manipulate. God has demonstrated in Jesus Christ the true divine nature. God is the loving God who overcame divine wrath toward us sinners. God sent the Son to die for our sins and raised him to life that in him we might have life. What we know about God in Jesus Christ is enough for us to understand God's feelings toward us so that we can trust God and love God in return. That is what counts. God makes faith possible by what God has done for us and made known to us, not what we can dream up about God as a philosophical formula. The fellowship of the Holy Spirit will be with us, says Paul. That is another way of saying that this great God whom the heavens and earth cannot contain has the ability to live with us and in us in Spirit.

How to Confess

The best way to confess the holy Trinity is simply to accept in plain and honest faith what God has done for us. We dare not permit the doctrine of the Trinity to degenerate into dry and empty formulas about God. To confess the Trinity is to experience daily the grace of Christ, the love of God the Father, and the fellowship of the Holy Spirit. As we do this, we recognize that our celebration of the Feast of the Holy Trinity is also the celebration of the mystery of God.

All illustrations and analogies of the Trinity fall flat and cannot even come close to suggesting to us the profundity of the mystery. The height of the mystery is suggested when our Lord Jesus Christ says, "I and the Father are one," or when he says, "If you have seen me, you have seen the Father," and again, "The Holy Spirit, whom the Father will send in my name, will teach you all things concerning me." This is the height of the mystery, because we cannot understand how it is possible. Yet it is also the mystery made simple and practical for us, so that we can experience it. That is the important part.

To celebrate the Feast of the holy Trinity is to know that the Father, Son and Holy Spirit reveal themselves as one in Christ that we might know the "grace of the Lord Jesus Christ, the love of God and the fellowship of the Holy Spirit." Dorothy Sayers, the English dramatist and lay theologian, described the Trinity in terms of drama. An idea originates with the Father, as the thought comes to the dramatist. That idea becomes incarnate in the actor, as the Word of the Father became incarnate in the Son. The idea is shared with people in the Spirit, in the same way the drama becomes a part of the audience who watches and listens. Wolfhart Pannenberg, the German theologian, wrote an excellent essay in which he explained the doctrine of the Trinity. Pannenberg noted, as in the lessons today, the doctrine of the Trinity is best understood as a description of the Father's revelation in the Son through God's Spirit. While all analogies are inadequate, we ourselves come close in our own complicated personhood. As individuals we are mind, body, and spirit. The heavenly Father makes it possible for us to trust God's relationships to us. Because God the Father has so revealed love and grace in the Son through the Spirit, our Lord urges us to share this experience. "Go therefore," Christ says, "and make disciples of all nations, baptizing them in the name of the Father and of the Son and of the Holy Spirit."

H.N.H.

SECOND SUNDAY AFTER PENTECOST

Unrecognized in Heaven
MATTHEW 7:21-29

An evangelical marketing report newsletter has come out to help Christian organizations learn from Madison Avenue. It gives updates on who's spending what, what secular publishers look for in new religious titles, which celebrities have recently accepted Christ. It reports on the development of smaller ministries over the one million dollar mark and advises readers about when to use a secular or a Christian ad agency. The *Wall Street Journal* began reporting on religious broadcasting when it became big business: Some TV religions take in $60 million a year, while others run up to about $75 million.

For all of these hucksters of religious soap, the body of Jesus Christ has become a market, the Christian is regarded as a consumer, the Christian ministry is converted into a business, and blessings are measured in terms of profits and material success. What obviously works is giving the people what they want. Offering a message that promises health and wealth will in turn receive support and big profits. No one has to ask whether the gospel preached is from God so long as the success formulas work.

Question Success?

All this money making, all this healing, all these mighty works and profits, however, may go unrecognized in heaven. In the Gospel appointed for today our Lord Jesus Christ says, "Not every one who says to me, 'Lord, Lord,' will enter the kingdom of heaven, but only the one who does the will of my Father in heaven. On that day many will say to me, 'Lord, Lord, did we not prophesy in your name, and cast out demons in your name, and do many deeds of power in your name?' Then I will declare to them, 'I never knew you; go away from me, you evildoers.' " Those are harsh judgments.

It is difficult for us to imagine that much of what is done in the name of the Lord Jesus on such a grand scale could be so wide of the mark as to merit his disapproval. We ourselves are accustomed to honoring the name of Jesus. When much is done in his name, it seems strange to think it all could go unrecognized. So little appears to be done in his name as it is. How could Christ possibly refuse these works done in his name? He does explain the basis for his judgment in the Gospel for today.

The Ten Words

The strong warning of Jesus comes as a conclusion to the Sermon on the Mount as we have it recorded by Matthew. Matthew's account of the Sermon on the Mount is one of our Lord's interpretations of the law of God. He did not give us a new version of the Ten Commandments. He did not give us something different from the Ten Commandments. He did not give us substitutes for the Ten Commandments. But Jesus did give us a radical interpretation of the commandments. He did this because religious people had worked hard to understand the Ten Commandments. The worshiping community had given elaborate interpretations, illustrations, and exhortations as to the way the commandments should be kept.

The people created their moral standards for behavior, their ethics for controlling behavior, on the basis of what they called the Ten Words. The former translation had it, "Everyone . . . who does my works." In doing this they taught not simply what they thought was right or wrong but what they believed was the righteous life. They taught people how to earn the goodwill and favor of God by their behavior. They came to believe that they would keep the commandments and do God's will.

Jesus exposed that notion as completely erroneous. He showed that each of the commandments, to be sure, is meant to control behavior. Yet each of the Commandments by its very nature also reveals that people are sinners in their hearts. They sin before they do anything. They lust in their hearts. The think evil. All bad behavior has its source in the heart. Misbehavior began in the garden, when Adam and Eve failed to trust the word of God. Sin was initiated with the doubt in the heart. It has been that way ever since.

Action Words

For this reason, Jesus said that to do something in his name was not necessarily recognized in heaven. It must be done as a "doing of the will of the Father who is in heaven." Now how does one do that? Not be doing commandments, because the commandments already condemn us as sinners. Thus Jesus said, "Everyone then who hears these words of mine and acts on them . . . " Now how does one act on them? That is a typically Hebrew way of speaking. It is perfectly logical, because in Hebrew, words are always action words. It is natural then to think of acting out words or doing them, because, in the Hebrew understanding of things, words are meant to be done.

Then Jesus rather fittingly used an analogy or illustration to make his point about acting on words. As we shall see from his illustration, however, this kind of doing is not something that we do on our own. It is doing his words. We draw on the words that come from him as the source for our acting, and they become the enabling power for acting.

An Illustration

Jesus' illustration is the parable of the man who builds his house on a rock and the foolish man who builds his house on sand. The house built on the rock, of course, withstands floods and torrents. The other house, naturally, is slated for disaster. The point of the parable is that one must build one's life on the Lord Jesus Christ. He is the Rock. All doing is meaningless if it is not built on the Rock, because all will be lost in the storms of life themselves or in the final judgment. All the materials and the energy are wasted if our life is not built on the solid foundation of the Lord Jesus Christ.

Christ is life. He is the spice of all life. Life is to be found in him. He not only gives live but redeems and saves it. By dying on the cross and rising from the dead, Jesus did not simply demonstrate that he could withstand the temptations of life, the terrors of death, and the captivity of the grave. He actually built for us a life that can withstand these same forces. Christ is the foundation, because he has been in our situation and has withstood all that beats against us. Adversity, guilt, shame, temptation, terror, and death may work against us, but Christ is the foundation that enables us to stand up against it all. There is no fury we cannot weather when Christ is our foundation.

What God Has Done

In the Fourth Gospel the evangelist John called Jesus the Word. He is God's revelation or self-expression. Over and over again in that same Gospel the Lord Jesus said that the words he spoke he had received from the Father, they were not words carrying his own authority. He wanted to make it clear that what he said came from the Father, was of the Father, and was the Father's doing. Likewise Jesus explained that the works he did were also of the Father.

Thus when Jesus urges us to do his words, he is asking us to do the words of the Father, or as he said, to do the will of the Father. The Lord Jesus is pointing us to the activity the heavenly Father performs for us. It is his helping and redeeming activity that he has worked out for us and that he continues to work for us. We are encouraged then to concentrate on what God has done for us. To do God's word is to take seriously what God has already done for us. Doing is receiving what God has done.

Too Easy?

The further we get into this subject, the more clearly we can see that an important difference exists between doing works in Jesus' name as some expect to do them and "acting on his words." In John's Gospel the people asked Jesus, "What must we do, to be doing the work of God?" Jesus answered them, "This is the work of God, that you believe in him whom he has sent" (John 6:29). People often say, "That's too easy." Some would also say, "That means people do not have to do any good works, and you will simply discourage people from doing good in the world." Jesus would answer, "If you say that, you do not understand either my Father or me." The whole point is that we do not have to try to manipulate God through what we do.

God does work a miracle in us when God gives faith. In one sense faith is easy, because God gives it. In another sense it is impossible on our part. It is impossible because we cannot have it without God. But with God we are free to do what has to be done. The commitment and the faith for work are essential. No work that we do will be perfect. Yet by faith our works are furnished with the righteousness of the Lord Jesus Christ. Even as we are made righteous by faith, so are our works made righteous. All that we offer up to God in Jesus' name by faith is acceptable to God. The freedom to live and work this way can never be emphasized enough. Knowing that through God's word of grace and forgiveness we are liberated, we do what has to be done without worrying whether it will be acceptable or not.

A Final Word

Jesus talks about works in other places and in other ways. In one such place he was speaking in regard to the last day, the day of judgment. He said that on that day many will be surprised that they are not among those who enter into his kingdom. They will go unrecognized in heaven just as Jesus says in this text (Matthew 25). Those who do enter into the presence of Christ, however, will be equally surprised. Jesus will commend them for good works they do not remember doing.

Christ will point out that the good things Christians did were the ordinary, everyday things that had to be done for their neighbors in need. So normal were their reactions to needs that they acted spontaneously and in live without thinking about how this would count with God. The dear children of God will be unable to recognize their own good works in heaven. But how pleased they will be to receive the commendation of the Lord Jesus Christ.

Our Lord therefore encourages us to act on his words, which is to do the will of the Father. This is simply to ask that we be bathed in his love and forgiveness in order to share his love with others.

H.N.H.

THIRD SUNDAY AFTER PENTECOST
Dealing with a Sick World
MATTHEW 9:9-13

Chaim Potok's novel *The Gift of Asher Lev* is every bit as sensitive and stirring as his previous novels concerning the tensions in the Hebrew community. Asher Lev is an outstanding artist who found in France stimulation and the quietude essential to his work. He is called back to America to attend his uncle's funeral. He is uncomfortable with the changes that have transformed his old neighborhood, and he is shocked when he tours the New York art galleries. What he views makes him think art has become a Mardi Gras. The ordinary has become king surrounded by popularization, shallowness, doubt, and cynicism. The real burden for Asher, however, is the attitude of his father, a rabbi. Asher's father complains bitterly that he does not understand his son's works of art. His confusion dates back to Asher's painting of two crucifixions of his parents.

In a painful dialogue Asher tries to explain that his art may be difficult for his father because life is difficult. His father replies that life is difficult and ambiguous only because we make it so. He asserts that the task of people who believe in God is to bring God into the world. Asher does not wish to contradict his father but indicates that the rabbi does not understand how pervasive the problem of evil is. Asher believes that people are not capable of redeeming themselves.

This is the kind of tension reported in the Gospel appointed for today. The tension is between those who in hope believe that we can change and redeem the world and those who rely only on God to redeem us. The calling of Matthew was a bold stroke on the part of Jesus that highlighted the manner in which God goes about redeeming the world.

Matthew Is Called

The story of the calling of Matthew is related simply enough in the Gospel According to Matthew. Mark and Luke do not add much besides calling him by the name of Levi. What makes this so striking is the evangelists' suggestion that it was almost by chance that Jesus noticed Matthew sitting in the seat of customs. Mustering his sovereign authority, Jesus said to the man, "Follow me." Jesus did not pick someone who was qualified for discipleship by piety or behavior. Jesus did not ask for credentials or references. Nor did Jesus use some gifts of persuasion to coax the man or to indicate his expectations for him. Just the opposite is true.

Matthew was anything but likely to bring prestige and character to the movement Jesus was organizing. The man was a public disgrace to his fellow citizens. Taxes were a controversial necessity. But to collect taxes for an alien and occupying government was nothing short of treachery, particularly when the tax collectors were known to profit personally from their collections. Moreover, if Matthew's name was Levi, he had disgraced the name of those— the Levites—who served the tables of God in the temple, serving instead the table of the enemy Caesar. Any man that collected his fees knowing full well how the people felt had to be most contemptible. Yet when Jesus commanded the man to follow him, Matthew rose from his table and did so immediately.

An Act of Forgiveness

The calling of Matthew was just like all the wonderful acts Jesus had performed for the benefit of others. The drama so obvious in the healing and helping of others is present here also. The kind acts that became standard in his ministry expressed the fullness of our Lord's compassion and grace. Yet as ordinary as the event of the calling of Matthew may appear to the reader, those who witnessed it must have been awed by the manner in which this man was taken captive by the love of our Lord. Matthew walked away from a way of life that had both enslaved and condemned him. Our Lord accepted and took under his wing one whom society could not tolerate. Jesus emphasized the completeness of his acceptance and forgiveness for Matthew when he went home with him.

The Gospel relates, "And as he [Jesus] sat at dinner in the house, many tax collectors and sinners came and were sitting with him and his disciples." From Mark and Luke we learn that "the house" was the home of Levi, whom we presume is Matthew. The incident underscores the fact that Matthew and his tax collector friends were lumped together socially with the other outcasts. They had to find their companions among the people who were labeled sinners. These people were flagrant violators of social mores. They were an embarrassment to the decent and upright citizens. They belonged to the company of skid row and red-light district. Worst of all, they did not appear to be serious at all about doing their part to usher in the kingdom of God by living righteously.

The Protest

Our Lord's willingness to associate with these dregs of society did not go unnoticed. Although Jesus' calling a tax collector to be one of his disciples was shocking, it was not out of character with the unusual things Jesus had been doing. At least the tax collector gave up his obnoxious and traitorous profession. The enemies might have had to concede one good aspect to this incident. However, that did not reverse their judgment on Matthew for having done what he did. Now Matthew gave further evidence of his unreliability by allowing the riffraff to celebrate his new relationship with Jesus of Nazareth. That put Jesus in a bad light too.

The evangelist noted, "When the Pharisees saw this, they said to the disciples, 'Why does your teacher eat with tax collectors and sinners?' " It appeared that Jesus had not raised Matthew to his level. Rather Jesus had stooped to the level of tax collectors and sinners. Jesus kept adding fuel to the fires of contempt that these official religionists were kindling for him. To greet these people on the street might be one thing. To sit at table and dine with them, however, was to show the highest form of respect for them. One dines with one's peers and intimate friends. Jesus was signaling that he accepted these social misfits as his friends and intimate companions. What possible explanation could the disciples give for such outlandish behavior?

The Response

Our Lord's response to the Pharisees who interrogated the disciples was forthright. We are not sure whether the question was conveyed by the disciples or if Jesus overheard it. At any rate, Jesus did not hesitate to state why he befriended sinners. Jesus said, "Those who are well have no need of a physician, but those who are sick." Jesus did not defend the life-style of the people he befriended. He did not approve of the things they did or cherished. He explained that they were sick. To be sure, they were sinners. To be sure, they needed help. They were afflicted with the condition common to all people born into the world. Jesus was the one who was willing to offer them help by being their spiritual physician.

The cure that Jesus brought was not all that easy. His cure required, first of all, the admission of one's sickness and need. Matthew, like his companions from the seamy side of life, responded to Jesus as one who recognized their sickness and as a physician who was also willing to do something about it. Jesus did not isolate them from society but brought to them the love and forgiveness necessary for their recovery. The Great Physician went among them that he might free them from the plague of sin and guilt that dominated and controlled their lives. Jesus was a true realist about what kind of people they were. He was also the one who could hold out the highest hope for their rebirth through the application of his love.

We do not have to succumb to the pessimism of Asher Lev, who was certain people could not reform themselves. We do not have to fall for the Pollyanna view of his father, who thought people could cooperate with God and make all things right. In Jesus Christ we experience the love, grace, and mercy by which we are reborn and through which we can make all things new.

H.N.H.

Needed: Compassionate Workers
MATTHEW 9:35—10:8

Mikhail Gorbachev addressed his people after the historic coup in August 1991 that failed to reestablish the rightist element of the Communist party in the Soviet Union as supreme authority. He had to make a painful confession. Gorbachev admitted that the coup was largely his own making. He had selected and trusted the wrong people. Consequently he felt compelled to dismiss the very people on whom he depended to support his causes. This is no isolated incident of betrayal in history, of course. Those who rule have always had to be wary of their confidants. "Et tu, Brute?" — "You too, Brutus?" — the last words of Caesar, addressed to his friend Brutus as Caesar lay dying from wounds inflicted by his enemies. The saying has been popularized to apply to any betrayal.

The experience and fear of betrayal or disloyalty is certainly rampant in the business world today. Buyouts and takeovers instigate wholesale firing by new administrations, fearful lest faithful employees of the sold company not develop loyalty to the new regime. Newly installed political administrations also practice firings or call for resignations fearing that persons outside their party will not perform well. The same kind of fear is rampant in academic and medical communities.

Thus it is not surprising that when our Lord chose his disciples, one among them would also betray him. It is worth noting, however, what was involved in the selection of our Lord's original cabinet of co-workers.

The List

The list of the twelve apostles collated by Matthew in our Gospel reading today is his own arrangement by choice and differs slightly from the other evangelists. All the evangelists agree, however, that Peter should be listed first. Simon Peter enjoys that priority because of his leadership activity. The evangelists also agree that Judas Iscariot should be listed last, because he is "the one who betrayed" Jesus.

No small amount of debate about this selection has taken place among sophisticated theologians as well as ordinary Christian lay people. The argument centers on the question of whether Jesus knew when he selected Judas that Judas would betray him. The question gets pushed further by those who ask whether it was not necessary for him to choose someone who would betray him in order to fulfill the plan of redemption as Jesus understood it. We need not get lost in a dither in discussing such questions. This Gospel offers absolutely no evidence that Jesus had a notion that Judas would betray him.

A Constant Problem

The motives, sincerity, and faithfulness of Judas may have been just as pure as those of the other disciples at the time of their calling. We have to remember that none of the disciples remained faithful to their master when he was taken prisoner in the garden, and Peter made a public denial of his association with Jesus. Furthermore, Jesus was just as careful to forewarn Judas of his fateful betrayal as he did Peter of his faithless denial. Also, when Jesus caught them in the very act of their fall from grace, he tried to regain them both—Judas with a word and Peter with a stare.

Jesus was not a fatalist. Jesus did everything in his power to win the hearts and affections of people. As we can learn from the holy Gospel for today, our Lord clearly intended to claim the world for the heavenly Father. Jesus chose co-workers to aid him in that cause.

However, just as one among them fell from grace and did not
return, so some among us do the same. Each of us has to blush
with shame when we recall the times we have betrayed or denied
the Lord and his cause; but in repentance we find comfort in his
grace and forgiveness. This is precisely why our Lord in a later parable urges the servants of the church not to make judgments about
who are the faithful and who are the faithless lest they misjudge
some (Matthew 13:24-40).

A Constant Need

What the Gospel relates to us is our Lord's dedication to sharing
the good news of the kingdom, which is to proclaim that God is
still in charge and truly does love the creation and the creatures
God has made. As a sign of this gracious rule and presence of God
within the creation, Jesus went about "curing every disease and
sickness." This was to indicate that God had reversed any judgment the world, the devil, or sinful beings had passed on the
human situation as being utterly hopeless.

As Jesus made this tour of gracious activity, he was utterly
amazed at the condition of the people he saw. Jesus "had compassion for them, because they were harassed and helpless, like sheep
without a shepherd." It was then that Jesus called the attention of
his disciples to the fact that the human predicament was beyond
human control. There was much to be done and too few workers.
"Therefore, ask the Lord of the harvest to send out laborers into his
harvest."

From all indications, we have not gained on the situation. Daily
we read and see the signs that the world is in pitiful shape. Whatever momentary recesses or interludes of hopeful behavior we
enjoy are always interrupted by the news that the world is out of
joint again.

The Kingdom Is Near

The world's sorry condition was no excuse for our Lord to give it
up to the domination of the demonic. The more pain and disarray
Jesus saw, the more he was convinced that he should do something about it. For him the answer was to proclaim "the good news
of the kingdom." To demonstrate the effect and the power of his
kingdom, Matthew enumerated in the previous two chapters of his
Gospel ten different mighty acts Jesus performed for the healing
and restoration of people. Matthew brought together these ten

signs to corroborate the completeness and fullness of God's gracious activity. Matthew certainly was no numerologist, but he employed these ten gracious deeds of our Lord to parallel the ten words by which God created the earth and the first creatures, the ten words or commandments spoken in the covenant, the ten plagues by which God exhibited his power to the Egyptians and the Israelites, the ten trials by which Abraham was perfected in his faith.

The revelation of God's grace in Christ was no less complete than what God had consistently manifested in the desire to reclaim the world. Matthew was not marshaling the evidence of our Lord's mighty deeds to prove what Jesus was. Rather the deeds were the signals of what God was revealing in this gracious activity. This was God operating in Jesus of Nazareth in a most wholesome and healing way in behalf of people. The range of healing and saving activities consistently pointed to the messianic character of Jesus, to his role in saving and redeeming people in need.

It Is the Work of God

If Matthew was sure that the ministry of Jesus was so comprehensive a display of the gracious activity of God in the world, we have to deal with a curious instruction Jesus gave to the disciples. Matthew reports that the instructions to the twelve began, "Go nowhere among the Gentiles, and enter no town of the Samaritans, but rather go to the lost sheep of the house of Israel." This sounds so limited, so provincial, so biased. Our Lord's design, however, was quite the opposite.

Our Lord had chosen the twelve as apostles that they might represent the new Israel. From the time of Abraham, God had promised to bless all the nations of the earth through God's special people. The people Israel were to be a model of the way God is willing to deal with all the nations of the earth. Israel was to be the depository, the fullness of God's promises for the world. Through Israel God would enable the peoples of the earth to experience the faithfulness of God's eternal love for humankind. The mission of the twelve to the house of Israel, therefore, was to ensure the global providence and grace of God for the world.

The Apostolate

It is important to note that the mission to the world that our Lord initiates is totally God's doing. It is God who ushers in the kingdom. The kingdom of God is God's rule, presence, and activity in the world. *We* do not bring in the kingdom, as some like to believe. Nor do we establish the kingdom of God on earth.

The proclamation that "the kingdom of heaven has come near" is the gospel, the good news that God is in Christ reconciling the world to himself and offering himself for the world. No one volunteers for this work. Jesus had said that we "ask the Lord of the harvest to send out laborers into his harvest." God has not only to call them through the Spirit but to equip them through faith and to confer on them through baptism the authority that God himself exercised in Jesus the Christ.

That is why Matthew calls the twelve "apostles." The apostle in the Hebrew community was a "messenger" who was considered a "proxy" for his teacher or master. The apostle was equipped to act on behalf of his teacher, not only making his work representative of but having the same power as the teacher. Hence Jesus could instruct his disciples to carry on the same kind of ministry they had witnessed and heard from Jesus.

At the moment it sounded so promising. Yet Jesus was to pass through the crucible of his passion, death, and entombment. The disciples would lose their way until their master was raised from the dead, had ascended to the Father, and returned to them in the gift of the Holy Spirit at Pentecost.

In *Man of the House,* Congressman Tip O'Neill has shared the memoirs of his public life of service. "Work and Wages" was the slogan that won O'Neill his first political seat in 1936. It was a recurring theme throughout his career. But in his later years O'Neill saw the idea fall into disfavor. The age of greed spawned a go-it-alone ethic. It allowed the young to neglect the aged, the healthy to forget the sick, and the wealthy to abandon the poor.

In the short time since his retirement in 1986, the wheels have come off the yuppie life-style. Given the present state of the national psyche, we cannot ignore one another. We have to rebuild our systems on loving and caring. All other systems self-destruct. As Christians we should understand this well. We all are now equipped by the Holy Spirit with the compassion to go about helping those who are harassed and helpless.

H.N.H.

FIFTH SUNDAY AFTER PENTECOST
Wanted: Bold Evangelists
MATTHEW 10:24-33

Damage, a first novel by Josephine Hart, has received acclaim as a powerful psychological study. The principal character in the story is a doctor, who had been born to wealth and married into wealth. The son-in-law of a member of Parliament, he also was elected to parliament. He was well regarded as a physician and political figure. His wife was beautiful. Together they boasted of a handsome son who developed a career in newspaper editing, and a lovely daughter who painted. One could not imagine a life more suitably and comfortably arranged.

Yet the good doctor complained that he never felt at home in this world, never felt fulfilled, and did not recognize himself. Then in a quick moment he thought he discovered himself in another. He became obsessed to the point that his life was totally damaged. Hence the title, *Damage.* At age fifty he ruefully acknowledged that those who knew him would have to regard as tragic his not having died in his fiftieth year.

This powerfully told story presents an insightful parable on the human condition. People can live shabby and dreary lives, but even those who appear to have everything in life may come up empty-handed or worse, may destroy their lives in a mistaken pursuit of fulfillment.

This is the heart of what Jesus was talking about in the holy Gospel appointed for today. The passage continues a discourse Jesus gave to his disciples to prepare them for an evangelistic mission. He was encouraging them to see the advantage they had in viewing life as it really is.

A World of Chaos

In the discourse on evangelism, Jesus pointed out that the disciples were not to be intimidated by what was going on in the world. Having been taught by Jesus, they were to be "like the teacher." Just as Jesus had been called "Beelzebul," that is, the devil, so would the disciples.

If anything, however, it looks to us as if the world does the work of the devil. Life is dreadfully cheap in our time. Hatred, terrorism, drugs, and murders spill into the streets. Children are abused and die. Families fall to pieces. Homeless people crowd the corners.

While we groan and rub our hands in hopelessness, we allow Hollywood to glamorize this escalating onslaught on life, to feed our horrendous appetite for the portrayal of more and more violence. We live in a period of chaos.

A World of Trouble

On the global scale, we still have not learned—after all the bitter human experience through all the ages of history—how to live in peace. After Desert Storm in 1991, we gave thanks that the war was short and that we had so few losses. We hoped that we could learn that no one can really afford modern warfare and that to invoke modern warfare means disaster. However, we know that as many as three hundred thousand Iraqis were lost, and we should grieve for the loss of humanity. The results were not all that good. A tyrant remained in power, and we shuddered when we learned of his nuclear capability. Yet we are concerned that the disarmament agreements of the superpowers still leave both Americans and Russians with arsenals that could end civilization.

At the same time that we worked to negotiate peaceful agreements between Middle East nations, we had to worry about competing with other nations in selling arms to them. Back home we also give weighty consideration to the kind of modern war machines we can build. The Catholic theologian Gregory Baum, in the *Ecumenist*, gave up in despair. He saw no signs that anyone seriously entertains the notion that we can truly work for peace.

So long as we believe that we are safe when we are superior or can make ourselves superior, we do not understand life. The issue of war and peace in our day betrays the fact that the world on its own does not understand the meaning of life. So long as the threat to the very existence of society is still harbored in the nuclear arsenals of the superpowers, the world has not given meaning to life.

Jesus observed that there is no reason to fear those "who kill the body but cannot kill the soul." The pervasiveness of violence and war shows that much of the world is in the hands of those who kill the body, and we may fear that the destruction will also harm the soul.

A Bankrupt World

Humanity comes up bankrupt in the search for answers to the major problems of life. We hear people decry the "absence of values." They lament that our children "are not taught values anymore." But how can we teach them when things are so out of balance? We have a horrendous military budget but cannot scrape enough money together to support adequate school systems. Our states encourage us to dream about becoming millionaires overnight with lotteries, and at the same time we support welfare systems that continue to lock the poor into poverty.

We pay outlandish salaries to sport heroes and then pay them more to advertise products that youngsters steal in order to feel accepted. We take our industry overseas to save a few dollars and close down thousands of factories, only to discover that we have lost our edge as an industrial nation. We find ourselves in a recession that does not seem to want to go away. We have allowed the family to disintegrate and yet wonder why children grow up feeling insecure and unloved. We created a sexual revolution, hoping everyone could be free, only to discover that we are slaves to the subject. The answer to all the problems? The law! Values? Who knows anything about values? If there are problems, sue somebody or something!

Jesus Is Pivotal

Jesus encouraged his disciples to take on the world of false power and delusions of grandeur. He said, "Have no fear of them." Whatever Jesus had shared in private or secret they could share openly in a large way. Jesus was going to make good on whatever he taught. We know that Jesus meant that he was willing to offer himself up as a sacrifice for the sins of the world.

Jesus was willing to die at the hands of unbelieving, distrustful, sinful people who thought they had to save their own lives by their own goodness. Jesus was willing to take this debate all the way to its conclusion. The people could force the issue by ridding themselves of a person who talked about God as someone who was so available as to be in the flesh. Jesus affirmed that it was so. God was present among them in this person of Jesus, and he was ready to die to prove it.

Prove it he did. Not only was Jesus so gracious as to offer himself up for crucifixion upon the cross, but he also rose again to prove that life is really and truly to be found in him, so that death itself could not deprive him of the eternal life that God offers and gives in him.

God Is Life

In essence Jesus was saying that God offers life to a death-infested humanity. In saying what he did in such a challenging way, Jesus was not unmindful of the power his enemies wielded. He knew that if they were capable of taking his life, they were also capable of making martyrs of the disciples. Yet Jesus continued to insist that the cause was worth dying for. The world was God's and worth dying for. The powers in the world were destroying it. We know that well enough today. Jesus could teach, however, "Do not fear those who kill the body but cannot kill the soul; rather, fear him who can destroy both soul and body in hell."

Even if the evil powers are bent on destroying the world and all that is good in it, you do not have to fear them. If they elect to destroy you over your protests against their evil and because you evangelize for good, don't fear them. Remember your allegiance is to the God who created and redeemed you.

An Integrated Life

Jesus encouraged his disciples to challenge the world with the gospel. Moreover, Jesus offered great consolation. "Are not two sparrows sold for a penny? Yet not one of them will fall to the ground apart from your Father, and even the hairs of your head are all counted. So do not be afraid; you are of more value than many sparrows." God dwells within us to protect us through our Lord Jesus Christ.

Donald Hands, a clergyman who is also trained in psychiatry, has proposed a definition of an "integrated life." He explains that the integrated life is one that makes sense out of one's total experience of mind, body, and spirit through the relationship to the incarnation of our Lord Jesus Christ.

People who try to control behavior only by repression are sure to have things backfire. Those who seek to control by suppression are apt to create all kinds of misery. People who believe their behavior is best served by gratification are asking for trouble. Sublimation, another form of behavior control, is likely to have all kinds of unwelcome eruptions.

As our lives are integrated by faith through our Lord Jesus Christ, however, we are able honestly to deal with our thoughts, feelings, and impulses in relationship to ourselves, to others, and to God. Although I have oversimplified Dr. Hand's theory, this process of integration by faith in Christ helps us to discover that we do not have to create our self-defense, self-esteem, self-worth, or righteousness. It comes as a gift of God in Christ. We do not have to be obsessed with self-concern, for we discover that the one who is the most concerned for us is none other than God. God is not too busy to take the time to count the hairs on our head.

A Life Readily Available

Our Lord's observation about the Father's intimate concern for our lives is fortified by his promise. We are the vessels of God's love and grace for redeeming a mad, mad world. Jesus assures us that if we engage with him in this redeeming work, he will acknowledge us before the Father in heaven. When we share the good news of God's grace in Christ, we are true to our discipleship.

On the other hand, to fail to share the good news is to allow the world to suffer the damage it brings upon itself and to endure the possibility of damaging ourselves eternally. We need not even consider that possibility. Far better that we accept all of the love, encouragement, and assurances of our Lord to become bold evangelists in witnessing to a world that is doomed without us.

H.N.H.

SIXTH SUNDAY AFTER PENTECOST
Who Said It Would Be Easy?
MATTHEW 10:34-42

David Halberstam, a Pulitzer Prize winner, has made it his calling to comment on political and economic power in America, and in the world, for that matter. Drawing heavily on his experience as a *New York Times* reporter in Eastern Europe and on research on the Japanese economy, in his book *The Reckoning* he helps us to understand what the future might bring. His little book *The Next Century* shares with us the secret we all know but do not like to admit: the American Century is past. The time of easy affluence in America is over. In a sense it has been over for a long time. While we were obsessed with the interminable war in Vietnam and the cold war with the Soviet Union, Japan was occupied with building itself as a nation of commerce. We poured all of our energies and resources into a war we could not win and built a nuclear arsenal to prevent a war no one wanted.

Now nations of the Eastern bloc have to learn how to live with freedom and how to create economies that work. At the same time, the Japanese worry if their next generation has gone soft and will not be able to compete at the same level that the generation that made Japan an economic power did. If America is to regain the place it once occupied as an economic power, we are going to have to work hard. We are going to have to energize ourselves in new ways and give up old assumptions about ourselves as a nation. In order to regain our position, we are going to have to lose something. That sounds somewhat like the words in the holy Gospel appointed for today when Jesus talks about losing one's life in order to find it.

The Paradox

In the Gospel we have a continuation of the instruction our Lord gave to the twelve whom he had chosen as apostles. He was preparing them to carry on the mission and ministry the heavenly Father had given him. He made this shocking observation: "Do not think that I have come to bring peace to the earth; I have not come to bring peace, but a sword." This hardly sounds appropriate coming from the one who was to fulfill the messianic hope as the Prince of Peace.

Can it be that the one whose birth angels celebrated with the declaration "Peace on earth" talks about bringing a sword? Yet this is what the evangelist records. Jesus is no softie, no teddy bear, no marcelled, pastel-colored shaman. Jesus knew that what he offered and what he called people to, was divisive.

The Prince of Peace can bring peace and make peace only if he can cut people off from the world that stands between himself and those whom he calls. We find this in striking human terms as people in Eastern Europe, South Africa, South America, and Central America struggle to install peace and freedom in their parts of the world. Civil liberty cannot come without pain. Peace most often comes when people have been willing to pay a very high price.

In spite of Jesus' claim that he had come to fulfill the law, which he explained was summarized in love, he knew he would put people at odds with one another, even within families. Jesus said, "I have come to set a man against his father, and a daughter against her mother, and a daughter-in-law against her mother-in-law; and one's foes will be members of one's own household." How does this happen?

Jesus represents and is the fullest expression of God's love and concern for the world. Therefore nothing and no one should jeopardize the relationship between the person and the Christ. Jesus explains, "Whoever loves father or mother more than me is not worthy of me; and whoever loves son or daughter more than me is not worthy of me." A parent or a child can be just as much a false idol as one made of gold if that person derails, falsifies, spoils, or hinders one's faith in Christ. This may sound harsh, but much of the divisiveness in families would not occur if our Lord Jesus Christ were the permanent, unseen guest of the family.

Cross Bearing

Jesus does not intrude in the lives of people to make things difficult for them. Jesus does not stand among people to see how many families he can make miserable, break up, or destroy. Jesus does, however, bring a cross. He encourages people to "take up the cross and follow" him if they are to be worthy of him. The cross means going the second mile, expressing love in its fullest dimension, being ready to die for the sake of humanity. Jesus did this as he taught and lived the genuine love of the creator God for God's creatures. Strangely enough, people did not like what they saw. They preferred to save their own skins, so they nailed Jesus to the cross.

Jesus knew, however, that to trust God's love in spite of the suffering that the cross entailed was to have life in the resurrection. Thus Jesus extended the invitation to others to take up the cross and follow him. In doing so, they would discover the true meaning of love, forgiveness, and grace. They would experience for themselves the blessings of Christ's love for them. They would also be empowered to express the same kind of love for others.

Jesus revealed the reality that God is found in suffering. Luther liked to say that if you want to find God, do not look for God where everything is peaceful and serene. That is obviously a charade the devil is playing on you. If we want to find God, we must look for him at the cross, where he suffers with us through the pain of our lives.

Lost: A Life

Jesus further explained that this commitment and cross bearing is fundamental to understanding and living life. He said, "Those who find their life will lose it." If people believe that life is to be found in what they can make of it and what they can do to protect, insulate, and prolong it, they will lose it. Eventually they will have to sing, "Is that all there is?" The answer to that is yes, and you will have to give it up.

The Day America Told the Truth is a book of surveys collected to discover what Americans believe about everything that matters. When asked what dreams they had to change themselves and how they hoped to fulfill their potential, people gave simple enough answers. The editors of the book, however, were amazed at the findings. People did not aspire to be better persons or to make this a better world. The top-ranking answers were "I want to be rich" and "I want to be thin."

Mike Yaconelli, senior editor of *The Door*, asserted that such findings reveal the bankruptcy of the American soul, the lack of responsibility, the absence of values, and the epidemic of violence. God, he pointed out, does not care if we are rich or poor, fat or thin.

If our best dreams are only to be rich and thin, we not only will lose our lives, but we have lost them already. Our Lord Jesus Christ calls us to a life of sacrifice and self-denial.

Found: A Life

Jesus not only warned those who have such small and petty dreams that they will lose everything, he also promised, "Those who lose their life for my sake will find it." Tony Hillerman has written an exciting mystery novel about a missing geologist in *A Thief of Time*. The drama takes place in the area of the Anasazi culture near the Grand Canyon. The story gets us involved in the unanswered questions about the Anasazi culture, which lasted about a thousand years: why the people developed the life-style they did, why they came to such a difficult place for habitation, why they left.

In a somewhat similar way, Jesus affirms that we will most certainly lose our lives and leave no clues as to what we were if we are merely self-serving. We do not discover ourselves when we live for ourselves. Luther said we discover ourselves and life when we live outside ourselves, that is, when we live in our neighbors in love, just as our Lord Jesus Christ lives in us. We have seen this demonstrated in our own lives. When we become overly concerned about ourselves, we tend to lose ourselves in obsessive depressions. When we become too self-satisfied and smug, our neighbors become absolutely bored with us, if they do not avoid and disdain us. Far better that we learn how to find our lives in Christ.

A Prophetic Task

As Matthew pieced together the instructions our Lord gave his friends for their discipleship, he showed Jesus explaining further what was involved in finding life in him. Not only were the disciples intimately bound up in his life as worthy companions who lose their lives for his sake, but they were also identified with our Lord. Jesus promised, "Whoever welcomes you welcomes me, whoever welcomes me welcomes the one who sent me."

The followers of our Lord will readily be recognized as those who are receptive to God's grace and providence. This is not worldly recognition or acclaim. More often than not it may be hidden, like the grandmas of Russia who kept the faith alive during the suppression of Christianity.

Jesus added, "Whoever welcomes a prophet in the name of the prophet will receive a prophet's reward." All too often the reward of the prophet was pain and martyrdom. Yet the memory of the prophet was celebrated, and those who failed to heed the prophet were the losers and serve as warnings of God's judgment. Jesus added, "Whoever welcomes a righteous person will receive the reward of a righteous person." This righteousness was not the self-righteous behavior of those who dared to think they could pawn themselves off as holy and innocent before God. This righteousness was like Abraham's, who was righteous before God because he trusted the heavenly Father who bestows righteousness by grace. The righteous belong to the family of God because they believe that God has made them the vessels of God's grace and that they are the very ones through whom God can act in and on the world.

Scattering the Good

All that our Lord shared with his disciples about discipleship was realistic. He offered them no false hopes about being able to win the whole world. He did not outfit them as salesmen who could win with the hard sell or as smoothies who could pose as soft, angelic messengers to the world. He gave them encouragement by assuring them that they were to be cut from the same cloth as his mission and ministry. They were to be poured into the same mold of sacrificial love and grace; they would be extensions of the high calling given to Jesus by the heavenly Father. What the twelve did would not be lost on the world. On the contrary, their ministry would never be in vain. "Whoever gives even a cup of cold water to one of these little ones in the name of a disciple—truly I tell you, none of these will lose their reward," Jesus concluded. That means that as the twelve took up the ministry from our Lord, they could offer the kingdom of God's love in Christ to the world with high delight. The people who gave them the slightest assistance in their wearying task as they made their way in the wilderness of the lost world would receive a blessing.

No matter how people get involved in the promotion of this work of God's grace, they can be certain of God's blessing. "The little ones," the disciples, welcome the help they receive. But even more, our Father in heaven welcomes that help with blessing. That's how we all fit in. In Christ we not only discover our own life, but we have the assurance that what we can do for his sake will be life for the world.

H.N.H.

SEVENTH SUNDAY AFTER PENTECOST

New Insights
MATTHEW 11:25-30

Gail Godwin's novel *Father Melancholy's Daughter* is the story of a young woman's struggle to discover herself. Another central character in the story line is her father, Walter Gower, an Episcopal priest who suffers from melancholia but who is also driven by an intense commitment to serve his people well with personal and tender care. As he goes about his ministrations in St. Cuthbert's parish, he is not unaware of the differences between his and others' approaches to ministry. The most obvious contrast with his ministry is the work of Jerry Hope, the Episcopal priest at St. Matthias across town. Walter grouses that Jerry was so busy attending to the requirements of his program director that he had to hire another Episcopal clergyman to take up the counseling duties. Together the counselor and Walter Gower realize that their approaches to ministry are not simply a contrast in style to the ministry of Jerry Hope. The differences result from their opposing theologies.

Lay people certainly are not oblivious to such differences. They can openly discuss the clergy's divergent interpretations of the gospel and their conflicting ways of serving. Knowing that, we can understand how tensions developed between Jesus and the religious leaders of his day as he preached and ministered to the people. The evangelist Matthew explains the tensions as he brings together some of the sayings of Jesus in the holy Gospel for today.

The Context

In Matthew these sayings follow Jesus' reproach of the towns for refusing to believe the "deeds of power" Jesus had performed in them. Before pronouncing judgment on these towns, Jesus had spoken about the ministry of John the Baptizer. John, languishing in prison, had inquired about the work of Jesus. Jesus sent an assurance that the work of the kingdom was being done. Then Jesus spoke about the contrasts in style between John's ministry and his own. The styles were different, but the message was the same: the kingdom of God had come. Jesus pointed out that the people refused both John and himself.

But at the same time, what was refused and rejected by some was accepted and trusted by others. The work and message of Jesus had not been ambiguous. It was not to be understood by one group one way and another way by another group. It was clear enough for both groups, and one group refused it.

The Hidden and the Revealed

In view of the rejection and the reception he was receiving, Jesus was able to pray to his heavenly Father, "I thank you, Father, Lord of heaven and earth, because you have hidden these things from the wise and intelligent and revealed them to infants; yes, Father, for such was your gracious will." The will and intention of God is not that people should not understand. The revelation was clearly made in Jesus Christ. If people use their intelligence and wisdom to pursue only what is logical, however, they miss the goodness of God. What is hidden to them is God's graciousness in doing for people what they themselves cannot do. Thus God's goodness and grace can remain hidden because of intellectual pride. The "infants," meanwhile, grasp what is being revealed to them.

Those who did receive our Lord were like little children who openly show their dependence on others. The "little ones" are not hesitant to confess their lack of understanding. The disciples did this over and over again and manifested an openness to Jesus' revelation or correction. What was a failure with the pious and the sophisticates of the religious community turned out to be a success with the naive and open-minded "infants," who were ready and eager to receive the fullness of the love that our Lord offered.

Jesus Is the Clue

Jesus explained why some people could accept him and others could not. Jesus did not come to reveal a debatable set of propositions about God. Jesus did not come to develop a new system of behavior by which people could win the affection of God. Jesus came to cement the relationship between God and people. Jesus said, "All things have been handed over to me by my Father; and no one knows the Son except the Father, and no one knows the Father except the Son and anyone the Son chooses to reveal him."

Jesus expressed the fullness of God bodily (Colossians 2:9). Jesus therefore could properly claim that he not only resembled the Father but that "all things had been handed over to him." Jesus was helping people to understand what God is like. The Father wants everyone to know that. The Son could show us concretely how God feels about us. Jesus made that his mission and ministry.

Jesus said, "No one knows the Father except the Son and anyone to whom the Son chooses to reveal him." This is exactly who Jesus was revealing when he did the deeds of power in those towns that rejected him. A meaningful relationship with God would be possible only for those who could first understand that Jesus was the only one to mediate it between God and us.

The Burden

As Matthew recorded it, Jesus capped these important insights into the tensions that had developed between him and the religious leaders with a most gracious invitation: "Come to me, all you that are weary and are carrying heavy burdens, and I will give you rest. Take my yoke upon you, and learn from me; for I am gentle and humble in heart, and you will find rest for your souls. For my yoke is easy, and my burden is light." Jesus applied to himself the words the rabbis used to refer to the law of God—*yoke* and *burden*. They promoted a fastidious attention to the law of God. They supplied detailed explanations of how the law of God could be kept. In doing so, they added minutiae to the law that made it a loathsome and impossible burden. They encouraged a rigid adherence to the law for people to win the favor and blessing of God.

If people did what was required of them, the teaching suggested they would be amply awarded. Their goodness and righteous deeds would achieve great blessing, and they would be assured good health and wealth. Such teaching transposed the law of God into a logical explanation for the behavior of both God and the people. If both coincided, all would be well, and the kingdom of God would certainly come.

Such teachers have never been in short supply in the world. They fill the airwaves with religious soap. They peddle their wares with intensity and place burdens on their hearers. Their success is remarkable. Their teaching seems logical and self-respecting.

But Jesus came to rescue us from the fallacy of our logic. Logic will not save us. Our best efforts will not redeem us from pain and the grave. That is why Jesus said, "Come to me . . . and I will give your rest. Take my yoke upon you, and learn from me." Our Lord Jesus Christ lived his life as a model for us. What he bequeathed to us was the true shape of life and death.

To live life as designed by God is to trust the Father. To die in peace is to trust the Father. We can trust God the Father because we know that God loves us. God created us in love and has never stopped loving us. That love does not depend upon what we do or even what we believe. We do not make God into a believer in us.

We, however, can believe in God in spite of what we are, what we do, and what happens to us. Jesus proved this. From the human point of view, things did not go well for Jesus. He was crucified for doing what was good, just, and holy. Yet he continued to believe his Father. Even when death came too early and undeservedly, he believed, and God raised him from the dead. Therein our Lord demonstrated that our daily lives are linked to eternity by the love God has for us. God gives our lives an eternal value, and we do not have to prove anything, earn anything, or deserve anything from God. That is the yoke Jesus hangs around our necks. He says, "I am gentle and lowly in heart."

An Easy Yoke

Jesus has sympathy and compassion for us as we deal with the daily burdens of life and death. Jesus cannot shield us from the judgments that the world lays upon itself. But he does assure us that we are not under the judgment of God. The yoke he lays on us is a call to trust the love of God. When the teachers of Jesus' day spoke of the law of God as a yoke, they used the best language they could to encourage the people to put off the yokes and burdens of the world and accept the yoke of God. Yet they failed to keep the people from becoming self-concerned and turned in on themselves. Such piety tended to make the people as self-centered as if they had been the children of the world.

Jesus, however, made it possible for those who came to him to experience the freedom and rest of knowing that their lives were in the hands of God. Jesus taught nothing new. Jesus taught what was evident from the dawn of creation.

The risen Christ was and is the living proof of how taking the yoke of Christ works out for us. How it happens in our lives has been worked out for us in Holy Baptism in which we die and rise with Christ. We experience no pain in that transaction. Yet in baptism we drown sin and death and are brought into the fullness of life with God. The taking of this yoke upon ourselves is accepting what God gives in love and grace. Faith discerns that such a yoke is easy to take, to be sure.

A Light Burden

When Jesus talked about an easy yoke or a light burden, he was not employing oxymorons. Oxymorons are words that are contradictions in terms. Both yokes and burdens are normally considered oppressive and worrisome. Yet Jesus changes that with the offer he makes to us.

How we discover the manner in which Jesus makes the yoke easy and the burden light is the subject of Susan Howatch's exciting novel *Glamorous Powers*. Jon Darrow, an Anglican churchman, experiences disappointment after disappointment in his marriage, his children, his vocation, his career in parishes and in a religious order. He is deeply pained over and over again as he pursues visions, hopes, and dreams. Finally one day in a chapel he comes to a sudden awareness of God's love. All of the past sorrows, guilt, and futile pursuits are swept away. It finally dawns on him that the divine love revealed in the crucified Christ is the boundless grace that makes the yoke easy and the burden light.

What we discover, as Jon Darrow did, and as Walter Gower preached, is that when our Lord talks about his yoke and his burden, he gives us not something new to do but the eternal gift of God's love, so that we can deal with the weariness and the heavy burdens that others lay on us.

H.N.H.

EIGHTH SUNDAY AFTER PENTECOST
Hey, You, Listen!
MATTHEW 13:1-9 (18-23)

The *Smithsonian* (August 1991) published a lively and exhaustive article on how the tractor sparked the industrial revolution on the American farm. Steam tractors arrived at the turn of the century to assist farmers in their quest for greater productivity. Only about 20 percent of the farmers took to the steam tractor, and the steam machines began to fade from the picture by 1910 when internal combustion tractors began to take over.

By 1919 tractors were being used quite widely. By 1932 more than a million farmers owned tractors, but the machines did not outnumber horses for farming until 1955. Eventually farmers trusted the machines enough to dispense with horses entirely. Not only did farmers increase their productivity, but they were able to cultivate marginal land that had been left idle or used only for pasture. The size of the average from grew from fewer than 140 acres in 1910 to about 460 acres today.

A generation ago John Steinbeck wrote about this transition, about tractors covering the fields like insects. In *The Grapes of Wrath* he described the plight of those who were driven off the land. One poor soul chatted with another about how one could not live on the land anymore unless one had two or five or ten thousand acres and a tractor.

The revolution of the tractor has been followed by other revolutions on the farm—hybrid seeds, irrigation systems, fertilizers, computers, and advanced agronomy. We stand in awe of these achievements. Of course, farmers still have to cope with the drought and other natural disasters. Still, they have moved a great distance from the primitive agricultural experience our Lord talks about in the holy Gospel for today.

The Sower

In order to appreciate the parable of the seed and the sower, we have to think in primitive terms. Most of us urban people know something about the American farming enterprise, because we read about it, are dependent on it, may have visited a farm or two, or may have invested in one. However, probably very few of us have grown up down on the farm. In 1920 nearly half of our population still lived in rural areas. By 1980 only 26 percent of the population was rural. For that reason it is important that we do not think of the parable out of our experience of American farming.

Most of the people of our Lord's day were farmers. The society was principally agricultural. Although the nature of the soil, the climate, and other factors made farming a life of constant toil and hardship, the industry was basic to survival. A large part of the land was desert and rock and could not be farmed. A typical farmer did not live on the farm but in a nearby village or town, most often near a fortified city. He owned no more land than he could manage with his family. He probably grew vegetables and herbs alongside his house. When the Israelites first came to the promised land, each household was given a plot of land. But as the rich engaged in buy-outs, it became difficult for the poor to hold on to their land.

If you can erase the images of American farmers and their farms from your mind, and can picture instead a hardworking farmer toiling in a small field with bare hands, you can begin to understand this parable. If you place this anxious farmer in the middle of a confined field surrounded by hard paths that separate his plot from those of his neighbors, and if you can see him marching over his stone-laden field trying to make rows with the seed he throws from his hand, then you can picture what Jesus was was saying. From the pulpit of a boat on the Sea of Galilee Jesus preached to the rural congregation that had gathered on the beach. He told them that a farmer went out to sow his seed, but as he threw out the seed, some fell on those hardened paths, and the birds came and devoured them.

Jesus later explained that the seed is the word of God that is snatched up by the evil one. The devil works overtime to convince everyone that the word does not have a chance. It is not difficult to find people who have been diverted from the word. The easiest place for that to happen is right in the church.

People can get concerned about all the wrong things. They can be persuaded that the church will fail if the congregation gets behind in paying its bills. They can be absolutely certain the church is not going to get the job done; compared to successful businesses, the church seems ineffective. They can point to the successes of the evangelists of health-and-wealth gospels, while the church in the central city does not grow. The seed always falls on hard ground when those who receive it have all the wrong expectations of what the word can and will do.

The Persecution

On the other hand, Jesus said there are some people who receive the word with great enthusiasm and are open to what the word can accomplish for them. Unfortunately they are often like the seed that Jesus said fell on rocky soil. The ground looks good on the surface, but it is not deep. The seeds quickly germinate, because they are exposed to the elements that cause growth. When they come under the continuing heat of the sun, however, the plants wither away. These are those who wilt under persecution or the threat of it. We think of the many stories that describe the church's suffering under the communist regimes in the Eastern bloc countries and in China, for instance.

We should not fail to note, however, the subtler forms of persecution that are going on in our own country, where we boast of our great freedoms. Christians can get greatly excited about someone else banning Christmas crèches on the town hall lawn or the square in the commercial district, or about prayer in public schools or Christian hymns on the program of the high school choir. The very same people, however, do not get excited about their own excessive commitments to little league, soccer, football, Girl Scouts and Boy Scouts at the expense of Sunday school or confirmation classes. At the adult level, the pressure of the affluent yuppie lifestyle carries the same force as outright persecution. Peer pressures, fear of not being fashionable, and the demand for conformity are forms of subtle persecution.

The Cares of the World

There are also built-in anxieties that distract people from the word. Jesus' analogy is the seed that falls among thorns. The seeds are quickly choked by the thorns, which Jesus identified as the cares of the world and the lure of wealth. The distraction in these instances is caused not by other people but by the things of this world that people think will make them comfortable and save them. Gretchen Ziegenhals, one of the editors of the *Christian Century*, wrote of her observations of the Amish people. She noted how difficult it is for the Amish to remain separate from the world. In their efforts to discipline themselves to do without material goods and even some of the basic freedoms, they have attempted to freeze their culture and remain aloof from the world.

We smile inwardly as we see how the Amish have made some compromises with the modern world. At the same time, they can inspire us to reevaluate our needs and wants. Ziegenhals quoted one tour group leader who was asked to describe what it meant to be Amish. He answered by asking the group how many in the tour group felt they would be better off without TV in their homes. All hands went up. Then they asked how many would now go home and get rid of the TV. No hands went up. Certainly TV is a major distraction, but it is only one of many in our age of affluence that can choke off the word in the lives of people who have been exposed to it.

The Good Soil

Yet Jesus said that the struggling farmer who throws out the seed is not to give up in despair over these failures of the seed to take proper root. Jesus said, "Other seed fell on the good soil and brought forth grain, some a hundredfold, some sixty, some thirty." The fault in each other case was with not the seed but the unproductive soil. The fault was with the soil that failed to give any kind of yield. The seed is the gospel, which gives life. But if the soil is not receptive, the seed cannot produce. Hence the gospel will not bring forth any fruit in the lives of people unreceptive to the gospel.

Fred Meuser, former president of Trinity Lutheran Seminary, in a lecture for the cassette series called *Resource,* spoke of Martin Luther's frustration as a preacher. Luther preached about two hundred sermons a year. In 1530, however, he became so completely discouraged at the response of the townspeople that he refrained for a considerable time from preaching and spoke in the harshest terms about the people's ingratitude. He complained that it was almost enough to make one quit. Eventually, though, he returned to preaching and never spoke again of his depression about preaching. Rather Luther emphasized the importance of thinking of preaching as the sowing of the seed, knowing that it is God's word, the gospel that will bring forth fruit. We are not to judge how and when that will be, but we are to share this seed of the gospel to the best of our ability.

Jesus Is the Seed

When Jesus told the parable of the sower and the seed, the twelve asked him why he taught in parables. Our Lord's answer is a clue to understanding the Gospel According to Matthew. Jesus explained that the disciples were given the gift of understanding by the power of the Spirit. Others failed to understand even though they heard the same message and were witnesses to the same ministry. A bond of understanding existed between Jesus and the disciples. Even though there was much they did not understand at this time, and much that they misunderstood or misapplied, they were bound by their common understanding that Jesus was sent on the messianic mission by the heavenly Father. Other people would not and could not understand his parables because they were resisting the work of the Holy Spirit.

When Jesus was quizzed about this parable, he explained the different kinds of soil that rejected the seed of the gospel. On another occasion Jesus further explained that he was the seed. At the Feast of the Passover prior to his passion, Jesus said, "The hour has come for the Son of Man to be glorified. Very truly I tell you, unless a grain of wheat falls into the earth and dies, it remains just a single grain; but if it dies it bears much fruit" (John 12:24). Jesus did suffer and die upon the cross and was placed into the earth that he might emerge victorious over sin, death, and hell. He died to bring forth the fruits of eternal life for us. He bore much fruit that we might have the forgiveness of sins and live in the certainty that eternal life is his gift to share with us.

So Hear!

The implications of this parable are clear. We are involved in the parable. Every one of us has to blush with shame when we hear the descriptions of the various kinds of soil that reject the word, the gospel. We are all guilty of being those kinds of soil that are distracted from a proper hearing and believing of the gospel. At the same time we should be encouraged by the news that the gospel inevitably brings forth fruit and does so abundantly. We have experienced this ourself. The gospel has taken root in our hearts so that we do believe this Lord Jesus Christ and we do respond to his love in faith.

A cautionary word is thrown out to us. Jesus began the parable on that note: "Listen," he said. Jesus closed the parable in the same way, "Let anyone with ears listen!" All of us have to take heed that we do not become indifferent to the hearing of this gospel. We should examine ourselves to see if we have a tendency to say no to all invitations to hear and to study this word of grace God has revealed to us. We have to wonder about ourselves if we keep saying this word is too hard for us, so we never take the time to master and study it. At the same time we should remember the promise that where this gospel takes room in the hearts of people through the Spirit of God, the gospel does work and brings forth fruit beyond our counting. No wonder then that Jesus says, "Hey, you, listen!"

H.N.H.

NINTH SUNDAY AFTER PENTECOST
A Good Hands-off Policy
MATTHEW 13:24-30

The parable in today's Gospel reading follows directly upon the parable of the seed and the soils. It is another parable drawn from the agriculture of our Lord's day, this time focusing on the final judgment.

Today it seems that the prophets who write and speak about the final judgment on creation are found among news analysts and journal editors. In 1982 Jonathan Schell published *The Fate of the Earth,* a book that resulted from a series of three articles he wrote for the *New Yorker.* Schell declared that human civilization was threatened with total devastation by a nuclear holocaust. The relaxation of the cold war has made us somewhat indifferent to this possibility. Yet America and Russia are still the custodians of nuclear arsenals that grew while they worked at the effort of mutual nuclear disarmament. The end of civilization by a nuclear confrontation remains a distinct possibility.

Meanwhile, we live in an age in which farmers handle the problem of weeds among the wheat with herbicides that raise serious concerns on the part of environmentalists. We are alerted regularly to the presence of radioactivity endangering not only the weeds among the wheat but the wheat, all vegetation, and the very marrow of our bones. An environmentalist like Jonathan Weiner, for instance, reminds us in his book *The Next Hundred Years* that our planet has no life insurance policy. Infants born today, he asserts, may experience more changes in their lifetimes than the planet Earth has since the birth of civilization. Much has to be done if we are to preserve the creation as we know it.

Jesus did not approach the subject of the final judgment like the doomsday prophets of our day. Certainly our Lord would encourage good stewardship of the creation. And Jesus did make it clear on many occasions that people will be held accountable for the way they respond, or fail to respond, to the revelation of God's loving concern for the creatures of the creation.

Jesus said in the parable that the kingdom of heaven may be compared to a man who sowed good seed in his field. In the previous parable Jesus had explained that the seed was the word of God. When the good seed is sown into the ground, it will yield good crops. The parable suggests to us that God sows the seed out of good grace. In a later explanation to his disciples, Jesus identified himself, the Son of Man, as the one who sows the seed. What is important to note at this point is that the seed is sown as a totally gracious act on the part of God.

The Enemy Comes

As certainly as God, out of good and perfect grace, works on behalf of the people, someone is sure to work to counter that divine activity. Jesus said, "While everybody was asleep, an enemy came and sowed weeds among the wheat, and then went away." The interpretation offered in Matthew is that the enemy is none other than the devil himself.

It is not difficult to document how assiduously the demonic is at work in the world. For every chapel erected to the glory of God, we can be sure the enemy establishes a crack house somewhere. The demonic is obvious when, as a superintendent of public schools complained, the defense industry gets a million dollars to build one smart bomb, but the school gets only twenty-six hundred dollars a year to create one smart child. One does not have to be extraordinarily perceptive to see something demonic about the fantastic amount of waste in this country while a good percentage of our population lives below the poverty line. There is something evil about the fact that Americans pay over $600 billion for health care, while fifty million Americans do not have adequate health insurance and some thirty million have none at all.

The demons, we should note, are at work among good people. The devil is an expert at using the mask of religiosity to tempt people. The work of God is often hindered by people who pass themselves off as upright and holy. The exposure of TV evangelists who peddled their religious soap makes this clear. However, they were not exposed until after they had bilked millions of people. Even after they were publicly censured, they did not lose their followings completely. To be sure, the enemy is clever in deluding people inside and outside the church.

The Problem of Detection

The presence of so much evil in the world prompts people to ask why God tolerates this situation. Why should not the evil be separated from the rest of the world in which the word has borne fruit? Jesus sought to answer that kind of question with the parable. The slaves of the householder ask permission to go pull the weeds sown by the enemy. The master restrains the servants for fear they will uproot the wheat along with the weeds.

Anyone who has worked a garden knows how easy that is to do. Good gardening or farming would seem to require that one take the risk in order for the good crop to flourish. But we often learn too late the difference between the weeds and the flower. Some weeds have their own beauty, and some plants have no beauty at all until the time of their yield. It can be difficult to see the difference between the weed and good yield of the earth. However, as in the parable, even when the person doing the weeding is capable of distinguishing the good from the bad, the good can be uprooted as one uproots the bad.

God's Tolerance

The parable discloses the gracious tolerance of God. The master says to the servants, "Let them both grow together until the harvest." In the kingdom God does not want the work of the final judgment to be rushed. The time before the harvest is a time of grace. People should have the opportunity to repent and to bring forth the fruits of repentance.

It is true that the faithful are apt to think that evil is winning out in the world. The scales appear to be tipped in the favor of evil. That is not the way it is, however. God is patient with sinners and is willing to wait for those who will repent. We all know instances of this phenomenon in people's lives. We know persons who had fallen out of the active life in the church and have returned. We know of people who had dramatic changes in their lives when they finally came to faith for the first time.

One pastor who visits prisoners in a state penitentiary told of one inmate who was living out a sentence of thirty-one years. When asked about his attitude toward imprisonment, the inmate expressed his gratitude. He had come to know the Christ within the prison. He he not been imprisoned for his wrongdoing, he may not have learned about Christ.

The time until the harvest is a time God allows for people to come to the knowledge of God's love and grace for all. We may not be aware of those who respond. In fact, we may be troubled at times because we see nothing happening. It may be we who are asleep and indifferent to the hand of God in people's lives. For God is careful not to withhold grace from those whom he still seeks to win.

God's Judgment

If the servants in the parable find the tolerant attitude of the master questionable, the master assures them that all will turn out right in the end. The master says, "At harvest time I will tell the reapers, 'Collect the weeds first and bind them in bundles to be burned.'" One is not to mistake the postponement of weeding out the bad as indifference on the part of God. In due time God will appoint that moment for the final judgment to fall upon the world.

In point of fact, there is no delay in the judgment. What appears to be a postponement is a sign of our own impatience with God. God does know what is going on in the world of people. God's direction concerning the final harvest reveals the constant presence of God in a world gone made. God offers grace and meaning to a graceless world when great minds have dubbed the age as absurd. Yet no one knows how evil and perverse this generation is more than God. God knows that not all will respond to God's genuine offers of love. In the end, what comes up as worthless will have to be treated as worthless. As weeds are thrown into the fire to be burned, those who have failed to respond to the best efforts of God will be excluded from the kingdom.

In the parable the master also orders the wheat to be gathered into his barn. The parable illustrates the magnanimous character of the gracious God who desires that all be saved and brought to the knowledge of the truth. God consistently makes every effort to see that all are safely brought into the harvest who at any time respond to the love God manifests for the world. There is no better expression of this patience than what God endured sending the Son to save the world from its folly. The one who tells the parable of God's patience had to live out this patience as he witnessed and experienced the hostility and animosity of the world toward that which is pure, loving, and holy.

Jesus himself became the victim of the impatience of the religious world that thought it could usher in the kingdom by weeding out the evil and establishing its own righteousness. The result was that sinful, impatient people crucified the Lord of life in the firm conviction that they had hastened the kingdom. Unwittingly they had played into the hands of the patient God, who raised the Son from the dead to proclaim to the world that it is God, and God alone, who has the last word. God has the last word not for the sake of dooming sinful people to perdition but the the sake of the elect, who will be gathered into the glorious kingdom of God at last to share eternity with the ever-patient God of history.

Hands Off!

The parable should demonstrate that God is also extremely patient with us. Each one of us can recall moments in our life when we were empty of faith or were guilty of unfaith. Our teen years may have included periods of alienated behavior. College years may have found us guilty of the common arrogance of those who think they are the first to dream up serious doubts about God. We may have found trust in God extremely difficult in times of depression and disillusionment.

Thank God for exercising extreme patience with us then and not moving in on us to weed us out as evil ones! Likewise we are challenged by God's example to demonstrate the same kind of patience and charity with our neighbors. Bigotry and intolerance will never do. As the parable suggests, we must practice a hands-off policy in judging who finally is to be lost. As we ourselves have experienced the patience of God, we should deal patiently with others in love.

H.N.H.

TENTH SUNDAY AFTER PENTECOST
The Treasure
MATTHEW 13:44-52

Listen to another story about finding a treasure:

The kingdom of heaven is like a widow who was nervous about going to church. She had missed several Sundays in a row before her husband passed away. He was sick, and she didn't want to leave his side. She expected God would forgive her, but now it was difficult to return. She felt so out of touch.

And not many days had passed since the funeral. The last time she was in church, the casket was there. She sat in the front pew. She was surrounded by her children. She cried. She didn't want to go to church and cry again. She had visions of sitting in the pew, Kleenex tightly clutched in her fist, tears running down her cheeks. She didn't want to make those around her feel uncomfortable. She didn't want people feeling sorry for her. She was afraid of what might happen if she went to church this soon after the funeral.

But in the kingdom of heaven, God breaks through fear and anxiety. The widow felt nudged, somehow encouraged to go to church. Beneath her fear an even stronger feeling stirred inside her. She recognized a powerful desire to be worshiping among her Christian brothers and sisters. She felt the need to be surrounded by those who embodied God's Spirit. She wanted to hear their voices filling the sanctuary with songs of praise. She longed to receive God's forgiveness and hear God's promises. The kingdom of heaven is like a widow who felt the Spirit of God encouraging her to go to church soon after her husband's funeral.

The widow gathered what little strength she had and made her way through the doors of the sanctuary. She greeted only a couple of people before settling into her pew. As the service began, she fought back her grief and claimed the strength God gave her. She heard the comfort of God's word as she listened to the hymns and the sermon. God's voice even came through her own when she heard herself joining in during the Nicene Creed.

As the worship service progressed, the widow was able to stay calm. She controlled her thoughts, not allowing herself to think too deeply about her sins or grief. She was even careful not to let herself be touched too intimately by the promises of God. That too could make her lose control. The widow managed to keep her composure . . . until Holy Communion. Until the pastor looked into her eyes and said, "The body of Christ, given for you."

She could no longer hold back the tears, but that didn't matter anymore. Her need to look strong in the eyes of others was gone. The tears were good. These tears were spontaneous. As they filled her eyes, she realized that the feelings she experienced were not primarily feelings of grief. These were tears of joy. In her hand she held the most magnificent treasure she had ever seen. In her hand she held the body of Christ. And as she placed the bread on her tongue, she felt closer to God than she had ever felt before. She felt close to the Christian family who joined her at the table. She felt close to her husband, who shared Christ's feast eternally.

As the pastor placed the glass of wine between her fingertips, she again heard God's words to her, "The blood of Christ shed for you." And as the wine washed down her throat, she felt cleansed.

In that moment she felt free—free from her sadness, her guilt, her loneliness. Through the tears in her eyes, she recognized the treasure she was receiving. Nothing else in all the world mattered. She was loved by her Savior. And he gave her hope.

Jesus said, "The kingdom of heaven is like a merchant in search of fine pearls; on finding one pearl of great value, he went and sold all that he had and bought it." That widow was one of God's fine pearls. You are another of God's pearls, great in value. You are God's treasure. God has given up everything for you. Jesus died on the cross for you. The kingdom of God is like the Savior of the world seeking you out, reaching down into your life, calling you his treasure, and giving you everlasting salvation.

In the kingdom of heaven, God gives you all you need—Jesus gives you himself. Today Jesus offers himself to you. He gives you his body through the bread of Holy Communion. He gives you his blood in the wine. As you partake of this special treasure, Jesus gives himself to you fully, so that you may know the forgiveness of all your sins. Jesus holds nothing back from you so that you may know the completeness of his love. You are God's great treasure, and God gives himself to you so that you may be God's own forever.

Jesus said, "Again, the kingdom of heaven is like a net that was thrown into the sea and caught fish of every kind." The kingdom of heaven draws all of God's people together in one communion. God unites us with himself, with one another, and with all the saints who have gone before us. As we receive the treasure of our Lord, we will know forgiveness and be empowered to proclaim God's love to others.

In, with, and under the bread and wine sitting on our table this morning is hidden the treasure of the kingdom of heaven. It is ready to be discovered by you. The Savior of the world is here to offer you forgiveness, hope, and unity. While you're at the table, partaking of the treasure, nothing else matters. All the anxieties, worries, and fears of your life are put into perspective. Compared to the treasure, the troubles of this life are minor. They are powerless next to the powerful one who has claimed you as his own.

Come to the table and discover the treasure. Come, be found by the one who loves you. Come, be a part of the whole kingdom of heaven.

P.F.W.

ELEVENTH SUNDAY AFTER PENTECOST
Giving Thankfully
MATTHEW 14:13-21

One cool summer afternoon, Anna stepped through the doors of the shelter for the homeless. She stood on the threshold for a minute just to enjoy the savory aroma escaping from the kitchen. Today the dining area smelled of turkey, dressing, and gravy. The delicious odor instantly reminded Anna of Thanksgiving. Childhood memories of that special holiday flooded her mind as she remembered the many Thanksgiving meals she and her mother and father had prepared together. She recalled feeling especially warm and happy inside as the three of them sat down to the feast they had all contributed to and gave thanks to the Lord for their many blessings.

Anna had a lot to be thankful for. She was blessed with parents who always loved and cared for her. Even though they were not rich, she always had a place to sleep, food to eat, and clothes to wear. But others in her neighborhood weren't so fortunate. Anna grew up seeing poverty all around her—in her school, among her friends, and at the shelter her church had begun. Yes, Anna had a lot to be thankful for as she stepped through the doors of the shelter. God had not only blessed her materially; even more, God had blessed her with the capacity to care and the ability to give. Each Thursday afternoon Anna spent her time at the shelter with her homeless and hurting neighbors. As she did, she became God's blessing to them.

Today, like Anna, we can give thanks to God for many things— our friends and families, our homes, our nation, plenty of food, our church, and our faith. Along with Anna we can give thanks to God for our ability to care and to give thankfully. What a privilege it is to be able to share cheerfully and compassionately what God has first given us.

When Jesus stepped off the boat, he saw a great crowd; and he had compassion for them. When Jesus looks at our world today, he sees people he loves who are hungry and homeless and in need of help. In Africa he recognizes thirty million people who need special relief. He sees millions more in the Soviet Union, hungry and afraid. Jesus knows each of the one out of five children who go to bed hungry in the United States. And in the crowd, Jesus sees many who struggle right here in Oelwein, Iowa. Jesus sees every one of them. But Jesus doesn't see them as a burden. He sees their need as an opportunity to show compassion.

"When it was evening, the disciples came to Jesus and said, 'This is a deserted place, and the hour is now late; send the crowds away so that they may go into the villages and buy food for themselves.' [But] Jesus said to them, 'They need not go away; you give them something to eat.' '' Jesus wanted to feed the crowd, but he also wanted to do something more—he wanted to give his disciples the joy that comes from giving thankfully.

The disciples wanted to send the great crowd of hungry people away. They didn't want to have to deal with them. Aware of their resources, they knew they couldn't feed over five thousand people. But Jesus had plans for his doubtful followers. He wanted to teach them to care. So he said, "You give them something to eat."

As Jesus looks at our world today, he turns to us, his disciples, and says, "You give them something to eat." Jesus tells you to give them something to eat, not just so that the hungry can be fed; Jesus turns to you so that you may know his compassion and be filled with the joy of being a blessing to others.

We might think the crowd is too large. Five thousand people seemed overwhelming to Jesus' twelve disciples, but today . . . today we face thirty million in Africa, another twelve million in America, as well as millions more across the entire world. Does Jesus really expect us to feed all these people? Yet today we've brought our canned goods. Today we're prepared to give our offerings to our denomination's Hunger Appeal. Today we listen to Jesus' words and are ready to respond. We're ready to experience again the joy and the blessing of giving to those in need.

A few years ago, the Evangelical Lutheran Church in America issued a challenge, a challenge that grew out of Jesus' mandate to his disciples, "You give them something to eat." Every member of the ELCA was invited to give two dollars a month to the Hunger Appeal to help feed the hungry of our world. Since that invitation, the funds for the ELCA Hunger Appeal have been growing. More and more of Jesus' Lutheran disciples are learning to give thankfully to those who are hungry. And more and more of our neighbors—at home and throughout the world—are being fed.

Jesus said, "You give them something to eat." Where Jesus is involved, five loaves and two fish will feed five thousand. Where Jesus is involved, two dollars a month will feed millions. If every confirmed member of this one congregation gave two dollars a month to the Hunger Appeal, we would be providing $1,970 a

month to feed the hungry. That's $23,640 a year! Just thin
many of Jesus' people who are hungry could be fed. And t
from just one congregation. As members of the body of Christ
powered by him, we really can feed millions.

This morning we do have much to be thankful for. We can thank
God for the many blessings we have and the many ways we are
provided for. We can thank God for the compassion God has for us
and for all the people of the world. And we can thank God for
teaching us to be compassionate and for granting us the joy of
giving thankfully in the name of Jesus.

P.F.W.

Little Boat on a Storm-Tossed Sea
MATTHEW 14:22-33

Jesus was probably exhausted. After hearing the news of
John the Baptist's death, Jesus needed some time away, some time
alone, to grieve, to pray, to be silent with God. But when he
stepped off the boat onto the shore of what he thought would be a
lonely place, crowds of people came running toward him. Yet
when Jesus looked out over the people, he didn't see just a crowd
of bothersome people; Jesus saw individuals. He saw individuals
who were sick and in need.

Instead of sending them away, Jesus healed the sick, gave them
hope, and at the end of the day fed over five thousand people with
only five loaves of bread and two fish. As the sun was setting, the
crowd was healthy, happy, and refreshed; but quite likely Jesus
was exhausted. Even more than before, Jesus needed to get away
for some quiet time with his heavenly Father.

Jesus turned to his disciples and told them to get into the boat
and go back to the city. He wanted to be alone. The gospel writer
suggests that the disciples may have been hesitant about getting
into the boat at that particular time. Matthew writes, "Immediately
he *made* the disciples get into the boat and go on ahead to the other
side."

The Sea of Galilee was a beautiful lake surrounded by hills, with
the snow-capped summit of Mount Hermon to the north. It was a
magnificent setting, but great currents of air would frequently roll

down from the surrounding hills and sweep the surface of the lake with a fierce storm. The disciples may have noticed that the conditions were looking just right for one of those powerful storms. Getting into a boat on the sea of Galilee may have been the last thing those twelve men wanted to do that night. But Matthew tells us that Jesus made them go.

After Jesus sent away his disciples and the crowds, Jesus found a place of solitude, where he spent the evening and stayed into the night. Meanwhile a storm had developed and the disciples were out in the middle of the lake battling the wind and waves in the deep dark hours of the night. As they were fighting to stay afloat, one of them pointed out a figure hardly visible through the spray of the water and the blackness of the sky. A ghost! Fear on top of fear. The disciples feared for their lives—the strong wind, the powerful waves, and now a ghost. Together they cried out in fear.

But immediately Jesus spoke to them: "Take heart, it is I; do not be afraid!" Peter, impetuous Peter, cried out, "Lord if it is you, command me to come to you on the water." Jesus said, "Come," and Peter stepped out onto the crashing waves. He wasn't there long when the water began to overcome him. But Jesus reached out his hand and pulled him up. Jesus pulled Peter out of the chaotic water and carried him safely to the boat, as the wind ceased and the storm miraculously disappeared.

That night, out in the middle of the Sea of Galilee, twelve men whose hearts were still pounding from fear, recognized the Son of God and realized he had saved them. That night, just before the rising of the sun, songs of praise were sweeping over the waters of the sea of Galilee. The Son of God had once again rescued his fearful, doubting people.

Matthew tells this story not only to let us know about something that once happened to Jesus and his followers. This story is also a parable about the church. It describes the church as a little boat filled with frightened, doubting disciples on a storm-tossed sea. It's not easy for us to embrace that image. We don't usually think of the church as a frail structure filled with faithless people. Our ancestors built our churches with stone and sturdy pillars so that they could withstand the wind, the rain, and the harsh realities of the elements. They built our churches with the hope that these buildings would stand forever so that the faithful would gather for worship and send the songs of praise sweeping over the lake or valley or prairie. We like to think of the church as a solid place, a sturdy physical building filled with people who have a firm faith in the Son of God.

Yet it is becoming increasingly clear that Matthew's picture is accurate. The church seems more and more to be like a fragile boat struggling to stay afloat in a world filled with dangers and disappointments. Rural decline is forcing many people to leave their small towns. Sickness and death are invading our congregations. Most rural churches are showing fewer and fewer numbers on their rolls. The number of people in the pews is dwindling.

Biblical literacy is lacking because people don't seem to have time to study the Bible in their homes or with others. Events in the world and in our private lives are threatening our faith and causing the faithful to wonder where God is. Right now the seas outside our boat are churning with a struggling educational system, a culture saturated with addictive substances, and threats of war.

Matthew painted a picture of the church as a fragile boat being tossed around by the fierce wind and waves. But it is into this picture that Jesus came. Jesus entered the dangerous waters. He walked on them. He felt the force of the spray against his face and the strength of the wind pushing at his back. Jesus knew the danger, but he went to join his disciples. Jesus went to accompany his loved ones through the storm and saved them from the waves.

This doesn't mean that the storm will stop if we keep our eyes on Jesus. The storm may continue for what seems a long time. But through the spray and the splash of the waves Jesus will be there. Jesus is there calling to you, "Take heart, it is I; do not be afraid!" As disciples of Christ, living in a sinful world, we are always serving in the midst of winds we cannot withstand alone.

We cannot meet the struggles of everyday life all by ourselves. We need our Savior to accompany us, and help us through. We need our Savior to give us a push now and then so that we dare to enter the struggles of others and the problems of the world. This is where he calls us. He calls us to speak a message of hope. He calls us to bring a calming presence to those who feel thrown to and fro by the waves of life. Jesus calls us to follow him.

In his parable of the church, Matthew wants us to experience the storm. He wants us to realize that Jesus doesn't come to take away all of our hardships, our struggles, or our doubts. As long as we live on this earth we will encounter problems; and like his disciples, we are called to enter into the problems of others as well.

But out of the midst of the storm, Matthew wants us to hear another sound. "Take heart, it is I; do not be afraid!" We cannot save the world. We cannot even save ourselves, but we are met by one who can and does save, both us and the world.

Angelo Roncalli, known as Pope John XXIII was the leader of the Roman Catholic Church during one of its most troubled times. It is said that when he went to bed at night, he would say to himself, "But who governs the church? You or the Holy Spirit? Very well then, go to sleep, Angelo."

As you encounter the strong winds and waves in your personal struggles in life and as you dare to enter into the problems of others, listen for the voice of Jesus. For he comes to you and says, "Take heart, it is I; do not be afraid!"

P.F.W.

THIRTEENTH SUNDAY AFTER PENTECOST
Great Is Your Faith
MATTHEW 15:21-28

I am a woman from the region of Canaan. Most people know very little about me. My name is never mentioned, but the Gospel writers, Matthew and Mark, do give a brief account of one of the most important events in my life. They tell about the first time I met Jesus. They share the first time I realized the depth of God's love for me.

I remember that day like it was yesterday. It was the third day of the week, and I began my morning as usual with a trip to the marketplace. The square was buzzing that bright, shiny morning. There was more gossiping going on than bartering. Something had happened.

It's just about impossible to keep a secret in a community like this one. Each morning everyone gathers in the marketplace and exchanges the latest information about their neighbors and friends. On this particular morning it was obvious that something had taken place in the Jewish community. Groups of Jews were huddled around, talking in hushed voices, passing on some confidential information. Others walked around slowly, pretending to be shopping, but concentrating more on the talk of the Jews.

As I milled around the marketplace, I overheard bits and pieces of separate conversations. The excitement stemmed from the arrival of a man named Jesus. I heard the word *messiah* being used. Being a Canaanite, I wasn't too familiar with the Jewish religion, but I did know that they were waiting for their messiah, a king to come and save them.

As I walked around, I felt the excitement of the crowd. I heard comments like "Jesus is the messiah. He healed my uncle," "Jesus is our Savior. He gave my blind cousin sight," "Jesus casts out demons," "Jesus teaches like no one I have ever heard before!" The Jews were ecstatic. Something stirred within me.

As I walked home from the marketplace, one of the comments I'd heard kept ringing in my ears. "Jesus casts out demons," "Jesus casts out demons." I wondered what they meant by that. Did they mean that Jesus was able to relieve people of their lifelong torment? Could he somehow get rid of demons? I should have been bolder and asked someone. Jews usually ignored us Canaanites. They have nothing to do with us; but I could have at least tried. I could have asked. Maybe in all their excitement, someone would have told me more.

"Jesus casts out demons." That phrase haunted me as I went about my morning chores. As I ground wheat for our bread, I imagined myself going back to the marketplace. I thought about the words I would use to inquire about Jesus. I imagined myself being bold and finally getting what I wanted. But that's as far as I got. In my dreams I could be assertive. But I could never actually go back to the marketplace and approach a Jew. They would not even acknowledge me.

Then my thoughts were interrupted by the fearful screams of my eldest son, "Mother, it's happening again! Come quickly! Come quickly! Mother!" I found my son standing over my daughter, whose body was jerking uncontrollably. She was silent as her arms and legs struck out involuntarily in every direction. She began to choke. Her deep brown eyes clouded and disappeared under her lids.

I couldn't just stand there and watch this happening to my daughter another time. "Get out of my house," I pleaded. "Get out of my daughter!" This demon had been haunting her since she was two. We never knew when it would enter her. There was never any warning. At times it seemed to stay for hours and other times it would last only a few minutes. But she was never herself for several days after a spell like this.

I couldn't take it anymore. I turned to my son and told him to stay with her. I felt desperate. My legs whisked me out the door, and the name Joanna entered by mind. Joanna's house, where Jesus was staying. I started to run hard in the direction of the Jewish section of town. My heart was pounding. My whole body trembled as my feet slapped against the ground. Only one thought filled my mind, "Jesus casts out demons," "Jesus casts out demons." The words echoed in my mind each time I gasped for air.

I ran harder and farther that morning than I had ever run before. I soon saw a commotion. My legs didn't stop until I reached the thick of the crowd, where I began screaming at the top of my lungs, "Have mercy on me, Lord, Son of David: my daughter is tormented by a demon." I had never realized the capacity of my voice. Never before had it exhibited such strength. Everyone heard me. Everyone turned toward me as I made my way to Jesus' side. "Have mercy on me, Lord, have mercy." It seemed I had caught the attention of everyone in the crowd. Everyone, that is, except Jesus.

All eyes were on me. All except Jesus' eyes. "Have mercy on me Lord," I pleaded. But Jesus didn't skip a beat in what he was doing. It seemed as if he himself were deaf and blind, oblivious to what was going on beside him. "Have mercy on me, Lord." Something was pushing me to continue. Something was keeping me from giving up.

Finally a couple of men urged Jesus to send me away. They were perturbed by my outburst and aware of the disturbance it was causing in the crowd. But Jesus calmly answered, "I was sent only to the lost sheep of the house of Israel."

Normally I would have been embarrassed by my own outburst, accepted my defeat, and turned toward home. But from somewhere deep within me came a courage that I had known only in my dreams. Instead of sheepishly excusing myself, I dropped to the ground on my knees, looked up into Jesus' eyes and begged, "Lord, help me." Finally Jesus spoke directly to me. But he said, "It is not fair to take the children's food and throw it to the dogs."

My heart sank. I knew I didn't deserve to be helped by the Jewish messiah. I wasn't a Jew. I worshiped a different god. Of course Jesus shouldn't help me. He had enough to do to help those who have been faithful to him. My heart sank, but my voice continued. "Yes, Lord, yet even the dogs eat the crumbs that fall from their masters' table."

I was shocked at my own assertiveness. Something was pushing me. But it was then that Jesus finally looked at me. It was as if his eyes penetrated into the depths of my soul. "Woman, great is your faith! Let it be done for you as you wish."

At that moment, my daughter was healed. At that moment, I knew unconditional love. At that moment, I experienced the Messiah's acceptance and knew that he was my Lord too.

On that special morning, the gift of faith was being born inside me. God decided to love me in spite of all the religious laws and traditions that declared me unacceptable. God decided to love me and give me, an undeserving Canaanite woman, the gift of faith. That's what was stirring inside of me. The gift of faith was that "something" I felt that moved me, encouraged me, and helped me to be assertive when I needed to be. It was faith that gave me the strength and courage to go to Jesus, to lay my problem at his feet, and to know his salvation.

Because you have gathered here this morning to hear the word of God and to worship our Savior, I know that you too have received the gift of faith. God has decided to love you. God has chosen to give you the special gift of faith. Follow your faith. It will lead you to Jesus. It will show you God's love again and again. Follow your faith. When you do, you will see the depth of God's love revealed to you.

P.F.W.

FOURTEENTH SUNDAY AFTER PENTECOST
Jesus Is the Answer
MATTHEW 16:13-20

I'd like to introduce to you a character created by one of my favorite authors, Jon Hassler, in his book *Jemmy*.

Jemmy was short for Gemstone. Her mother had named her that. Jemmy had straight black hair that hung down to her waist. The soft bronze color of her skin seemed to be a reflection of her deep brown eyes. The intensity of her stare revealed the sorrow in her life. Jemmy's mother was Chippewa, and her father was white. Her family didn't live in town, but they didn't live on the reservation either. When Jemmy was of elementary age she want to school on the reservation, but after completing the eighth grade, Jemmy was bused into town, where she went to high school.

Roxanne was the only other freshman student at Eagleton High who had Indian blood. Because her mother and father were both Chippewa and she lived on the reservation, Roxanne never fully accepted Jemmy. Jemmy wasn't white, but she wasn't Chippewa either. Still, Roxanne would use Jemmy's friendship to get a free cigarette, a stick of gum, or to borrow Jemmy's brown suede purse with the leather fringe. One day after school, Roxanne and Jemmy were sitting in their usual place at the back of the bus. Roxanne was chattering as always about unimportant things. But Jemmy, absorbed in her own thoughts, was paying no attention.

Then, out of the blue, Jemmy interrupted Roxanne with a question, "What do people say about me? Who do they say I am?" Roxanne was stunned for a moment. The glaze in her eyes indicated that she was searching. She was contemplating the answer to Jemmy's question. But she didn't have to search long. "Well," Roxanne said, "you know what they say. You've heard the names. Some say half breed. Other say you're an easy date. Other say you and your Dad smoke opium together all night long."

Jemmy looked into Roxanne's eyes and said, "What do you say about me to others? Who do you say that I am?" Roxanne was silent for an unusually long time. Then Roxanne broke the stare and said, "Well, I jist say that you're Jemmy." And she changed the subject.

Jesus asked his disciples, "What do people say about me, who do they say that I am?" When the disciples conveyed to Jesus the gossip of the day, they were careful to avoid the cruel titles they had heard. They didn't mention blasphemer, glutton, or wine lover. They said, "Some say John the Baptist, but others Elijah, and still others Jeremiah or one of the prophets."

But Jesus wanted to know more. Jesus asked his friends, "Who do you say that I am?" A deafening silence replaced the eager voices of the disciples. They were happy to report the titles they had heard from others, but they were unsure about their own understanding of who Jesus was, and they were reluctant to reveal their uncertainty.

Peter may have searched his thoughts and feelings for what seemed an eternity before he broke the silence. "You are the Messiah, the Son of the living God." I wonder if Peter knew what he was going to say before he said it. "You are the Messiah, the Son of the living God." Did Peter understand what he was saying? Did he know what he meant by that?

As I worked with this text, a strange thought entered my mind. I wondered what would happen if instead of giving a sermon, I gave a pop quiz. What if I had read the Gospel and then passed out to each of you a piece of paper with one question on it? The question would have been the same for all of us. "Who do you say Jesus is?" Could you have answered that question? In agreement with Peter, some of you might have thought to write down the same words used in our Gospel: "Jesus is the Messiah, the Son of the living God." Others might have said, "Jesus is my Lord and

Savior." And still others, "Jesus is my friend." Who do you say Jesus is? Could you answer that right now?

Yes, Jesus is the Messiah, the Son of the living God. Jesus is your Lord and Savior. But what do you mean by that? What do we mean by those titles? Our answers might be more complete if we simply list words that describe what we mean. Jesus is almighty, loving, gentle, compassionate, understanding, forgiving. Jesus is my helper, my guide, my God. Using the words of a popular Christian phrase, "Jesus is the answer!"

Children often ask wonderfully deep religious questions in simple language. Will my dog go to heaven? If Jesus is in heaven, how can he be here too? My grandpa never went to church with us before he died; is he in heaven now? Did Noah really live to be six hundred years old? How would you answer these questions?

Adults also have questions of faith. Many of us talk about the list of questions we want to ask God when we get to heaven. If Jesus is the Messiah, the Son of the living God, then why is there so much pain in this world? Why is there suffering? Why is there hunger? Why do people fight with one another?

Susan's closest friend died last month. Her daughter came home drunk last week. When Susan, on her way home from the hospital after having a lump removed from her breast, noticed a bumper sticker that said "Jesus is the answer," she thought to herself, "The answer to what? To my loneliness, my feelings of inadequacy as a mother, or to my fear of cancer? If Jesus is the answer, then why is all of this happening to me?"

Sometimes we are too quick with our answers. We don't want people to know that we just aren't sure what we mean when we say Jesus is the Messiah, the Son of the living God. We don't want people to think we aren't strong in our faith. We don't want to seem illiterate when it comes to the Bible. As people of God, we feel that we need to know the answers to questions of faith.

We think we should be able to give Susan a Christian remedy for her suffering. We feel we should be able to answer all of our children's questions about God. We think that if we are good Christians, we should know exactly what we mean when we confess that Jesus is the Messiah, the Son of the living God. And so when difficult questions of faith arise, we are tempted to say Jesus is the answer and then change the subject. If we say any more, someone might realize we don't have all the answers.

Who do you say that I am? Jesus is the Messiah, the Son of the living God. Yes, Jesus is the answer. The gift of faith places that confession on our lips and engraves it in our hearts. But how is

Jesus the answer? How is Jesus the answer for Jemmy, a girl shunned by others because of her race? How is Jesus the answer for Susan as she finds herself dealing with one tragedy after another? How is Jesus the answer for the little boy who is concerned about his grandfather who never went to church? When questions like these arise, God doesn't expect us to have all the answers. We can confess our faith. But it's also OK to say, "I don't know. I don't completely understand how God works. I'm searching too. Can we search together?"

One day it will all be clear to us. One day we will be able to explain fully what it means that Jesus is the Messiah, the Son of the living God. But until then we must continue our search. We must not be afraid to ask questions and to admit to one another that we don't know all the answers. We must continue to search the Scriptures, watch for God's presence in our lives, and look for the answers together.

As you search, as you struggle with questions of faith, God will bless you with the faith to proclaim, "You are the Messiah!" even when you don't completely understand what that means. God will bless you with a faith to search. God will bless you with the answers to your questions. Because Jesus is the Messiah, the Son of the living God!

P.F.W.

FIFTEENTH SUNDAY AFTER PENTECOST
Blessings, Peter!
MATTHEW 16:21-26

Blessings, Peter! Jesus called you blessed. You seemed to be the only one who understood who Jesus really was. Some thought he was John the Baptist, others Elijah, and others Jeremiah or one of the prophets. But you, Peter, you got it right. When Jesus asked, "Who do you say that I am?" you were the one who blurted out the answer Jesus was hoping for: "You are the Messiah, the Son of the living God."

It must have been truly a blessing, Peter, to be the first one to recognize Jesus' identity. What excitement you must have felt when you realized who Jesus was. Jesus, the Messiah that all of Israel had been awaiting for generations. Jesus, your companion, your teacher, your mentor, was the Messiah. Jesus was the one sent by God to save Israel. Finally God's Messiah had appeared to rule God's people and restore the great nation of Israel. And Jesus was the one. It must have felt tremendous to be in the presence of the Messiah and to be the one who recognized him.

Blessings, Peter! You know you didn't do it on your own. Without God's help you would have seen Jesus just as everyone else did. Without God's favor you too would have answered Jesus' question by naming one of the prophets. But God had chosen you. God had chosen you to be the one to identify Jesus as Israel's king. You were important to God, Peter, a crucial character in Jesus' life and in the life of the whole church. You, Peter, were blessed with a rocklike faith, a strong faith on which Jesus built the whole Christian church.

Blessings, Peter! God blessed you with a wonderful privilege and a huge responsibility. Jesus gave you the keys, Peter, the keys to the kingdom of God. Whatever you bound on earth was bound in heaven, and whatever you loosed on earth was loosed in heaven. You, Peter, were given the responsibility to forgive. And that responsibility was shared with the church. God makes forgiveness known through you, Peter. God makes forgiveness known through the church—the church built on the faith you professed.

Blessings, Peter! You were the strong one among the disciples. You were always ready to take the lead. Risks seemed to energize you. Your impetuous response in so many situations revealed your excitement, your energy, your willingness to take steps in faith. When Jesus said that he was going to suffer and die, you were ready to do whatever it would take to protect him. You were insistent on not letting anyone or anything get in the way of Jesus doing his work as Israel's Messiah.

You even rebuked Jesus himself when he spoke of traveling to Jerusalem, where he knew he would suffer many things from the elders, chief priests, and scribes and eventually face his death. You wouldn't hear of it. The Messiah of God was to rule a long time, bringing peace and justice to God's people. Yes, Peter, you were a strong, faithful leader with honorable intentions.

Blessings, Peter! Or should I say, Curses? Did you hear what Jesus called you? He said, "Get behind me, Satan!" Which is it Peter? Are you a rock on which Jesus can build his church, or are you the devil through which the church could fall? What happened, Peter? You were chosen by God to reveal the identity of God's Messiah. But now God's Messiah is calling you Satan. With just a few short words you reveal to Jesus that you in fact do not understand who he truly is. Jesus accuses you of setting your mind on human aspirations rather than the will of God. Which is it Peter? Do you know who Jesus is or don't you?

Curses, Peter! How can Christ's church be built on Satan? What happened to your rocklike faith? If Jesus says he must go to Jerusalem to suffer and die, why do you doubt him? If you believe that Jesus is God's Messiah, can't you put your arrogance aside and trust that Jesus knows what he is doing? Peter, I guess God's ways are not your ways. Maybe Jesus is not the Messiah you were expecting.

And Peter, you talk so big. You indicated that you would be willing to protect Jesus. When Jesus said that there was no other way, that he must suffer and die, you said that you would die with him. You promised that you would never deny him. You promised that you would always claim him as your Lord, your friend, and your teacher. You promised. Yet right at the time he needed you most, at the very moment of his trial before the high priest, scribes, and elders, the cock crowed. You had denied Jesus. You denied him, not just once but three times. Peter, how could you reject Jesus like that?

Curses, Peter. Or should I say, Blessings? Yes, Peter, you did misunderstand. You had the right words that afternoon when Jesus confronted you with the question, "Who do you say that I am?" But your understanding of the Messiah's mission was all backward. Jesus wasn't the Messiah you had expected. No, Jesus didn't become the earthly ruler of the Jews. Jesus didn't sit on a throne and lead the people in successful battles against the Romans and others who threatened them. Jesus didn't become the Messiah you had anticipated. Yes, Peter you did misunderstand.

And Peter, your faith didn't always prove to be rocklike. Your commitment to Jesus wasn't always secure. But Peter, you are blessed. You are blessed, because Jesus is God's Messiah. Jesus is the Messiah who died for you. Jesus is the Messiah who didn't reject you even when you denied him. Jesus is your Savior who will always love you, forgive you, and claim you as his own.

Blessings, Peter! Out of your misunderstanding, Jesus helped you to understand. When your faith was weak, Jesus never gave up on you. Jesus held you up and gave you strength to meet each day. Even though you denied your Savior, he will never deny you. You have the keys to the kingdom, the power to forgive sins; and now you know the freedom and joy of being forgiven. Because of Jesus' death and resurrection, your sins are now behind you, and each day brings a fresh new start.

Each day brings new occasions to express your love for Jesus. Each morning promises chances to help someone else to understand God's grace. Each dawn carries the possibility of opportunities to take Christ's loving presence to those in need.

Blessings, Peter! Because of Christ, you are the rock on which the church is built; you are a chosen one of God. You are forgiven, loved, and saved by the Messiah who died on the cross for you. Blessings, Peter, blessings!

P.F.W.

SIXTEENTH SUNDAY AFTER PENTECOST

A Gathering of Three
MATTHEW 18:15-20

Nina had always been an active woman. Every morning she'd thank God for her health and her energy. Because Nina enjoyed people so much, she made it her goal to get a good visit in at least once a day. She played bridge once a week and attended the senior citizens club whenever they gathered. She also enjoyed a variety of activities at church, including quilting, circle, and women of the church. Every Tuesday morning Nina would rise early to tidy up her apartment and make fresh cinnamon rolls for her Bible study group. (She always insisted that they meet at her place.) She looked forward to the smile on her friends' faces as they stepped through her kitchen door and took a deep breath. Enjoying the aroma of Nina's cinnamon rolls and fresh-brewed coffee had become a tradition for this gathering of Bible students.

In the evenings Nina crocheted afghans for her children, her grandchildren, and now her great-grandchild, who was expected to arrive in March. Sometimes she'd give her fingers a break from the hook and yarn so that she could curl up under her own tattered blanket and spend a few hours with one of her favorite authors.

One morning in early fall, Nina was awakened by the sun peeking in through her curtain. Before opening her eyes, she pushed her hair net up away from her eyebrows where it had fallen during the night. She felt the warmth of the sun on her cheek. Her first thought that morning was a prayer: "Thank you, God, for your creation—for the bright, cheery sun, the clear blue sky, the people I call my family and friends. Thank you for my health, my energy, and the gift of being your child."

As Nina sat up to put on her "gear" (that's what she called her elastic stockings), she began looking forward to her day. This afternoon the women of the church were meeting. It was her circle's turn to bring the lunch. Even though she had just made cinnamon rolls yesterday morning for her Bible study group, Nina decided that this would be a perfect day to make another batch. She thought it might be a nice treat for the women that afternoon.

After her usual breakfast of oatmeal, toast, juice, and coffee, Nina got to work on her cinnamon rolls. She decided to make them small and make enough for everyone to try. While her rolls were rising, Nina took a break. She poured a fresh cup of coffee and sat down at her desk. After glancing at the newspaper, she made a few phone calls to visit with some friends and find out the community news.

Nina was good at staying on top of things. She always knew who was in the hospital, who was celebrating a birthday, who was planning a Tupperware party, and whose turn it was to read in church on Sunday. If anyone wanted to know the latest gossip, Nina was a good one to phone.

Her cinnamon rolls were ready to come out of the oven at one o'clock. That was perfect timing. While they cooled, Nina changed her clothes and got ready for the women's meeting.

As she drove to church, Nina organized in her mind the things she needed to bring up at the meeting—the quilters needed more fabric, the food pantry had plenty of canned vegetables but was short on tuna, the communion ware needed to be polished, and it was time to decide on a fall cleanup day.

Nina parked her car next to the pastor's spot and carried two pans of cinnamon rolls into the kitchen. When she returned with the third pan, Rebecca was just setting her pan of bars down on the counter. Rebecca looked at Nina with her third pan of fresh cinnamon rolls and said, "What are you trying to do? Take over the women's group too?"

Nina felt as if a knife had just been stabbed into her back. She was hurt and angry, but she wasn't going to give Rebecca the satisfaction of knowing how bad she felt. Nina ignored Rebecca the rest of the afternoon, and when it was time to serve lunch, Nina made sure she was working at the opposite side of the kitchen from Rebecca.

On Sunday morning Nina enjoyed a quick exchange with the greeters and accepted a bulletin from an usher. She glanced at her pew, the third row from the back, and noticed that Rebecca was sitting in the spot right behind hers. Nina quickly looked around for another empty place, walked about halfway up the aisle and slid into a pew on the opposite side of the church.

A week had passed, and Nina was still feeling hurt and angry at Rebecca. So she decided to confide in a friend. A bit more time had passed, and one Tuesday morning, during Bible study, she relayed the incident to her group. Nina also mentioned Rebecca's rude comment when she spoke to her friends on the phone or as they visited over coffee. She didn't talk about it intentionally, it just happened to come up.

But it didn't take long before almost every woman in the church knew that Nina and Rebecca weren't getting along. Everyone was careful not to put Nina and Rebecca in the same serving group, on the same altar committee, or together on the janitor's list. The community did their best to keep Nina and Rebecca separated from each other. No one wanted any hard feelings to surface. The longer Nina and Rebecca ignored each other, the deeper the chasm grew between them.

The new pastor at St. Peter's came over to visit Nina one afternoon. They had a good time looking at the pictures of Nina's children, grandchildren, and great-grandchildren. Nina showed Pastor Jan the latest afghan she was working on and asked her opinion about adding one more color.

During their visit, Pastor Jan mentioned that she had heard that Nina made the best cinnamon rolls in town. That embarrassed Nina a bit, but it also made her feel proud. Pastor Jan went on to tell Nina about a youth event she was planning and asked Nina if she would make some of her cinnamon rolls for the kids. Nina was delighted to help. "I'm expecting quite a few to show up," explained Pastor Jan. "Do you think you could make three pans?"

A blank look came over Nina's face as she stared at Pastor Jan's lips and thought: "Three pans of cinnamon rolls?"

Pastor Jan noticed Nina's hesitation and began to retract her request, "If three is too much . . . "

"Oh, no," Nina replied, "it's just that I haven't made three pans of cinnamon rolls since the last time I brought them to the women's meeting." Tears started to well up in Nina's eyes, and she told Pastor Jan what had happened between her and Rebecca. Nina talked about the hurt, the anger, the feeling of a knife being stabbed into her back. The pain was so intense. Pastor Jan asked Nina when this happened. Nina said, "Eight years ago, this October."

"Have you and Rebecca ever talked about what happened?"

"Oh, no," Nina said. "She hasn't talked to me since, and she's even quit coming to church activities. She knows what she did. She knows how much it hurt."

"But if you've never told her, how can she know?"

It took some time, but Pastor Jan finally convinced Nina to go talk to Rebecca. Nina agreed only after Pastor Jan offered to go with her.

That night Nina had trouble sleeping. She really didn't want to talk to Rebecca. It happened so long ago. Why couldn't she just forget about it?

When morning finally came, Nina got dressed, dusted off her family pictures, and put on a pot of coffee. She got the pot out for her oatmeal but then replaced the lid and set it back neatly in the cupboard. She wasn't really hungry. She tried to read the newspaper but couldn't concentrate. She didn't even have the desire to make her morning phone calls. The morning seemed to drag. Nina's head ached, her stomach was turning, and when she reached for her coffee cup she noticed her fingers shaking.

At ten o'clock Pastor Jan came to pick Nina up. The ride to Rebecca's was quiet. Nina didn't even feel like commenting about the weather. All she could think about was Rebecca. She really didn't want to do this. How are you supposed to tell someone they have hurt you?

Rebecca took a few seconds to reach the door. Even though Nina knew Pastor Jan had phoned ahead, Nina still hoped that Rebecca wouldn't be home. When she finally came to the door, Rebecca greeted Pastor Jan and invited them in. She led her guests into the living room, where they all found a place to sit. The air was thick. If anyone had walked into the room at that moment, they would have been able to feel the nervous vibrations. Pastor Jan looked at Nina and then at Rebecca before she broke the silence. "Rebecca, do you remember the last time you served at church with Nina? It's been about eight years now?"

Rebecca turned her head slightly and began to stare at a spot on the floor. "Yes, I remember. I'd been baking all morning. I got up early to make a special pan of bars. I was looking forward to trying this new recipe. While they baked, I decided to get my laundry done. But when I came up from the basement, I heard my timer buzzing and I saw smoke seeping out from the oven door. My bars were black. All I had time to do was mix up a package of brownie mix and take it to church. I was disappointed and embarrassed. That's when I saw you, Nina." As Rebecca looked up at Nina, a tear ran down her face. "I'm sorry."

Nina reached over and squeezed Rebecca's hand. "I'm sorry too, Rebecca."

In Rebecca's kitchen that morning the coffee and cinnamon rolls were transformed into a sacramental meal. As Nina, Rebecca, and Pastor Jan broke and ate the spiraled bread, they experienced forgiveness and reconciliation. The talked about their gardens, their latest craft projects, their families. They laughed, they drank two pots of coffee, and Nina invited Rebecca to ride with her to the next women's meeting.

Jesus said, "For where two or three are gathered in my name, I am there among them."

P.F.W.

SEVENTEENTH SUNDAY AFTER PENTECOST

On Counting and Forgiveness
MATTHEW 18:21-35

Have you ever noticed our society's enthrallment with calculation? We seem to be fascinated with statistics and numbers. We talk about bushels per acre and price per bushel. We measure the rain in hundredths of an inch and can tell within a few drops if we got more or less than our neighbors. We count each other, sending out elaborate census forms to every home in the country. We even know the number of people who die each day from starvation. Counting intrigues us. It seems to be a matter of great consequence.

But sometimes counting can interfere with what we're about, with who we are called to be as God's people. We can keep our noses buried so deeply in our ledgers that we forget to enjoy life and care for one another. We're so busy counting that we miss the beauty of the world around us. Have you ever known a golfer who is so wrapped up in her score that she forgets to enjoy the game? Or a fisherman who is so intent on catching a big one that he misses the fun and relaxation of the sport? For all the value of numbers, sometimes it's just better to let a star be a star.

I think that is where Peter was off base in today's Gospel. He asks Jesus, "Lord, if another member of the church sins against me, how often should I forgive?" Peter wants to count something that's better left uncounted. He wants to keep track of reconciliation, love, forgiveness. But like the stars in the sky, once you start keeping track, you've already lost some of the wonder. You begin to think that forgiveness is something that belongs to you, that you can own it and dispense it at will, and you forget that it is a gift. So when Jesus tells Peter he should forgive seventy times seven, he doesn't mean to count up to 490. He means to stop counting, and to let forgiveness flow freely.

Then Jesus tells a story that goes something like this: There was a rich banker who decided to go over his books. He found that one of his employees had borrowed $25 million and hadn't paid it back. He called the man into his office and said, "Unless you can come up with the money today, I'm going to have to turn you in."

The employee started sweating bricks and asked if he could have a little more time to come up with the cash. "Well," said the banker, "I'm feeling pretty generous today." He took his black pen in his hand and wrote across the employee's file, "Credit to this account $25 million." "Don't worry about paying me back," he said. "Just consider it a gift."

But soon after the employee left, the banker heard a scuffle outside his office. He went out and found the forgiven employee pounding on one of the tellers, yelling at the top of his lungs, "You owe me two dollars and I need it right now. If you don't pay up, I'm going to break every bone in your body." I'm sure you can remember the rest of the story.

The point Jesus is making is that if you want to start keeping ledgers on forgiveness, you're always going to end up in the red. If books were kept, we'd find, like the employee, that the debt we've been forgiven by God is insurmountable. What we have to forgive each other can't compare to what God has forgiven us. If God kept track and counted, we'd never be out of debt.

But God doesn't keep track. Books aren't kept in the kingdom of heaven. Forgiveness flows freely. Like the rains that water the earth, forgiveness brings new life where there are signs of death. It makes relationships new again. In fact, forgiveness is the basis of our life together. Without it, we couldn't function as a church, as families, or as a society. Forgiveness changes us as individuals and as a community, because we learn, by forgiving and being forgiven, to live with others.

Forgiveness doesn't mean ignoring sin or letting evil go unchecked. Instead it means dealing with sin together, so that evil no longer infects our relationships. Forgiveness is hard work. It's risky. And it won't be accomplished while we're busy counting.

But as wonderful as forgiveness is, we can't always do it. Sometimes people are too badly hurt. A victim of abuse might say, "I'll never be able to forgive my abuser." Or you may have heard survivors of Nazi concentration camps talk about refusing to forgive their tormentors. The wounds are still too deep for them to forgive. Sometimes distance or death can keep us from forgiving. Reconciliation is often more difficult when it's too late to right the wrongs that have come between us. And sometimes forgiveness isn't accepted. It misses the mark. It is misunderstood. It becomes just too hard to try again. All of us have times when, for one reason or another, we just can't forgive. At those times, our question isn't, "How many times should I forgive?" but "What if I can't forgive at all?"

It is then that we once more throw ourselves on the mercy of our God. At these times we can pray, "I can't forgive this, Lord. Do it for me. Take this hurt into your own hands and bring your gift of healing."

People often say, "Forgive and forget." But that's not always healthy. True forgiveness doesn't necessarily forget. Often the wrong has to be addressed, not forgotten, in order for healing to take place. Maybe we should say instead, "Forgive and remember." Remember that *you* have been forgiven a debt you could never pay. Remember that forgiveness can overcome the curse of sin in our lives. And remember that even when your well of forgiveness runs dry, God is there to forgive and renew. God's love is beyond our counting, more than the raindrops that water the earth or the stars that fill the sky.

How many times should I forgive someone who sins against me? Do it until you lose count. And then give it over to God, whose forgiveness knows no end.

P.F.W.

EIGHTEENTH SUNDAY AFTER PENTECOST
The Incomprehensible Goodness of God
MATTHEW 20:1-16

Picture the scene that Matthew painted. It's set in the marketplace, the spot where people from all over the city congregated. Children were running around, playing games, and calling to their friends. Shoppers were squeezing the fruit, handling the goods, and bartering with the merchants. Dotted around the marketplace were scribes in long robes, who were saluted by those who passed. Amid all the commotion were those who stood idle, hoping to find work. Some stood in groups, talking to friends and sharing the events of the day before. Some were quietly contemplating their situation.

A loud cry interrupted the thoughts of the quiet and the chatter of friends: "The grapes are ripe and ready for harvest! Come, everyone willing to work! There is plenty for all to do!" The unemployed eagerly gathered around the householder to find out what there was to do and how much they would be paid. The householder negotiated with his new employees, and it was agreed that everyone would be paid a denarius, which was the average daily wage. The workers were sent off into the vineyards to begin harvesting in the cool morning air.

Three hours later the householder returned to the marketplace. There was not as much commotion as there was earlier, but there were still people standing around who were willing to work. In fact, they were so willing to work that they didn't even inquire about wages. They were content to accept that the householder would pay them a fair sum.

Twice more during the day, the householder returned to the marketplace, and each time he employed all who wanted to work. One hour before the end of the day, the householder gathered all those standing idle in the marketplace and encouraged them to work for him during that final hour.

When evening came, all the workers were called in from the vineyard to be paid, beginning with those who worked for only one hour. Those people were paid a denarius for their hour of labor. The next group was paid a denarius for their three hours, as were all the people who had worked that day, regardless of the amount of time they gave to the harvest. Those who worked a full day were confused, hurt, and angry that they had not received more for the time they had given and the burdens they had endured. But the householder reminded them that they had agreed upon a denarius, they had a contract. He also said to them, "Are you envious because I am generous?"

Jesus told this parable in response to Peter's question, "Look, we have left everything and followed you. What then will we have?" Peter was pointing out to Jesus all that he and the other disciples had given up in order to become his followers. They had given up their homes, their families, their jobs, their security. Peter had given up his whole life for Jesus, and now he wondered what he would receive in return. In response, Jesus told him this parable. Peter would receive salvation, eternal life, a place in the kingdom of heaven. "And," Jesus says, "so will everyone else!"

As a disciple of Christ, as one who has given your life to Jesus, how does Jesus' response to Peter make you feel? How does it make you feel when Jesus says that every Christian, everyone, no matter how much they have given to Jesus in their lifetime, will receive the same wage—salvation? How does it make you feel to hear that some who have wasted their lives and not until the last hour before death confessed Jesus as Lord, receive the same as you do— eternal life with God? It doesn't seem right. It doesn't seem fair. Won't we receive something more than the others for giving far more than an hour of our life to Jesus?

As active Christians, we give ourselves to God. We resist the desire to sleep in or to work on Sunday mornings. We give away our hard-earned money in order to support the work of the church. We spend time in prayer and the study of Scripture when we could be getting our work done or enjoying some sort of recreation. The confirmation students spend an hour every Wednesday after school at church, as well as study at home with their Bibles, while others play basketball, watch TV, or do something with their friends. As followers of Jesus, we accompany people through illness and even death. As active Christians, we follow Jesus into the vineyard, where we are called to do the work of Christ.

For us, the ones who faithfully do the work of Christ, this parable still doesn't make sense. It doesn't seem fair. We are the ones who have done most of the work. The laborers that began working the first hour of the day picked many more grapes than those who began working the last hour. Yet they all received a whole day's salary. If that were to happen today, there would be labor strikes. The unions would be in an uproar. It would turn our whole economy topsy-turvy. Those who work for only one hour should not receive a whole day's wage. It is only right that the reward for our labor should be consistent with the time we put in.

But this parable has nothing to do with fair labor laws. It is not a prescription of how employers should treat their employees. It is a description of how God works in the kingdom of heaven. In our first lesson today we heard that the Lord said to Isaiah: "My thoughts are not your thoughts, nor are your ways my ways." God's goodness is incomprehensible to us. We cannot fully understand it. We are so concerned with making everything fair that we can't understand generosity.

According to our understanding, God doesn't act fairly. In fact, by putting ourselves in the place of the laborers who started at sunrise or midmorning or even early afternoon, we have missed the point of the parable. Jesus is the one laborer who works from sun up till sun down. Jesus is the one who has borne the burden of the day and the scorching heat. Only Jesus has earned salvation. Yet God calls us to himself and gives to us the full wage. God gives to you the promise of salvation, not because you have worked hard enough but because Jesus has done it for you.

God gives us much more than we can ever earn. The wages of sin is death, but God gives us life. The laborers in the vineyard all received a full day's wage regardless of the hours they worked. We have all been given salvation, regardless of the sins we've committed.

And God continues to trust us with God's work. God chose us in our baptism, renews us at the table, sends us out as laborers to plant and harvest, to speak to those who have never heard and to proclaim the word anew to those who have fallen away. We have been accepted by God. We have all been made equal and are all recipients of God's grace.

Let me suggest an alternative ending to the parable. And when evening came, the owner of the vineyard said to his steward, "Call the laborers and pay them their wages beginning with the last, up to the first." When those who are hired at five o'clock came, each of them received a denarius. And when the laborers saw that they would all be given a day's wage, they all cheered, thanking the landowner for his generosity. Each worker went home smiling, happy for one another and praising God.

Unlikely ending? Maybe. Impossible? Not at all. When your life is focused on Christ, when you are giving thanks for your own blessings instead of complaining to God about what others get, God's generosity and indiscriminate love still may not look fair, but they sure look great!

P.F.W.

Where Are the Real Christians?
MATTHEW 21:28-32

Today's Gospel text raises a thought that is not comforting. In fact, it is a troubling thought. It disturbs me personally as a Christian. But it also disturbs me as one who is called to be a pastor in the church.

In this Gospel passage Jesus is telling a story. It's one of those clever stories Scripture scholars have labeled a "parable." A parable is tricky. It's meant to be; that's what it's for. A parable, if we let it work, will shock us into seeing our life in a whole new light.

A preaching teacher wrote a book about Jesus' parables in the Gospel of Matthew and called the book *The Divine Trap*. The tasty bait in this divine trap is the story told about someone else. We sniff and follow the bait. Then, bam! The trap springs. We discover that the story is not about someone else but about ourselves. So what is the "bait" here?

Jesus begins: "So what do you think? What is your opinion? Come on in," he says. "Enter into this." A man had two sons . . ." It could just as well be "A woman had two daughters . . . "

A parent had two children and said to them both: "Go work in the vineyard." The first refused. She said, "No, I won't." But later she thought better of it, and she went and worked. The second daughter responded by saying, "Sure, I will. I'm on my way." But she never went. Which child did the will of her parent? The first? The one whose first response was no?

Now, if the parent, if the vineyard owner in the story, is the maker of heaven and earth, and we are the children, which one are you? If the shoe fits, put it on. If the shoe pinches, it's the right one. It's meant to pinch, for the sake of revealing the truth about us.

In today's reading Jesus made no bones about applying this parable directly to those to whom he was telling it. Jesus had arrived in Jerusalem, the capital city. He was not in the streets. He was teaching in the temple. His audience was made up of those you would be sure to find in the temple: the good religious folk and their leaders. Jesus was not addressing himself here to the riffraff, to those who were excluded from the temple. He was speaking to you and me. At least that's what we would like to think. Or is it? For what he said is that those who were out selling their bodies in the streets and those who were out extorting money from other people would get into the kingdom before the hearers of this parable would.

This is what led me to the troubling thought: Perhaps the *real* Christians are out there, in the world; not here, in this church building. Of the two daughters sent out to work, which one actually did the will of her parent? Isn't it the one who said no, but did yes? This parable is a warning to those of us who say yes.

On a recent flight, the 747 in which I was riding sat a long time on the tarmac at the airport waiting for clearance to take off. I decided to pull out my little traveling pocket Bible and reflect on upcoming Scripture texts.

I hardly noticed the flight attendant coming down the aisle making one last check that all seat belts were fastened, all headrests upright, and all carry-on baggage safely stowed overhead or under the seat ahead of you. The flight attendant was already saying something before I realized that she was talking to me and that it was a question.

"Pardon me?" I queried.

"Are you a Christian?" she repeated.

"Yes." I heard myself say.

"I am too," she said. "That girl over there is too," she added. Then she passed on down the aisle.

"Are you a Christian?" As my questioner continued down the aisle, I sat there with my answer. "Yes," I had said. I had said it unambiguously, after barely a moment's hesitation.

Today's parable comes as a warning to those of us who say yes.

As I sat there, I thought that perhaps a more honest answer would have been, "I'm trying to be."

I felt a little irked, but more amused, at the implication that being a Christian made me one of a select group of three on that crowded jumbo jet.

Am I Christian? Oh, I've been baptized. My baptismal certificate, signed by Pastor Arthur F. Steinke, is framed on my study wall. Not only have I been baptized, but I go to church *almost* every Sunday.

But today's Gospel suggests that that is not what it's all about. It takes more than being baptized and being a card-carrying church member to be a Christian. It's about something else.

What is it?

The parable implies that it is not those who say yes to God who find life, but those who actually in their lives *do* what God wills. Not verbal assent but obedience is what counts. What makes a difference is not only what we do on Sunday, but what we do on Monday and Tuesday and Wednesday and . . .

This emphasis on obedience was a passion with Jesus. "By their fruits you shall know them," Jesus said. And "Not those who say, Lord, Lord, but those who do the will of my heavenly Father shall enter into the kingdom of heaven."

After all the teachings that Matthew gathered into the Sermon on the Mount, Jesus says "for who hear these teachings and don't act on them, it's just like building a house on sand. But if you act on them, it's like building on rock."

So what determines a real Christian is not what we say but what we do. Is that it? It is tempting to reduce today's Gospel parable to actions speak louder than words. But there's more to it than that. There's the matter of repentance. It may escape our first notice, but the child who actually fulfills her parent's will is the one who repents. The one who said no but then thought better of it is the one that Jesus commends to us. The one who changed her mind. On the other hand—and shockingly—Jesus identifies the good religious folk in the temple as those who have not repented.

What is it, to repent? Perhaps the best image of repentance is that of the first child in the story: She was marching away from work in the vineyard but then turned around and walked back in the other direction. To repent is to realize that we have to change—and to actually change. To repent is to recognize that there are places in our life where we have to change our direction or we will become destructive, of ourselves or others.

The source of spiritual danger may be great or it may be small. Repentance may mean recognizing that you are addicted and seeking to put the addiction behind you, putting your feet on the road to recovery. Repentance may mean reneging on one commitment (for example, to attend a church meeting) in order to fulfill a deeper commitment (for example, to attend to one's family). Repentance may mean telling someone you are sorry for something that you did or didn't do. Repentance may mean sending 250,000 troops half way around the world, and bringing them home again without a war. Repenting is being different the next time. It isn't easy.

Doing this begins with facing some truth about ourselves. Perhaps you've seen the poster that reads, "You shall know the truth," quoting the Gospel of John, "And the truth shall make you free. But *first* it will make you miserable." Repentance is moving from not having a care to being miserable for the way we've been to the newness of life and change of heart that God offers—the "new heart and new spirit" that Ezekiel spoke of in today's first lesson.

The one who fulfills God's will is thus the one who repents, like the daughter in the story who realized that her no was wrong, thought better of it, turned around and did yes.

But there is one more thing: The time to turn is now. Ezekiel proclaims that what matters is not what the fathers or mothers have done but what we do. What we have done is not what matters. Whatever we have done or failed to do in our lives up to now is of no account. Only the present matters.

In an election campaign an incumbent will say, "I stand on my record, on what I've voted for and against." But as we stand before God now, our record is of no account. God doesn't give a hoot about our record. Whether it's good or bad, whether it's something we're proud of or something we're ashamed of, doesn't make any difference at all. All that matters is what we do *now*. What we do now—not what we have done in the past—will determine whether we receive fullness of life or miss it.

A parent had two children and told them both to go to work in the vineyard. The one who said no, then repented and went, is the one who actually did the parent's will. This is a disturbing parable to those of us who have said yes. It places our lives in a totally different—and not immediately welcome—light. Perhaps those who are actually doing God's will are not those who have said yes. Perhaps the real Christians are out there, in the world; not in here, in this church building.

Let me ask you: On your next flight, if the flight attendant should inquire, "Are you a Christian?" what would you say? Are you? If you have second thoughts about it, then, God willing, you may be closer to God's kingdom than you think! For it may be as Luther has said that "it happens—indeed, it seems to happen consistently in this matter of faith—that the person who thinks she believes finally does not believe at all, and the person who thinks she does not believe and despairs actually believes most of all."

We have reason to be unsure about ourselves. But we need not be unsure about God: God is waiting with open arms. On the palms of God's hands we may see the marks of the nails. We may see them because, whether or not we are turned toward God, God is turned continually toward us. Toward us and toward all.

Thanks be to God!

R.L.S.

TWENTIETH SUNDAY AFTER PENTECOST
Whose Kingdom?
MATTHEW 21:33-43

Today Jesus invites us to "hear another parable."

In this portion of Matthew's account of the story of Jesus, Jesus tells many parables. Parables are slices of daily life. Often the stories Jesus tells have an exaggerated twist that forgoes realism in order to heighten the drama. Parables are like alternative worlds into which we walk and, at the end, suddenly see something about ourselves and about God that we had not seen before.

Hear then this parable:

One afternoon a shopper at a local mall felt the need for a coffee break. She bought a little bag of cookies, put them in her pocketbook, and got in the line for coffee. She found a place at a table, took out a magazine to read, and sipped her coffee. Across the table sat a man who was reading a newspaper.

She reached out and took a cookie. As she did, the man seated across the table reached out and took one too. This put her off, but she did not say anything.

A few moments later she took another cookie. Once again the man did too. Now she was getting a bit upset, especially since only one cookie was left now.

Apparently the man also realized that only one cookie was left. He took it, broke it in half, offered half to her, and proceeded to eat the other half himself. Then he smiled at her, arose, put his paper under his arm, and walked off.

Was she steamed!

Her coffee break ruined, already thinking ahead of how she would tell this offense to her family, she folded her magazine, opened her pocketbook—and there discovered her own unopened bag of cookies!

All the time she had been unwittingly helping herself to the cookies of her gracious host!

Actually it was the person with whom she shared the table who had every right to be offended, for she had taken what belonged to him without asking or even acknowledging it with a word of thanks.

The same mistake—but with decided vengeance—was made by the vineyard tenants in the parable told by Jesus. The tenants did not own the vineyard they were working in. Nor did they own its fruits. As tenants, they had only leased the piece of ground. They had not paid a purchase price; they paid only rent, and the rent took the form of a portion of the harvest.

If you have ever rented a house or apartment, you know that legally the renter's first obligation is to pay the owner. This is the obligation the tenants in the story had assumed in entering into this agreement with the vineyard owner.

But when the owner sent to collect the harvest from those who had leased the land, the tenants failed to acknowledge their proper obligation. Instead they took a mean-spirited and grasping tack. "Let us make the vineyard our own," they said to one another.

Then they proceeded not only to deny the owner the rent that was his due but to mistreat and kill those whom the owner sent to remind them of their obligations.

Like the weary shopper on coffee break, the vineyard tenants took to be their own what belonged to someone else.

So it may be with us. All our lives, as I once heard in a sermon, we've been helping ourselves to God's bag of cookies.[1] Whether we realize it or not, whatever cookies we may have are cookies that come from God.

What have we returned to God for the gifts, the life, with which we have been entrusted? I believe that this is the fundamental challenge to us in this parable of Jesus.

In whose kingdom do we live: in our own or in God's?

"The earth is the Lord's and the fullness thereof," sang the psalmist. The earth is the Lord's. We are tenants of the earth but not its owners. The earth has been entrusted to our care and keeping, but we do not possess it. The earth belongs forever to the one who made it.

The mystery is that we are responsible for what we do not own.[2] If we are parents and have children, we are responsible for them, but we do not own them.

If we have a house, even if we have a deed that says that we own it, we will not live in that house forever. We are only passing through as a lingering guest. We are responsible for the house; but we do not really own it in any permanent way.

And the life of our body—the air we draw into our lungs, the beating of our heart—we have this life and we are responsible for it. But we do not possess it. We have it only temporarily as a gift, a trust, from the source of life.

We are tenants on this earth, stewards of what has been entrusted to us.

A second theme in Jesus's parable—a theme noticeably absent from the winsome story of the unintentional cookie thief—is the element of judgment. The tenants in Jesus' story were held accountable for their actions. Jesus invited the hearers of the parable to pronounce the judgment concerning the tenants: "Now when the owner of vineyard comes, what will he do to those tenants?"

"He will put those wretches to a miserable death, and lease the vineyard to other tenants who will give him the produce at the harvest time," the listeners declared.

Then Jesus made it plain that his listeners had pronounced this harsh judgment on themselves. "Therefore, I tell you," he responded, "the kingdom of God will be taken away from you and given to a people that produces the fruit of the kingdom."

Here are words to make us sit up and take notice. This is not merely a sweet appeal to our good intentions. This is not simply wooing us to do what is right. Jesus is more truthful than that. Jesus makes it clear that as tenants, not landowners, in a kingdom that is God's and not our own, we are accountable to the owner for what has been entrusted to us.

What does it mean to produce "the fruits of the kingdom"?

The fruits of the kingdom are pointed out in the passage from the prophet Isaiah that is the first lesson on this Sunday. This passage, so familiar to Jesus' original hearers, is the scriptural source for Jesus' biblical figure of the vineyard:

> For the vineyard of the Lord of hosts
>
> is the house of Israel.
>
> and the people of Judah
>
> are his pleasant planting;
>
> [The Lord] expected justice,
>
> but saw bloodshed;
>
> righteousness,
>
> but heard a cry! (Isaiah 5:7)

The expected harvest of the kingdom is to be "justice" and "righteousness." But these have been lacking.

An indication of the harvest the vineyard owner expects is given in the Lord's words elsewhere about how we have treated the least of our fellow tenants: "I was hungry and you gave me food, I was thirsty and you gave me something to drink, I was a stranger and you welcomed me, I was naked and you gave me clothing, I was sick and you took care of me, I was in prison and you visited me" (Matthew 25:35, 36).

This is the "rent," the harvest, we are to return for the privilege of living and working in God's kingdom.

An element of judgment exists in Jesus' parable. But judgment is not the fundamental quality of God that the story reveals. The underlying reality of the story is that the vineyard owner has given over his well-prepared and fruitful land for the use of the tenants. The tenants are not slaves, but independent yet cooperative partners in the enterprise.

Even when the tenants turn against the owner, the absent lord is impossibly patient. After the tenants murder the first envoys, the lord sends not a military force or assassination team but merely a larger party of envoys seeking the harvest. When they too are murdered by the still unrepentant tenants, the owner remains undeterred in seeking to win them over. Like a smitten lover who cannot say no, he sends even his own beloved son. The son too is killed. But by the death of this Son we are saved.

We in the church, as a kind of tenants' union, now gather weekly on the anniversary of that Son's victory over death in order to offer back to the owner of the vineyard a portion of the grain and wine his land has yielded.

We offer up the sweat and tears and laughter of our lives. As we do so, we receive back as our food the body and blood of the Son who was slain that we might be redeemed. The Son was offered that we might be nourished and saved by the God who will not leave us alone but sends continually to save us from ourselves in order that we might live with him in his blessed kingdom now and forever.

R.L.S.

---

1. Bob Sims, sermon, June 2, 1991, Lutheran Church of the Redeemer, Atlanta, Georgia.
2. See Evelyn and James Whitehead, *Seasons and Strength: New Visions of Adult Christian Maturing* (New York: Doubleday, 1984), 50.

TWENTY-FIRST SUNDAY AFTER PENTECOST
Just Say Yes
MATTHEW 22:1-10 (11-14)

"Almighty God, source of every blessing, your generous goodness comes to us anew every day. By the work of your Spirit lead us to acknowledge your goodness, give thanks for your benefits, and serve you in willing obedience."

(Prayer for the Twenty-first Sunday after Pentecost, *Lutheran Book of Worship*)

A certain congregation that is known for its fine liturgy and music also has a reputation for having one of the best coffee hours going. Immediately after the worship service, worshipers stream over to the coffee hour to enjoy the fellowship and the bountifully provided refreshments. In this parish the attention paid to what happens after worship gives credence to the belief that among Lutherans coffee hour is the third sacrament. The secret behind this weekly spread is that all members receive a coffee-hour assignment when they receive their membership certificate. So everyone has a share in this second-order "work of the people."

Each Sunday the fare is rich. There are home-baked cakes and cookies. For those who are hungrier, there are open-faced sandwiches and chips and dips. Once a month there is even pizza! Then there is the fresh fruit for the calorie-conscious and a children's table where punch is served in unbreakable cups and kids can reach some less-sticky offerings. There is coffee and tea—both caffeinated and herbal—and punch. While this weekly post-Eucharist banquet does not quite offer the extravagant menu mentioned in today's reading from Isaiah—"a feast . . . of rich food filled with marrow, of well-aged wines strained clear"—it does offer a pretty good resemblance. It is a real party.

The coffee hour takes place right after the eleven o'clock worship service, and of course everyone is invited. Virtually all the worshipers participate. Some people who did not make it to the service even come to the coffee hour!

This latter situation, however, is a source of consternation for some of the church members—and for one strong-willed Dutchman in particular—who feel rather strongly that this coffee hour should not become an open house party for the whole city. In particular, they feel, it should not be a free feeding station for some of the street people who come ill clad and strong smelling to fill their faces with the lovingly prepared food. The coffee hour, they protest, is for those who have been to worship, so they may enjoy their fellowship with one another on this special day of the week.

Other members of the church by contrast—and another outspoken Dutchman in particular—say, "If we cannot give some food to these people who are hungry, what good is it that we come here and pray? What does it mean if we pray in the church and then right afterward we cannot even accommodate ourselves to feed these people? All have to be welcome. We cannot turn them away."

So the lines are drawn.

Who is welcome to the feast?

The question of who is welcome at the feast seems to be the issue in Jesus' parable. Jesus tells a story about a king who pulls out all the stops to throw a tremendous party to celebrate the wedding of his son. This is not what some people think of as Sunday worship, a come-whenever-you-are-able affair. Rather this is a once-in-a-lifetime chance. This is the social event, not of the week, but of a lifetime. It is a party to end all parties. After all, how many times in a lifetime does the chance come to attend a royal wedding feast?

Because Jesus begins his story with "The kingdom of heaven may be compared with . . . ," we are alerted to the fact that the wedding behind the wedding of which Jesus speaks is nothing less than the wedding of heaven and earth, the betrothal of God to humankind and humankind to God in the Son Jesus Christ. Jesus is speaking of "the great and promised feast" for which we pray weekly, "when Christ will come again in beauty and power."

For this unprecedented extravaganza the king sends out servants to invite the privileged guests. Apparently only certain persons are to be so honored.

"Aha," I can hear the strong-willed Dutchman mumbling in the back pew, "You see? Only certain guests are invited! Not everyone!"

"Yes," his compatriot retorts, "but watch how the privileged intended guests responded!"

Those on the official guest list who received personally delivered invitations, Jesus says plainly, "would not come."

When a second, more urgent invitation was extended, those on the original royal guest list acted with even greater contempt. Some simply ignored it. Others, Jesus says, responded to this golden opportunity by seizing the king's servants, treating them shamefully and killing them. Against these the angered king retaliated in kind, destroying them and burning their city.

This last, troubling turn of the story was no doubt understood by the early readers of Matthew as a reference to the destruction of Jerusalem, "the city that murders the prophets and stones the messengers sent to her" (Matthew 23:37).

As Jesus' story continues, however, the contemptuous behavior of the originally invested guests has an extraordinary consequence: the king decides to make the party an open house. This is a ruler who when deciding to throw a party will not be deterred by refusals.

Now everyone is invited. Now the doors of the kingdom are thrown open. The invitation to the marriage feast is extended to everyone who will come, without exception. Now your name need not appear on an official list. You need not check in at the door— "Anderson, Sarah? Ah, here it is. Please come in." Rather the door to this lavish affair is thrown wide open.

Here is a party that you do not have to deserve. The dignitaries have lost their privilege. Protocol is thrown to the wind. It is a state dinner in the East Room of the White House, but it might as well be a soup kitchen in its clientele. There is no questionnaire to fill out, no inquisition about your moral behavior. Jesus says that the hall is packed with guests, "both bad and good." There is not even the usual intake interview required by the community emergency food pantry.

And—amazing!—it is completely free.

It is not like one of those fancy balls or banquets you would love to go to but the tickets are $150 a couple.

Now, you know as well as I do that an invitation to a wedding and to the reception as well carries with it an understood social obligation to bring a gift. But here even that obligation is set aside in the extraordinary largesse of a royal wedding feast.

An invitation is presented with your name on it. All you need do is to say "Yes, of course!" and come. Just say yes!

God is throwing a party. It is already under way. The band has finished tuning up and is getting into swing. The hot hors d'oeuvres are fresh out of the oven. God is throwing a party. You are invited.

Just say yes.

But what does it mean to say yes, to accept God's invitation?

The president says, "Just say no!" Bumper stickers, billboards, and milk cartons carry the same message aimed primarily at youth: "Just say no to drugs!" When you are offered drugs or they are forced on you by others, just say no! This motto of the national antidrug campaign, however, has been criticized for being naive. When you recognize the intensity of pressure put on adolescents to conform, you understand the courage it truly takes to refuse and actually say no.

Jesus would have us reflect today on what it might mean to actually and truthfully say yes to God's invitation.

You remember that Jesus' parable concludes not with the whole world making merry at the feast but rather with the ejection from the party of a certain guest. The king's bouncers throw out a person who came to the feast but did not wholeheartedly enter into the occasion. Here was a guest who, like the vineyard owner's son in Jesus' previous parable, said yes but did not do yes. He or she came to feast—after all, everyone was invited—but presumed upon the king's graciousness and failed to enter fully into what the occasion called for. The missing wedding garment was a sign of a missing commitment, a lack of wholeheartedness.

How are we today responding to God's invitation? Have we said yes? Have we said a yes that really means yes?

The party that Jesus has in mind is open to all, without exception.

This is not to everyone's taste. I remember a mortally ill woman protesting to me that if people who had been mean to her were going to be in heaven, then she did not want to go there. But the party is God's, not ours. At God's party we do not get to choose our fellow guests. I do not doubt that we would be far more stringent than God is.

After the South African government had finally opened up negotiations with banned opponents, Lutheran pastor T. Simon Farasani found himself riding in an elevator in a downtown Lusaka hotel with the very same South African military officer who had five years before presided over Pastor Farasani's brutal and body-breaking torture in a South African prison. "Well," the white officer addressed him, "perhaps we are brothers after all, what do you think?"

"When Jesus said that 'in my Father's house are many rooms,' " Pastor Farasani now preaches, "if you would be able to visit some of those rooms, you would be surprised to see who some of those people are! Perhaps I would find that white officer there. And you might be surprised who you would find."

We do not get to choose our fellow guests. All we get to choose is how we ourselves will respond to God's invitation.

When our response to the invitation is, "Hell, no, we won't go," God takes us at our word. This is the word of judgment in Jesus' parable. This is a judgment, it is important to notice, that we pronounce on ourselves. After all, everyone is invited.

When by our lives we say no, God suffers our refusal. Unlike Luke's version, Matthew sets this parable of contrasting responses to the king's invitation in Holy Week, between Jesus' entrance to Jerusalem and his crucifixion. The world's no takes the form of Jesus' cross. But this refusal to accept is forever countered by the implacable yes that God uttered on Easter.

All our excuses for refusing to accept God's gracious invitation have not kept God from extending the invitation to us again and again. Indeed, as long as we are alive, the invitation is allowed to stand. But we do not have forever.

The hour is late, but it is not yet too late. There still is time. There is still the present moment.

Again today the invitation is extended.

I am not the king. I am only the king's servant. I have been sent to invite you—each one of you—to a party that has no end and has already begun.

Will you come?
I mean, will you really come?
The table is spread. The band is already playing. It is the supper
of the Lamb who was slain.
Everyone is invited without exception.
Will you come?
Just say yes.

R.L.S.

Giving God the Things That Are God's
MATTHEW 22:15-21

I have heard of a person who makes such a point of saying thank you that every time he writes a check to someone, he writes on the bottom of it, "Thank you very much!"

He began this practice some years ago and continues to this day. I suppose that he wants to become a more thankful person, and this is part of his discipline toward achieving that. Perhaps he once heard a sermon about cultivating an attitude of gratitude. He also realizes that we do not often let other people know how grateful we are for what we receive from them. This is one way he tries to let them know.

When he pays the monthly utility bill, he pauses for a moment before doing so to reflect on the many benefits he has enjoyed from the electric power he has received—the convenience of electric lights, the power that runs the furnace, the electric coffee maker and microwave and television and carpet sweeper. Then he makes out the check for the proper amount, and in the space on the bottom of the check for indicating its purpose, he writes, "Thank you very much for the electricity!"

When he pays the telephone bill he notes on the check, "Thank you for the phone service!" When he settles up with the department store, he does similarly, and likewise all the rest. To each their due.

Then each year comes April 15. Time to pay taxes.

One would think that the obligation of having to pay taxes might lead in quite a different direction.

But not so.

Here too, once he has calculated how much his tax bill is, he pauses to reflect on the benefits he has received by living in this country—the freedoms not enjoyed in some other lands, the relative personal security, the social benefits. Then he picks up his pen, fills in the proper amount on the check, makes it out to the Internal Revenue Service—just as you and I do—then in the space on the bottom of the check he puts his social security number—don't forget that!—and then adds a note: "Thank you *very* much!" I suspect that the people at the Internal Revenue Service who open these checks do not see many notes like that one!

Imagine: it is possible to pay one's taxes not grudgingly but with an attitude of thankfulness. At least, it is for some people, sometime.

In today's Gospel the question that is asked of Jesus is not whether taxes should be paid gratefully or grudgingly. Rather the question put to Jesus is whether in his opinion it is right and proper to pay taxes at all.

The political situation in the time of Jesus was quite different from our own. The land was under military occupation. A foreign power extracted taxes from the citizens. One might compare it roughly to living fifty years ago in Nazi-occupied France and being forced to pay taxes to the Nazi's puppet government. Or to living under apartheid in South Africa and being forced to support an all-white, racist regime. If you were living in circumstances like these, would it be right and proper for you to pay these taxes or not? This is the issue that faced Jesus and his contemporaries.

Jesus recognized that the question asked of him was a trick. Just like the question put to candidates for public office in the United States today, "Are you pro-life or pro-choice?" the divisive question put to Jesus admitted of no universally popular answer. The question about taxes was intended to get him into trouble with one group or another.

In any such situation of foreign oppression, one has two primary options: to cooperate or to resist. The two groups of people who approached Jesus represented two conflicting alternatives. The Herodians were Jews who were partisans of the ruling Roman royal family. The Pharisees, on the other hand, were religious purists who would have liked to avoid paying taxes to the gentile overlords.

Thus, in putting to Jesus the query, "Is it right to pay taxes to the emperor or not?" the Herodians and Pharisees meant to trap him.

They challenged Jesus. But Jesus gave a response that did more than merely foil their trick. Jesus gave a teaching that left them with a challenge that rings down through the centuries.

"Show me the coin used for the tax," Jesus said.

They gave him a piece of Roman currency called a denarius. Some of the Roman coins from Jesus' day have survived and are on display in museums. As our American coins today bear the heads of dead presidents, this small silver coin was minted with a likeness of the currently ruling Roman emperor, Tiberius. On the denarius Jesus held, Tiberius's head bears a laurel wreath, a token of the emperor's claim to divinity. Around the head on the coin runs the inscription "Tiberius Caesar, majestic son of the majestic God, and High Priest."

No wonder the more zealous and sensitive Jews took offense at having to pay taxes to so idolatrous a regime. No wonder the Jews scorned those who made contracts with the Romans to collect taxes. Yet the account of the good news that we proclaim today bears the name of just such a tax collector: Matthew, whom Jesus called to be one of his disciples.

"Whose head is this [on the coin] and whose title?" Jesus asked.

"The emperor's," they responded.

"Give therefore to the emperor the things that are the emperor's," Jesus replied, "and to God the things that are God's."

What belongs to the emperor?

Certainly the coin belongs to the emperor. In those days money was commonly considered to be the property of the ruler who had minted it. After all, it had his name on it, and his picture.

If Jesus was speaking only literally, all that he may have meant was to give the coin back to the one from whom it comes. That would be the extent of it.

But of course Jesus' original hearers as well as we today know that the government asks its subjects or citizens for more than money. The government asks also for allegiance. In time of war, the government asks for military service, which may require the taking of other people's lives or the sacrificing of one's own.

In giving us the teaching "Render to Caesar what is Caesar's and to God what is God's," Jesus does not provide us with a clear criterion for deciding what is rightfully due the government and what is rightfully due God. But Jesus framed the question very clearly. Jesus was clear that such a line is to be drawn. In placing duty to state in the context of duty to God, Jesus affirms that no claim on us by an earthly power is to be considered absolute. Only the claim of God on us, mediated by conscience, is absolute. We are not to give to Caesar what is God's.

Discerning what is right and proper in this respect is up to each one of us. Paul asserts repeatedly in writing to early Christian communities that believers are to respect governmental authority. God can work even through ungodly governments. In today's first reading, the prophet Isaiah showed how even the heathen ruler Cyrus could be an instrument of divine purpose.

Nevertheless there have always been times in the past and shall be in the future when government goes afoul of what God asks or allows. When this happens, government is to be changed, or, in the extreme, resisted. Thus in every generation and in many different countries, there have been people of faith who sometimes at great personal sacrifice have withheld from government their money or obedience when their conscience has led them to do so.

A recent example of such a stance was that of the United States Marine Private First Class Erik Larsen, who applied for, and was refused, status as a conscientious objector to war during the war in the Persian Gulf. From his cell in the military prison at Camp Lejeune, Erik wrote:

> Many folks say I was a threat to the government and that was the reason for my imprisonment. I disagree. It is Christ's message of nonviolence which frightens the government. . . . The scriptures and our Lutheran heritage teach me that there are times when a person must take the risk of imprisonment. Prison is not a place to be avoided but is a place where the spirit is alive. Each day I am here my faith and my commitment strengthens. I have learned that happiness resides within my soul and not in the possessions I gather around me.[1]

Whether or not one personally agrees with this particular stance, such witnesses to conscience challenge each one of us to be equally courageous and clear in discerning where we ourselves are to draw the line between what is legitimately due to Caesar and what is due to God alone.

Jesus' teaching in today's Gospel goes far beyond any quandary we might have about paying taxes. In fact it goes beyond any questions about military service or other obligations due to the government.

If Jesus had just let it go at "Render to the emperor the things that are the emperor's," then we might still hold back. While not always easy—especially when April 15 comes around—we might at least fulfill this part of what is asked. But Jesus went on to give a much farther-reaching commandment: "Give to God the things that belong to God."

This is the hard part.

This saying of Jesus places *everything* we own and everything we are in the context of our relationship with God. For example, when it comes to our spending that coin that Jesus is holding up in his fingers, we have so many choices to make. How much should we give this year to United Way? How much should we put away for our children's education? How much for our own retirement? Don't we deserve to be able to go out to dinner once in a while? How about the appeal to help feed the starving people in the horn of Africa or in Russia? How much shall we pledge to our congregation this year?

All these decisions. All these legitimate claims on us.

"Give to God the things that belong to God," Jesus tells us.

What belongs to God?

The Roman coin that Jesus held bore the image of the emperor. Therefore it rightfully belonged to the emperor.

What bears the image and name of God?

What, indeed, but our very self.

"Let us make humankind in our image," God had said, "according to our likeness" (Genesis 1:26). So God created us in God's image; in God's image God created us.

We are the coins of God's realm. Then let us "give to God the things that belong to God." There is a limit to what we owe Caesar. But there is no limit to what we owe God.

In the early centuries of the church's missionary activity in what is now Germany, entire tribes of warlike, barely civilized peoples were converted to Christian faith. In those days groups of people were sometimes baptized en masse by immersion in a body of water. But when some of the warriors were baptized, they held their right arms over their heads so that the hand in which they wielded their battle-axes would not be baptized. They still wanted to be free to use these hands as they wished. They did not want to subject their whole self to the covenant they were entering with God.

What may we be reluctant to place in the context of our covenant with God? Our wallet, our career, a relationship, our weekend, our work? But God's claim on us in our baptism is total. No part of our life is excluded from our fundamental covenant with the one who is our creator and redeemer, in whose image we were made.

Yes, it would have been much easier if Jesus, when he was approached by the Herodians and the Pharisees, had just let it go

with "Give to the emperor the things that belong to the emperor."
But Jesus did not stop there.

Jesus did not stop there in speaking with us without first directing our lives and our hearts to what is central.

Jesus did not stop there without first showing us what it means
to "give to God what belongs to God." Jesus rendered fully unto
God what was God's, and did so on behalf of us all.

The reason we give God what is God's is that God first gave us
God's own self. We remember this anew each time we repeat the
words "This is my body given for you; this is my blood poured out
for you."

God has given us what is God's.

Can we return less?

R.L.S.

---

1. Erik Larsen circular letter to friends, February 4, 1992.

TWENTY-THIRD SUNDAY AFTER PENTECOST
Love, Love at the End
MATTHEW 22:34-40 (41-46)

Do you remember what it was like when you first came to
this congregation as a visitor? Probably during that first visit, and if
you were interested enough to make subsequent visits, you were
trying to get a sense of the congregation. You may have been
asking yourself, "What would it be like to be a member here?"

One of a pastor's most stimulating tasks is teaching the class for
those visitors who are exploring membership in the congregation.
Newcomers see things with new eyes. Because they come with a
fresh perspective, newcomers tend to ask the best questions.

One question asked of me two years ago in a new members class
still has me thinking. "I had some upbringing in the church when
I was little," the prospective member began, "but I have been away
from the church for quite a few years. I really do not know much
about it. I am just coming back." After this preface, she put her
question: "I would just like to know, what will be expected of me if
I join this church?"

She sincerely wanted to know what it would mean to become a
disciple of Jesus Christ in and through this congregation.

What should I tell her?

What would *you* tell her? How would you summarize what it means to be a member of the local, face-to-face body of Christ?

I am still thinking about her question and trying to come up with an adequate response.

I find the question so provocative that I now address it to every class of new members. "What do you think it should mean, what do we have reason to expect from one another, when we become a member of this congregation?" I ask them. Then they share and discuss their responses with one another. The variety of perspectives is fascinating.

Different people emphasize different things. For some, regular worship attendance is paramount. For others, it is financial stewardship. Yet others give precedence to committee work or other "hands-on" involvement in congregational ministry. Others stress caring for one another or witnessing to our faith in our daily lives.

At some point in the discussion, I share with them the constitutional minimum requirement for active membership in the institution, which is a financial contribution or participation in Holy Communion at least once each year.

I wonder what Jesus would say?

If a prospective member of the body of Christ were able to ask Jesus himself what it would mean to be a member, how might Jesus respond?

I believe we can get a pretty good idea of Jesus' own perspective by attending to how Jesus replies to the question, Which is the greatest commandment in the law?

This question, I suspect, has a similar concern. The issue is, What is *most* important? Among all the things that are asked of us, what is truly essential? What can we not do without to be a disciple of Jesus Christ?

We should note before going on that in Matthew's distinctive description of this encounter, Jesus' questioner may be less than entirely sincere. Like the other two questions put to Jesus on the same occasion concerning paying taxes to Caesar and concerning the resurrection, this question about the greatest commandment is characterized by Matthew as a test, a trap, a trick to draw Jesus into unfavorable controversy.

But judging from how Mark and Luke relate the same incident, there is no indication that, were the questioner anything but totally sincere, Jesus' answer would be any different. In fact, Jesus' response to this question forms the core of the early Christian community's understanding of the gospel. To this all four Gospels and the writings of Paul bear unanimous witness.

The question put to Jesus is phrased in terms of commandments. We may think immediately of the Ten Commandments,
which we may have memorized along with Martin Luther's "This-
is-most-certainly-true" Small Catechism explanations in our confirmation class days. But Jesus' questioner undoubtedly has in mind
something more challenging than merely choosing one from
among the "Ten Words" Moses received from God on Mount
Sinai.

By the time of Jesus the multitude of imperatives in the five
books of the Torah, the "Law," had been counted, numbered, and
systemized to 613 commandments. Aren't you glad that Luther did
not deal with all 613? If he had, I suspect that many of us would
still be unconfirmed. The 613 commandments had been further
broken down into 365 negative, "Thou shall not," commands—
one for every day of the year—and 268 positive, "Thou shalt,"
commands—one (or so the rabbis calculated) for each of the 268
bones in the human body. Perhaps, as Robert Smith has com-
mented, this was to suggest that God's commands should fill every
moment and every movement of our lives.[1]

The spot on which the representative Pharisee sought to put
Jesus was framed by this question: Which, of all the 613
commandments—remember that Matthew mentions that this
fellow was a lawyer as well as a Pharisee—do you, Jesus, rank as
first and foremost?

We might hesitate to answer this probing question ourselves
had we never before heard Jesus' reply. What is it, after all, that is
most important of all? Do you have a ready answer?

Jesus seems not to have paused a blink before quoting back to
his interrogator two of the 268 positive, "Thou shalt," commandments. Which two?

They are two that begin with the words "You shall love. . . . "
Deuteronomy 6:5, "You shall love the Lord your God with all your
heart, and with all your soul, and with all your might." In other
words, you shall love God *totally*, with all your being. And Leviti-
cus 19:18, "You shall love your neighbor as yourself." That is, you
shall love your neighbor as totally as you love yourself.

Everything, Jesus says, not only in the Law but also in the
Prophets, turns on this hinge of "You shall love."

I wish that I had thought of this when the prospective member
asked me what would be expected of her if she joined this church?
This would have been a good and adequate reply.

After all, what Jesus says is true, is it not?

These words of Jesus put all 613 little rules and codes and norms of our lives and church into perspective. If what Jesus says is correct—that above all we are to love totally, both God and our neighbor—then everything else is secondary.

A story about the fourth evangelist, Saint John, seems to lead in the same direction as Jesus' encounter with this lawyer. Among the twelve original apostles, John alone is said to have lived into old age. For the commemorations of all eleven of the other apostles, the paraments are red, the color of martyrs' blood. But for John, the church is dressed in white, not red, for he alone of the original twelve did not meet with violent death in the pattern of our Lord. Saint John, it is said, lived to a ripe old age, most likely in the city of Ephesus in Asia Minor. In his later years not only his body but also his mind became somewhat enfeebled. Like my wife's grandmother, who in her advanced age was reduced to her mother tongue of Swedish and even in Swedish was limited to repeating over and over again a few simple, stock expressions, so the aging evangelist John was eventually pared down to but a few words—indeed to a single expression—which he would repeat constantly.

One may imagine the esteem and great reverence accorded this last surviving apostle of our Lord. On the Lord's Day he would be carried into the midst of the congregation that had assembled for worship. The people would fall silent to hear his words. Then the old man would open his mouth. This is what the aged apostle would say: "My children, love one another. My children, love one another. My children, love one another."

Over and over again. Just this.

It was as if in the crucible of Saint John's own experience of the Lord and of discipleship he had distilled the entire meaning of his eloquent witness to the gospel into these five words: "My children, love one another."

Saint John's distillation of our only fitting human response to God's grace is in accord with Jesus' own condensation in today's Gospel. The early Christian community shaped by the witness of the apostle John likewise expressed its understanding of Jesus' words in today's lesson when it wrote that "Those who say, 'I love God,' and hate their brothers or sisters, are liars; for those who do not love a brother or sister whom they have seen, cannot love God whom they have not seen. The commandment we have from him is this: those who love God must love their brothers and sisters also" (1 John 4:20, 21).

Jesus binds these two commandments into one: total love of God and total love of neighbor, so that one becomes the measure of the other.

"When the Son of Man comes in this glory, and all the angels with him"—so Jesus will say to conclude this time of teaching before entering upon his passion and death—the one upon the throne will indicate that those who fed, welcomed, clothed, and visited their neighbor did it also unto God. Those who did it not for their neighbor, did it not for God. For God and neighbor are one in love.

"You shall love," Jesus tells us today.

If we should ask Jesus, "Which is the greatest commandment?" or "What is it that is *most* important?" or "What would it mean for me to become a follower of yours?" Jesus' response is: "You shall love."

"With all your heart and with all your soul and with all your mind," you shall love. God and neighbor you shall love.

You shall love, Jesus tells us, as I have loved you. You shall love as totally as I love you still. "This is my body, broken for you. This is my blood, shed for you, for the forgiveness of sins."

In the end, there is love. Love at the end. Not our love, whether for God or for our neighbor. But rather, God's love for us. It is on this love alone—not ours, but God's—that we stake our salvation.

R.L.S.

---

1. *Augsburg Commentary on the New Testament* (Minneapolis: Augsburg, 1989) 265.

TWENTY-FOURTH SUNDAY AFTER PENTECOST
Keep Your Lamp Lit
MATTHEW 25:1-13

When Jesus talked about the ten virgins and their lamps, he was talking about a crisis. He was talking about an event in their young lives that was important not only for them but for the bridegroom and everyone connected to the wedding. The bridegroom was supposed to come and take the bride from the father's house to his father's house for the ceremony. The bridesmaids were to wait for the groom and accompany him and the bride to the wedding. If the wedding was at night, lamps would be needed to light the way. If there were no lamps, the bride and groom might stumble around or arrive late from having to travel in darkness. It was a big deal, this business about lamps.

In Jesus' story there were five wise maids and five foolish ones. The foolish ones didn't have enough oil to keep their lamps lit while the bridegroom was delayed. When the bridegroom finally showed up, they discovered their lamps were going out. It was a crisis. It was like forgetting to order your dress until a day before the senior prom or neglecting to put gas in the car for that trip across the desert. It was a crisis, and the five foolish bridesmaids were in a panic.

But this crisis was not just a social calamity. It wasn't just a few teenage girls in a tizzy about their performance for one wedding. This is the crisis of Jesus' second coming, his return to earth. This is a crisis of immense proportions, and the consequences are monumental. If the bridesmaids are prepared, then the joy of the wedding feast will be theirs. If unprepared, then their sorrow will be bitter beyond words.

Jesus had just finished telling his disciples about the signs of the end. Not that he was all that specific, mind you; he didn't give them any dates. But he impressed on them the necessity of being prepared. He said his coming would be unexpected. Then he compared the kingdom of heaven to this story about the wedding and the bridesmaids. Make sure you're ready. Make sure you have what it takes to follow the groom. Make sure you're prepared for the second coming of Christ or you may find yourself locked out of the wedding feast. Don't wait until the last minute to put your lamps in order. Long before that great and terrible day arrives you have something to do:

Buy oil, lots of it! Go to the store with your checkbook, and empty your account for one item. Hock all the family silver and jewels and sell Aunt Martha's antiques to get more money to buy more oil. Make sure your lamps are the best in town, and then store them where the devil and all his angels couldn't find them even if they had X-ray vision. Then you'd be ready. Then you'd have what it takes to meet him when he comes, and you'd be able to follow him through the door to a place where lamps no longer are needed. "Keep awake therefore, for you know neither the day nor the hour."

When you set up a business, first you go to friends, bankers, and family to get financial backing for your enterprise. You work long and hard hours to set things up so that when opening day comes you are assured of success. When you are getting ready for Christmas, you make sure you have the presents, the food, the silverware, the room, and everything all set up for that grand day. When you are preparing for the final Christmas, you make sure of your supply of oil.

The oil you need is the Word of God. The oil is the gospel and the sacraments. The flame is faith, which burns within us when we have the Word in the lamp of our hearts. If you rarely open the Bible and hardly ever study God's Word to find in it the fuel for life, you won't have to worry about trimming your lamp; it'll be burned out. If you don't read Bible stories to your children or ask questions about God, or if you take communion only on Christmas and Easter (if then), are you a wise or foolish bridesmaid?

Many people consider their religion to be only one small facet of their lives, a small part, like a lamp. They won't put anyone else's light out, but they won't bother to take care of their own, either. These are the foolish maidens who presume upon God's grace and say, "Well, God's a nice guy, surely he'll understand about me." They are willing to bow their heads in prayer out of deference to the pastor, but they never compose one on their own. Call them fair-weather Christians and summer soldiers, or call them foolish maidens, they are the ones who take care of the oil in the furnace for winter but never bother with the oil in their hearts. They are penny wise and pound foolish.

Jesus is not demanding that we take care of our own salvation here. Don't get the idea that he is telling us we have to work feverishly for our own salvation or he won't accept us. God's grace is in this parable, not works righteousness. Jesus is warning us not to behave like those foolish girls. That warning is itself a word of grace and hope when it tells us of the trouble we could run into if we neglect God's Word.

When we get ahold of this Word, we understand more clearly our position in the world. We find ourselves in the twilight of history between the day of earthly existence and the night of Christ's coming. Being forearmed about his coming, being told to be ready at all times, creates in us the desire to be as serious about meeting Christ as any bride would be about meeting her husband. Preparing seriously for Christ's coming is not a scary thing. He is the groom. The wedding is a feast. It's an occasion for joy and laughter. Don't we want to be ready for that?

When Christ tells us the truth about himself and us and the future, that's grace. When he warns us, it's also from grace. When he impresses on us the necessity of preparation, that's grace. It's grace because of what it does to us. These words are supposed to stir up our sense of anticipation, a holy hope. They are designed to create in us a serious attitude toward the kingdom of heaven. When we are seriously anticipating Christ's return by paying attention to God's Word here and now, when these words have been imbedded in our hearts and we believe that getting ready is necessary, then we know that we are touched by the Holy Spirit and truly expected at the feast. We are accepted into the festival hall already; otherwise we would be lazy, unconcerned, or foolish, and take God's love for granted.

Don't make the same mistake those five foolish virgins made. They found themselves shut out in the cold of night with the chilling sound of the Lord's voice ringing in their ears, "I don't know you." They had excluded themselves by their foolishness. It really hadn't mattered that much to them before, and now that the crisis had exploded with full force, they were caught short.

Our Lord is delayed. Perhaps this is good, because it gives us time to buy more oil. Perhaps this is for the best, because it gives us time to spread the warning. His delay gives us a chance to trim our lamps and prepare more seriously for his coming. We worship, we celebrate the sacrament, we study and discuss God's Word, we pray and meditate on his gospel. That is how we keep our lamps lit until he comes again.

Fools will disregard the warning and assume that they can handle any crisis that comes their way. They will flippantly expect that all will be well in the end, no matter whether or not they are ready. They will mock us as we buy up all the oil in town. They will dismiss us as fanatics and religious radicals. But when evening comes and the bridegroom suddenly appears, the foolish will be seen for what they are, and they will have no time to relight their lamps.

But the wise will follow the one for whom they had prepared. When he comes they will follow him into the wedding. They will put out their lamps and candles, their torches and lights, not because they have run out of oil but because the light of life that pours from the face of the bridegroom will be more than enough to illumine eternity.

R.A.H.

A No-risk Investment
MATTHEW 25:14-30

Someone might get the false impression from the story of the ten virgins and their lamps that we are supposed to take care of our own spiritual needs and feel satisfied with that. We could mistakenly think that if we have filled our lamps with oil, we have prepared for the coming kingdom and can sit back in our recliners all snug and smug, smiling to ourselves when we think of how well-stocked with fuel our cellar is.

But then comes the parable about the servants who were entrusted with large sums of money. Here Christ tells us that after we have been given what we need, after we have received the gifts we now possess, we are to use them for the kingdom. No time to rest on our laurels; there's work to be done until the master comes again and settles all his accounts.

The man of the house left to go on a long trip, Jesus said. So he entrusted his slaves with huge amounts of cash. The first slave got almost five hundred pounds of silver, worth about a lifetime wage. This was an incredible sum for any master to hand over, let alone to a slave. The others also received large amounts. He must have trusted them very much indeed. Two of these slaves made even more money than they had been given. They had been put in charge of a lot, and the majority took the risk of investing the money; when they had made more, they were given greater responsibilities.

All except one. One didn't do anything. He was scared. He was afraid, I suppose, of what his master would do to him if he tried to invest the one talent and then lost it. His security and safety depended on how he managed this great lump of silver, and so he was afraid.

His fear motivated him to dig a hole and bury the money. It was kind of like stuffing your mattress with a half million dollars. Now the money was secure. So was he; at least that's what he thought.

A lot of people, I suspect, think they're safe when they do things like that slave. Some church folks probably think they're secure when they take all the gifts and talents God gives them, enjoy them for their own benefit, then sit back and wait for the auditing day to come, assuming that if they've got their little heavenly bank account full or at least the coupons tucked safely away, then everything will be properly transacted when the day of accounts arrives.

Some of us may think the church is like a hole in the ground or a mattress. We just stuff the gifts God has given us into the mattress and feel content when it bulges like a mountain, convinced in our own mind that since we've gone to church and done a few decent acts of charity now and then, God must reward us for amassing all that heavenly currency. So at the pearly gates when they try to find our names in the book of life, we will proudly declare that it must be there since we've got this enormous padded bag filled with cash. We plunk it down at Saint Peter's feet demanding entry and say, "Here you have what is yours!"

Of course, Jesus isn't talking about money. He's talking about faith, love, hope, charity, kindness, abilities, life, work, and using all of them for the kingdom. He's talking about people and the way they live. Those who think they can pile up credits in heaven for themselves simply by hoarding the gifts God has given had better re-enroll in the spiritual economics class and learn a few things about divine banking procedures.

The first thing to learn is that God likes risks. If ever there was a risky thing to do, it was the risk God took in sending his only Son, his only beloved Son to earth to be crucified and die. Yes, God had planned that salvation would come through it all, but from a human point of view it was a pretty foolhardy thing to try. Most human stockholders would not have voted for such a scheme to save the company. More likely they would have retrenched and laid off a few workers and hoped for better economic times.

That's pretty much what the worthless slave did. He retreated from the challenge and hid from the responsibility. He probably thought he was being prudent or conservative when all the while the master had wanted him to be bold and advance beyond accepted practices into risking all for the kingdom's sake.

When we do risk all for the kingdom, we find that the return on our master's wealth is more wealth. Not more money, but people. Investing for people, gaining interest in human terms, that's our business. When we invest the gifts that God has given us and risk talking to someone about Christ, or when we serve someone who can never repay us, then we realize that all the talent that has been given to us is not for ourselves but for someone else. When we use the good things we have for someone else's benefit, we find out why we had them in the first place. Then we discover a feeling of worth the likes of which we can't calculate and we won't ever find buried in the ground.

To some it looks like bad business, but with God at the head of the corporation, there's nothing that can go wrong; setbacks and downturns yes, but no crashes and total failure. God has things well in hand, even though we think God's investments are pretty risky, even foolhardy. The investment is safe.

That's precisely why we can afford to risk everything ourselves. That's why we can afford to risk name and reputation, fortune and fame, in our efforts to serve the kingdom. We are assured by the chief executive officer that our account in heaven has been paid in full by the son, and that when the day of reckoning comes, the books will be in perfect order. When we don't think we can risk offending our guests by praying in a restaurant, when we are shy about telling our neighbors where we go to church, when we think that we have to play the pagan game of keeping religion out of business, then we can remind ourselves that there is no risk, no real risk, in using the talents God has given us. We can invest them in public, in private, in old businesses and fledgling companies without having to worry about what the Joneses think; for we already know what God thinks.

We don't have to be scared of God's reaction. Nor should we be ashamed of our Christianity and keep it for ourselves. If decent ethics are being violated at our place of business, we can find a way to address the problem. If some people have no church home and don't know about Christ, walk across the yard and tell them.

What have we got to lose? We have brothers and sisters to gain with the talents we've been given. Instead of burying them, use them for the kingdom. Don't be afraid of losing God's gifts but of not using them. Use those gifts to spread the wealth around to as many people as possible. Let someone else benefit by our good fortune. Christ never kept anything to himself but emptied himself for us. Since he has done that, we have the luxury of risking all for the sake of someone else.

Wouldn't it be great to spend someone else's money, especially if it's a lot of money? Wouldn't it be great to know that if we invested that money, we couldn't lose any? Wouldn't it be great if somehow, some way, we knew that taking risks with that money would pay off in billions?

Risk God's gifts and gain everything! Nothing will be lost with God's wealth, but there is a world to gain. And we can count on that!

R.A.H.

TWENTY-SIXTH SUNDAY AFTER PENTECOST
Not to Us the Glory
MATTHEW 23:1-12

Did you ever have a big sister or brother who always got you into trouble? You know the kind—they get their little brothers or sisters to do things for them but never lift a finger themselves. These autocrats force others to go into darkened alleys first or to touch dead birds or to repeat a lie to Mom and Dad about what happened with the lamp. Then again, maybe *you* were the big brother or sister?

There will always be manipulators and scapegoats, fall guys and puppeteers. Humans have a certain natural inclination to control and use others. There have been and will be con artists who, like the snake in the Garden of Eden, are willing to ply their trade on an easy mark.

When we read Jesus' denunciation of the scribes and Pharisees in Matthew 23, we clap our hands in delight as these charlatans get their comeuppance. Jesus had just spent a whole chapter arguing with these types about taxes, the life to come, the commandments, and the messiah. He had met every challenge and silenced every would-be examiner. These religious experts with their inflated self-importance had been deflated by a carpenter's son from Galilee.

When the dust of the conflict had settled, Jesus was able to comment on his opponents in a no-nonsense fashion. Matthew said no one dared ask him anything else. That was the first half of the contest.

Then came the second half, and Jesus went on the offensive. We cheer as we see our hero advance yard by yard toward the goal of truth and right.

The scribes and Pharisees were religious professionals. These fellows dressed in distinctive clothing so everybody could see who and what they were. When they went to synagogue on Saturdays, they sat right down in front with the other prominent men. They greeted the less fortunate in the marketplace with the proper greeting of a superior to an inferior, and they insisted on being addressed as rabbi or teacher. Why not? They had their master's degrees and their Ph.D.'s from the best Ivy League schools. They held their seminars in big halls and gesticulated with the flair of the best orators of the time. They were wise and learned, pillars of the community and guardians of the traditions.

But they didn't follow their own advice. They were talkers and not doers. They would tell people what to do, but if you asked for a demonstration, they would insist they were not in the practical theology department, and couldn't you go down the hall for that sort of thing? They enjoyed the privilege and pride, but when it came down to the basics, they wouldn't get on their knees for anybody.

Jesus fixed them all. There wasn't even one young smart aleck left who thought he could take a shot at him. Just great! Wonderful . . .

. . . Until we realize that Jesus was talking to his disciples. He was talking to the people who wanted to listen to him, to follow him. "What does that matter?" you ask. It makes all the difference in the world, because Jesus is not concerned with Pharisees and scribes, he's worried about us, his church, his people, his kids.

Jesus had made a lesson out of the teachers. He was not trying to tell us that the Pharisees and the Jewish religion were pompous windbags and that we should disregard all of their teachings as inferior. Jesus was using the bad apples in the basket to give a lesson to the new fruit that was being added. He was talking to his church and telling us, you and me, all of us here, that we have to beware of putting on airs and sticking our noses high in the sky when we've memorized the whole Catechism or gone to Sunday school without one absence the whole year or written a dissertation on the Bible. What do we think we're accomplishing when we insist on titles and honors and privilege? Who benefits? Christ reminds us, by pointing to the scribes, that human nature is manipulative and self-serving and that we have to watch out for that.

Jesus says we are not supposed to be called rabbis, fathers, or instructors, and teachers. Those titles meant something of rank back then. These titles had honor attached to them, position, and snob appeal. "Not so among you!" Jesus cried. "The greatest among you will be your servants." Why? Because we are all brothers and sisters. We have equal standing when it comes to God. No one is higher in rank than the others in this church. There is only one Lord and teacher, and he died and rose again in clear and concrete demonstration of his love. He enables us to serve; he makes us all one.

For Jesus the issue is clear. Our allegiance, our attention, our honor go not to humans who fill important spots but only to him. O, yes, there are plenty who function in select offices of ministry within each congregation. These God has called to certain significant tasks, like preaching, teaching, nurturing, leading. But they are not to be the objects of our adoration. Many men and women fill important positions in the church and, like Pharisees and scribes, have something worth saying and listening to.

But when they abuse that office or position for their own selfish pride, the office has been stained by hypocrisy, and some may stumble and fall because of it. Let the recent developments with popular TV evangelists be lessons to us not to put our faith in self-appointed leaders in the church. Any passive dependence on faces and names other than Christ is to be shunned, and no groupies are allowed to develop other than those who cry for Christ and his grace. When a pastor fills the important office of ministry, it is only to point to Christ, not to himself or herself.

This text is hard for all those of us who stand up in pulpits Sunday after Sunday, who administer the sacraments, who call on the sick and dying, marry and bury, and baptize young and old. We have no right to an exalted status in the community, and whatever distinctions are made between us and others is only for the sake of the community at large and has nothing to do with us personally. Anyone who is in the position of teacher and Christian mentor is occupying a place of spiritual leadership. Beware those who abuse that privilege; they shall be judged more harshly.

The message is simple: Forewarned is forearmed. When lies and deceit are exposed for the hypocrisy they are and told out loud in the temple precincts or in church, we know that we can continue to work in strength and courage, for we have been given a signpost that directs our feet, not down the path of ruin and self-aggrandizement, but to the true road of honor and humility.

The only true authority that any church leader has is the authority that comes from the Word of God, the Word of Christ, the gospel. Any other authority is false and misleading. That's why pastors need to hear this gospel. Somebody has to speak the Word, but that Word is always about somebody else. That Word always points beyond the preacher. That Word always draws attention to the only true rabbi and teacher, Jesus Christ. As the psalmist says, "Not to us, O Lord, not to us, but to your name give glory!"

R.A.H.

TWENTY-SEVENTH SUNDAY AFTER PENTECOST
The Only Thing That Will Endure
MATTHEW 24:1-14

If you've ever seen the Taj Mahal or Buckingham Palace or the Parthenon, or if you've been to the Pyramid of the Sun in Teotihuacán or the Great Wall of China or the pyramids of Egypt, maybe you can understand how the disciples felt when they walked through the gate of Jerusalem and looked back on the temple that Herod the Great built.

It was the third temple of God to stand on that site. The first had been built by Solomon and was destroyed by the Babylonians. The second had been built by Zerubbabel and was destroyed by the Romans. This was the third and most magnificent of all. It was said that on a clear day you could see it shining in the sun all the way from the coast. It was built on a platform area of thirty-five acres. There were roofed colonnades surrounding the temple. There was gold inside and outside, gold and silver over the gates, gold lampstands, and it took ten thousand men to build it.

It was begun in 20 B.C. and never really finished before the Roman legions returned to Palestine and destroyed it in A.D. 70 This time they plowed the temple mount and left nothing of the temple standing. They built a temple there to one of their own gods.

An old Jewish proverb said, "Anyone who has not seen Herod's building has not yet seen anything beautiful." Why shouldn't the disciples marvel at such a huge and beautiful structure? It was perfectly natural to stand in awe before the temple of Herod. But the temple, the great and most beautiful temple, is no longer standing. All that remains is a retaining wall on the western side of the old temple platform, the Wailing Wall. Everything else is gone, either destroyed or carried off.

Of course, with the temple went the sacrificing. The priests were out of a job. The Levites, the tribe from which the priests came, could no longer function as keepers of the temple. All the factions and subgroups within Judaism had lost their one central, uniting focus. The Pharisees, the Sadducees, the common folk, and all the rest had lost the one thing that held them together. All had been part of this grand building, and when it was gone, gone too were the Pharisees, the Sadducees, and the rest. When Jesus said that not one stone would be left on another, I think he was talking about more than just masonry.

He was talking about people. He was talking about how people focus their lives, their religious lives. If your faith life is dependent on this building, then look out. If your faith life is based on the way we organize ourselves, then look out. If your faith life is focused on the pastors or the leaders of the church, then look out. Beware that you don't put your faith in structures, either of stone or of organization. Because one day, this lovely house, this beautiful organization, and everything that goes along with it will be gone. The center of life does not consist in the houses you live in or the way your set up your daily schedule. The focus of life should be Jesus Christ and his cross, because in the end the only thing that will endure is the love of Christ.

That's an important message for all of us who have grown lazy and complacent and put our faith in the here and now. There might be quite a shock waiting for us one day soon when Jesus Christ comes in the clouds with his holy angels to reclaim once and for all his people and his world. If you've put your faith in peace and justice issues, ideological causes, social ideals, or the myth of human progress, remember that one day the whole world will be judged and all our precious offices and pieces of paper and our high-priority issues will be nothing; gone! The only thing that will remain is Christ's love and what we did in that love.

Watch then, because no one knows when he's coming, not the angels, not us, not even Christ himself knew when he will return. Only God the Father knows.

Some people put their faith in things here on earth; they focus only on what's happening now and forget that Christ is coming again. But there are also folks who pay no attention to this world but always keep their gaze on the world to come. These are the folks who like to predict when Jesus will return. They think they have more wisdom than Christ and all the angels put together.

One of them was Charles T. Russell, who predicted the end of the world and Christ's return in 1914. He had to change that, of course, and then said that what really happened was the casting out of Satan from heaven. "Millions now living shall never die!" his followers proclaimed. He died in 1916. His organization, the Jehovah's Witnesses, still tries to predict the end.

There have been others as well, including some Lutherans, but their predictions failed. These days we have Hal Lindsey and John Ankerberg and all kinds of seers to give us a scare every now and then. They have "experts" on their shows who read from Daniel and Ezekiel and Revelation and try to match Gog and Magog with Russia and China. Goodness knows what they do with Russia these days!

One thing I do know: If we get all caught up in matters that not even Jesus knew and get all bent out of shape wondering when the next world is coming, we won't have much time to pay attention to this world. We won't have much energy left to take care of orphans and the poor and focus our Christian eyes on our neighbor because we'll be too busy fussing with graphs and charts and beasts with ten horns. Love can grow cold in many ways.

He is coming again, but we don't know when, and it really doesn't matter. All we know is that he's coming, and one day all our misery and pain and disappointment and grief will be wiped away like your mom used to wipe your tears when you fell off your trike. It will all be gone, vanished in an instant at the sound of the last trumpet. When doesn't matter—the hour, the date, the year. All that matters is Christ's assurance that we will be saved from this vale of tears and that nothing can snatch us from our good fortune in his kingdom.

When he does come again, he won't come in through the back door. He'll rip open the heavens. Everyone will see that Christians were right to worship him. For those who have lost faith in that coming, here is a call to endurance in the faith. Here is a call to focus your eyes on Christ alone and not on anything else. Why? Because only his love will endure to the end and beyond.

All our calculations and causes, our buildings and organizations, will have nothing to show for themselves at the last day, unless they were founded on the love of Christ. Through persecutions from within and without, through false teachers and preachers, and through the hatred of all the nations, only one thing will endure, the love of Christ and all those connected to that love.

The love of some will grow cold, because they will care nothing for anyone but themselves. False prophets will lead some down dead-end roads. Some will reject the church and scorn it. Christians will be treated with contempt in the most respected circles and locked out of positions of power. It will seem as though everything has failed, and the worst part about it is that the church itself will have contributed to its own persecution by being ashamed to proclaim the faith.

But proclaim we must. That is our task. Proclaim Christ in word and deed. That's how we live in his love, and in the end that's what will endure. When we proclaim Christ in word and deed, by telling people the story, by showing them how to live as Christ says, by treating our neighbors like brothers and sisters, that's how we keep our love warm and vital until the end. Our power doesn't do this; Christ's does. It has always been Christ. His love first, then ours, and finally on the last day, his love forever.

R.A.H.

CHRIST THE KING, LAST SUNDAY AFTER PENTECOST
Lord, When Was It That We Saw You?
MATTHEW 25:31-46

Sometimes Jesus makes people squirm. When he talks about the sheep and goats, the separation, and eternal punishment, it gets a little too close for comfort. In fact little comfort is offered in this passage if you look at it a certain way. But when you realize that the king is Jesus, not some vindictive monarch from the Middle Ages or a blood-thirsty autocrat from the twentieth century, you realize that these few verses from Matthew are filled with hope.

Still, there will be a reckoning. There will be a day so incredible and unimaginable that to think of it now is to do it injustice. We can't comprehend it or project ourselves into it. When it comes, it will be like nothing we have ever dreamed. The king will sit upon his throne. Jesus the King will return to this fractured planet and establish his reign once and for all. Nothing hidden this time, like slipping into Bethlehem. Nothing unfathomable, like the Author of life hanging on a cross. This time the reckoning will come for all to see, and the sheep and goats will go their separate ways.

Yes, there will be a reckoning, even if we don't care to hear about it, even if it makes us sweat. And why is that? Why should this passage make a few of us shift our positions in the pew or in our chairs?

The answer is that this passage can convict us. It can indict us for not having lived up to our faith. It can bring us face-to-face with the fact that we aren't sure if we have fed, clothed, visited, or served anyone but ourselves. When we find out that only goats neglect such service, our collars get a little warm, our clothes a little scratchy, and we feel a creeping stricture in our throats and a shortness of breath. There we sit in a kind of nightmare, wondering if we're on the right side of the pulpit or the left.

Why did Jesus have to say all this? Why couldn't he just have said that everybody was ok, that he was a nice guy and no one should worry about anything at all? Why couldn't he have been a slick TV preacher and told everybody that he saves us just as we are—murderers, molesters, thieves, and all? Then we could continue in our sin unabated, unashamed, and unconcerned about our fate, believing that "God's business is forgiveness." It would have been a lot simpler.

But that would have been dishonest and misleading. Jesus would have been tricking us into a false sense of security if he hadn't pointed out that Christ the king takes sin seriously and will not hide it with a heavy coat of cheap paint.

Jesus wants us to be uncomfortable. He wants to prick our consciences, and he wants us to sit up and take notice that this whole life on earth now and in heaven forever is not something trite and simple; it cost him, the king, his very life, and in the end that death will be the determining factor for the future of the world. Salvation is no small thing, and the punishment predicted for those who couldn't care less for Christ and his sheep is not to be trivialized or expunged from the record.

It makes us realize that God is deadly serious about us and our world, about our lives and the lives of those around us, and that God will not deny the divine nature and goodness by doing away with justice. This leaves us confronted and convicted by God's truth and right, squirming in our pews and chairs, praying for this passage from Matthew to end.

When the passage does end, it ends abruptly. The goats on the left are sent to eternal punishment, while the sheep on the right, to eternal life. With that finale Jesus the preacher has ended his sermon. The point is clear: Life is serious business, and how you live it has a bearing on life forever. But that kind of message can seem small comfort to those who worry that they will go with the goats. If we are left to our own devices with no divine assistance, we may as well start facing God's field of wrath right now.

After all, what we really want to know is who are the sheep and who are the goats. Who are *we* in this story? Knowing that our love is never as great as that of Jesus and that our obedience is a pale shadow of his, are we the sheep or the goats?

Remember, though, what those on the right and the left of the king asked? They both asked the same question. "Lord, when did we see you . . . ?" They were not aware that they had done anything special or failed to do it. The righteous didn't seem to care who the hungry were or where they came from, and so were unaware that every time they served someone's need, they served Christ himself. They never thought about it as something to boast about. They were being true to their faith in Christ and following his command of love and didn't mind whom they served.

The evildoers weren't aware of anything special either; not because they were trying to follow Christ but because they didn't care. Goats couldn't care less about this passage and eternal life. Goats don't listen to Jesus' command of love. Goats are apathetic toward serving their neighbors. Goats always come up with some lame excuse for keeping their own treasures and talents and never mind about the stranger and the poor. Goats don't experience the anxiety of conviction. They don't feel like squirming in the pew or chair because they are convinced nothing is wrong.

This passage ought to affect us in the same manner as the story about the foolish bridesmaids (Matthew 25:1-13) or the parable of the talents (Matthew 25:14-30). Are we challenged by this story to live a life worthy of the calling to which we are called? Are we repentant for not having done so, asking forgiveness to begin again? Or perhaps we are only watching out for ourselves and are oblivious to the fact that one day all opportunities to serve will be gone.

If Christ has left us alone without these words, without this and other warnings, then we might be content to keep living lives of selfishness. If Christ had never said the king would return to separate the sheep and the goats, then all of us might fall over the bottomless cliff for lack of a shepherd to herd us to safety.

As it is, we do have a shepherd, a royal shepherd. We have a divine Savior capable of preserving entire flocks. For with these very words of stern warning and serious judgment, Christ presents to us, instills in us, and places in our hearts the truth of life's serious nature and leads us to safety. We listen to Christ's words and take them seriously and are indeed troubled by them or even convicted by them. But even then, precisely then, we realize that Christ truly loves and cares for us. Otherwise he wouldn't bother telling us a thing about bridesmaids, talents, sheep, or goats. If he didn't care about us, he would never have bothered to warn us about anything.

But warn us he did. Love us he did. And he has promised that his love would affect us on earth now and last through eternal life. These very words are designed to transform goats into sheep, sinners into the righteous, and the hopeless into the fortunate, and to shepherd us to his kingdom in safety.

The shepherd is coming, the crucified one, the beaten one, the one who endured slander and torture, who aligned himself with the powerless and the outcasts, who spent his days in ministry to folks who didn't have a spiritual dime to their names, the one who emptied himself of his divinity and took on human flesh. This one is king! The one who knows what the inside of the slaughterhouse is like and who is capable of shepherding us away from it—this one is our king who bothers himself with creatures like us.

If you have faith and Christ's love, then you will take these words to heart and act on them. If you have no faith, then you won't. When you hear such words again and again, when they become part of you, you'll wake up on the last day to discover that you, even you, had done some things out of faith and love that you yourself were not conscious of. You will learn the final lesson that true love and faith do not ask the cost or circumstances but only perform their duty to others as needed, just as the great shepherd of the sheep did.

We can squirm in our pews or chairs, then. It's good for us. It means we are alive to Christ's words. It means we care. It means that we belong to that great flock of sheep destined for eternal life, who listen to their master's voice, follow him now, and one day will flock to the kingdom prepared for us from the foundation of the world.

R.A.H.